Also by Robert Lyman

Slim, Master of War: Burma and the Birth of Modern Warfare
First Victory: Britain's Forgotten Struggle in the Middle East, 1941
The Generals: From Defeat to Victory, Leadership in Asia 1941–45
The Longest Siege: Tobruk – The Battle that Saved North Africa
Japan's Last Bid for Victory: The Invasion of India, 1944
Operation Suicide: The Remarkable Story of the Cockleshell Raid
Into the Jaws of Death: The True Story of the
Legendary Raid on Saint-Nazaire

THE JAIL BUSTERS

THE SECRET STORY OF MI6, THE FRENCH RESISTANCE & OPERATION JERICHO

ROBERT LYMAN

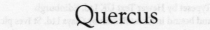

Quercus

First published in hardback in Great Britain in 2014 by
Quercus Publishing Ltd

This paperback edition published in 2015 by

Quercus Publishing Ltd
Carmelite House
50 Victoria Embankment
London EC4Y 0DZ

An Hachette UK company

Copyright © 2014 Robert Lyman
Maps © William Donohoe

A CIP catalogue record for this book is available
from the British Library

PB ISBN 978 1 78429 017 7
EBOOK ISBN 978 1 78206 538 8

This book is for Major Gordon Graham, MC and Bar,
with gratitude and admiration.

It is dedicated to the memory of those *résistants* and other
prisoners who fell during the RAF raid on Amiens Prison on 18
February 1944 as a result of the attempt by the RAF to free them
from Nazi captivity, and to those who were executed subsequently,
by German bullets either in France (some in an anonymous mass
grave at Arras Citadel and the Bois de Gentelles) or in the concentration camp system inside the Reich itself; as well as to the four
gallant flyers who were killed in the operation:

Group Captain Percy Charles Pickard, DSO and two bars, DFC RAF
(Mosquito Pilot)
Flight Lieutenant John Alan Broadley, DSO, DFC, DFM RAF
(Mosquito Navigator)
Flight Lieutenant R. W. 'Sammy' Sampson RNZAF
(Mosquito Navigator)
Flight Sergeant Henry Brown RAF
(Typhoon Pilot)

The rearward-looking photograph on the title page was taken by a fixed camera in the belly of the New Zealand Mosquito flown by Pilot Officer Max Sparks RNZAF and his navigator, Pilot Officer Arthur Dunlop RAF, at 12:03 p.m. on Friday 18 February 1944. The small amount of dust and smoke indicate that the photograph was taken immediately after the first strike, in which bombs were successfully placed against the eastern wall of Amiens's *Maison d'Arrêt* in a superb display of flying by three New Zealand aircraft of No. 487 Squadron RNZAF. The dust and smoke were caused caused by Sparks and Dunlop's plane, their bombs exploding in the German quarters close to the front gate. Frank Wheeler, a pilot in one of the protecting RAF Typhoon fighters high above the action, later reported how astonished he was at the flying skills of the Mosquito crews who, flying at about 200 miles per hour and at 30 feet above the ground (the walls were 20 feet high), placed their bombs directly in the target equivalent of the eye of a needle. The aircraft behind is the third of the New Zealand Mosquitoes undertaking the first run at the prison's eastern wall, flown by Flight Sergeant S. Jennings and navigated by Warrant Officer J. M. Nichols. The aircraft are already in the process of pulling over and above the prison, gaining height before making their getaway towards the coast, and the safety of home.

At least two indistinct figures can be seen standing on the opposite side of the road. Were these members of Dominique Ponchardier's support team? Possibly, although the likelihood is that they were hidden down a side street. In the minutes following this photograph, the two remaining New Zealand Mosquitoes of No. 487 Squadron, flown by Pilot Officers Merv Darrall and Bob Fowler respectively, flew north–south over the prison, crossing the road where Ponchardier waited to help escaping prisoners flee the prison.

The best men are not often left to build the future:
they have bought it with their lives.

Gilbert Renault ('*Colonel Rémy*')

Contents

Abbreviations and Glossary

Abwehr   The Wehrmacht's military intelligence organisation,
            which dealt exclusively with human intelligence,
            especially reports from field agents.

AEAF   Allied Expeditionary Air Force, commanded by Air
            Chief Marshal Sir Trafford Leigh-Mallory RAF. 2nd
            TAF was part of this organisation, and No. 2 Group a
            part of 2nd TAF.

AOC   Air Officer Commanding.

BCRA   Bureau Central de Renseignements et d'Action
            (Central Bureau of Intelligence and Operations), the
            Free French Secret Service.

Bodyguard   Overall Allied strategic deception plan for 1944.

'C'   Chief of the Secret Intelligence Service (MI6).

CD   Chief of SOE (Major General Colin Gubbins).

C-in-C   Commander-in-Chief.

Circus   The RAF term for bomber attacks with fighter escorts
            in the daytime. The attacks were against short-range
            targets with the intention of attracting enemy fighters
            and keeping their fighter units in the area concerned.
            The light bombers therefore acted as bait.

CIU   Aerial reconnaissance was the role of the RAF's
            Central (Photographic) Interpretation Unit (CIU)
            based at Danesfield House, near Marlow at
            Medmenham on the Berkshire and Buckinghamshire
            border, a sister organisation to Bletchley Park.

CND	*Confrérie Notre-Dame*, the *réseau* established by Gilbert Renault.
CNR	Conseil National de la Résistance.
CO	Commanding Officer.
Crossbow	The overall strategy to identify and destroy flying bomb (V1) supply and launching sites in France.
Deuxième Bureau	The Deuxième Bureau de l'État-major général (The Second Bureau of the General Staff) was the French Army's external military intelligence agency.
DSO	Distinguished Service Order.
FFI	Forces Françaises de l'Intérieur, formed in February 1944, the official French Resistance organisation representing the combined efforts of the previously disparate Resistance groupings and organisations.
Fortitude South	The tactical cover plan for Operation *Overlord*, designed to induce the Germans to believe that the Pas-de-Calais was the assault area (formerly *Torrent*, then *Mespot*).
FPU	The RAF's Film Production Unit.
FTPF	The French Communist Party was banned in 1940, and thereafter operated underground. The *Francs-tireurs et Partisans Français* (FTPF), founded as its military branch, became active in the Resistance after the German invasion of the Soviet Union in 1941. They considered their job to be the destruction of railway lines carrying men and materials to the eastern front, and hence waging war on their communist brothers in the Soviet Union; to sabotage factories working for the Germans; punish traitors and collaborators, and kill the occupying soldiers. In February 1944, the FTPF agreed to merge with the Forces Françaises de l'Intérieur (FFI).
Gilbert	MI6 *réseau* operated from Geneva by Colonel Georges-André Groussard.

Jedburgh	The name given to the three-man American-British-French teams parachuted in uniform into German-occupied France to train and assist the French Resistance in the months leading up to *Overlord*. The first Jedburgh teams were dropped into France in early February 1944, before the raid on Amiens Prison.
GIS	Geheime Staatspolizei (Gestapo).
MGB	Motor Gun Boat.
Milice	The pro-German French Militia, established in January 1943 specifically to counter the Resistance, and which began operating in the previous Zone Occupée in early 1944.
MI9	The escape lines organisation of MI6, responsible for facilitating the escape and evasion of Allied servicemen in Europe and their return to the UK.
Noball	The RAF term for air operations against V1 'ski' sites in Northern France from which the Germans began to launch flying bombs.
Overlord	The code word denoting the operation to liberate north-west Europe by Allied Forces through landings in Normandy.
OBE	Order of the British Empire.
OC	Officer Commanding.
OCM	*Organisation Civile et Militaire*. Northern zone Resistance movement, founded in 1940.
OSS	Office of Strategic Services, the US forerunner of the CIA and equivalent of MI6.
RAAF	Royal Australian Air Force.
Ramrod	The RAF term for short-range bomber attacks to destroy ground targets, similar to Circus attacks.
réseau	Resistance group
réseau d'evasion	Resistance group that existed expressly to rescue Allied servicemen on the run

RNZAF	Royal New Zealand Air Force.
Samson	An intelligence-gathering *réseau* reporting to the BCRA through the *OCM*. Run by the lawyer Maurice Rolland (*Renaud*).
SASO	Senior Air Staff Officer.
Sipo-SD	Sicherheitsdienst (Security Service of Himmler's Schutzstaffel [SS]).
SIS	Secret Intelligence Service (MI6).
SOE	Special Operations Executive
Sosies	A *réseau* run by Dominique and Pierre Ponchardier working to MI6.
Starkey	An amphibious feint to force the Luftwaffe to engage in intensive fighting over a period of fourteen days in the autumn of 1943 by building up a threat of an imminent large-scale landing in the Pas-de-Calais area.
STO	The Service du Travail Obligatoire, Vichy laws enacted in September 1942 and February 1943 in which men of working age were conscripted and sent to undertake forced labour in Germany.
2nd TAF	The Second Tactical Air Force, established to provide support to the battlefield across which Operation *Overlord* would be fought.
Todt Organisation	Named after the German Minister for Armaments and Munitions who established a massive labour organisation that undertook large-scale civil engineering projects across Germany and occupied territories during the Second World War.
Zone Libre	Free Zone (Unoccupied 'Vichy-ruled' France). The Germans occupied this zone in November 1942.
Zone Occupée	The Occupied Zone. The distinction between the two faded in 1943.

Dramatis Personae

The Secret Intelligence Service (MI6), Broadway House, St James's, London

Major General Sir Stewart Menzies, KCB, KCMG, DSO, MC (C)	Chief of MI6.
Lieutenant Colonel Sir Claude Dansey	Assistant Chief of MI6, responsible for running MI6 operations in Europe (with an exclusive focus on France from 1943).
Lieutenant Commander Kenneth Cohen ('Z1', 'Keith Crane'), CB, CMG	Late RN. European head of the 'Z' Organisation of MI6 until 1940, and then head of the Free French section (A4). Also Chief Staff Officer, Training, MI6, and in 1944 responsible for Operation *Sussex*.
Commander Wilfred ('Biffy') Dunderdale	Head of the Vichy Section (A5), MI6 until 1942, after which he was the MI6 controller for a number of *réseaux* as part of the P1 (France) Section. He reported directly to 'C'.
Professor Reginald V. Jones	Officially the Air Ministry's Chief Scientist, but also Chief Scientist to MI6.

Major James (Jimmy) Langley, MBE, MC	MI6/MI9 (P15) – London.
Major Airey Neave ('Saturday')	MI6/MI9 – London.
Michael Creswell ('Monday')	MI6/MI9 – Madrid.
Donald Darling ('Sunday')	MI6/MI9 – Lisbon/Gibraltar.
Lieutenant Neil Whitelaw ('Captain Thomas')	Ponchardier and Charraudeau's MI6 case officer.
Victor Farrell	MI6/MI9 Berne. Farrell 'ran' Michel Hollard of *réseau Agir*.

BCRA, 10 Duke Street, London

André Dewavrin (*Passy*)	Head of the Free French Intelligence Service, the BCRA.
Colonel Gilbert Renault, DSO, OBE (*Colonel Rémy*)	Established the *réseau CND* between 1940 and 1943, and managed other networks in France for the BCRA 1943–4. He was effectively Ponchardier's BCRA case officer, as well as the BCRA representative for Operation *Sussex*.
Captain André Manuel (*Maxwell*, *Pallas*)	A lawyer, and Dewavrin's deputy in London.
Jean Moulin	The architect of unity amongst Resistance groups. Arrested in June 1943, he died under torture.
Pierre Brossolette (*Brumaire*)	*Résistant* leader who worked with Gilbert Renault to establish the civilian wing of the BCRA, designed to create political unity across the Resistance following the loss of Jean Moulin. Arrested when attempting to return to Britain in February 1944, he

threw himself out of a garret window in March 1944 rather than face the threat of talking under German torture.

The Resistance in France

Dr Antonin Mans
Public Health Officer, head of the Civil Defence organisation in the Somme Department, and the secret head of the *réseau OCM* in the region, and of *Century*. Arrested 12 November 1943, and incarcerated in Amiens Prison before being deported to a series of concentration camps in Germany in May 1944. He narrowly survived.

Marie-Madeleine Fourcade (*Hedgehog*)
Leader of the *réseau Alliance*, an important MI6 intelligence-gathering network, badly damaged by the Abwehr in 1943.

Raymond Vivant
Sous-préfet of Abbeville, and head of the *réseau OCM* in the region after Antonin Mans's arrest in November 1943. Arrested and imprisoned in Amiens Prison on 12 February 1944. Escaped, and survived.

Captain André Tempez
Amiens Sector head, *réseau OCM*. Imprisoned in Amiens Prison. Executed at Arras in April, his body was found in a mass grave in October 1944.

Colonel Alfred Touny (*Lacroix*)
Based in Paris, head of the *réseau OCM* in north-eastern France.

Arrested at his home in Paris on 25 February 1944, a week after the release of some of his *OCM* colleagues from Amiens Prison at the hands of the RAF, Colonel Touny was shot in the moat of the Citadel of Arras at the end of April 1944. His body was found in a mass grave in October 1944, along with that of his friend and colleague André Tempez.

Dominique Ponchardier, MBE (*Elizabeth*)
Joint head of the *réseau Sosies*, responsible for operations in the *réseau* across northern France, principally focused on intelligence gathering for MI6. Survived (see Appendix 7).

Lieutenant Pierre Ponchardier (*Geneviève*)
Dominique's brother, and head of the *réseau Sosies* in the south of France. Survived.

Gendarme Lieutenant Marceau Laverdure
Member of the *réseau Zéro* in Amiens and author of the 'dossier' Ponchardier presented to Groussard in Geneva. Survived.

Vice Admiral Edouard Rivière
Member of the *réseau Sosies*, and right-hand man to Dominique Ponchardier. He was arrested in April 1944 and imprisoned in Caen. In May 1944 a heavy raid by the RAF enabled Ponchardier and Chapelle to help a number of prisoners to escape from the rubble of the prison, including Rivière.

Major Gustave Bertrand
A member of the pre-war cryptography department of the Deuxième Bureau, and a key player in France's pre-war

	intelligence war against Germany. Until late 1942 he was head of a covert intelligence network, run within the Vichy regime but working against the Germans and codenamed 'Kléber', led by Colonel Louis Rivet. In 1943 he worked closely with MI6.
Colonel Georges-André Groussard (*Eric*)	Head of the *réseau Gilbert*, based in Geneva, and Dominique Ponchardier's monthly contact in Geneva. He was a key MI6 source.
Captain Paul Paillole	Head of Vichy's Counter-Intelligence Service and a close contact of MI6.
Lieutenant André Devigny (*Valentin*)	A member of the *réseau Gilbert*, and right-hand man to Groussard.
Georges Charraudeau (*Chobière*)	Head of the *réseau Alibi*. It was his radio transmitters that Dominique Ponchardier used to send messages to MI6.
Dr Odile Catherine Regnault	A colleague of Dr Antonin Mans in the Civil Defence organisation, and a secret member of the *OCM*.
René (*Pépé*) and Maria Chapelle	Local leader of the FTPF *réseau* and Ponchardier's accomplice in the *Sosies*. Both were active in sabotage, intelligence and escape line operations. Maria Chapelle was arrested on 13 April 1944, tortured and deported to Germany. Maria survived the war, and died in September 2012. René died in 1970.
Georges Broussine, MC	BCRA agent and leader of the *Burgundy* (*Bourgogne*) *réseau*

d'évasion. The *Burgundy* line is estimated to have arranged the escape of more than 300 Allied airmen.

Joseph (Joe) Balfe, OBE	Leader of a *réseau d'évasion* at Hornoy-le-Bourg, 22 miles east of Amiens. Married to Madeleine Gaudière.
Robert Bibaut	Member of the *réseau OCM* and author of information on Amiens Prison sent to London. Sentenced to death for sabotage, but killed during the raid.
Jeannie Rousseau (*Amniarix*)	The *Alliance* agent who discovered the secrets of Peenemünde, later the Vicomtesse de Clarens. Sent to Ravensbrück women's concentration camp, but survived.
Michel Hollard, OBE	The independent agent and head of *réseau Agir* ('Act!') who discovered the details of the V1 deployment programme in north-east France and furnished them to MI6 in Switzerland. Arrested in February 1944, he was tortured and imprisoned first at Fresnes Prison and then sent in June 1944 to Neuengamme concentration camp, near Hamburg. He was freed on 20 April 1945.
Maurice Genest (*Henri*)	*Résistant* and prisoner in Amiens, who began sending details of the prison regime to René Chapelle in September 1943, urging him to arrange an attack to release the inmates.

Raymond Bonpas	Member of both the *OCM* and *Alliance*, and imprisoned in Amiens on 4 January 1944.
Roland Farjon (*Dufor*)	A leading member of the *OCM*, who was arrested on 23 October 1943 and turned by the Gestapo. As a *collaborateur*, he was responsible for the subsequent arrest of Dr Antonin Mans, Captain André Tempez and other leading *OCM* figures in north-eastern France in November 1943. He committed suicide following the Liberation.
Jean Beaurin	A young member of the FTPF who developed during 1942 a fine technique for derailing German troop and freight trains by the simple expedient of removing the bolts to railway tracks (see Appendix 4). Arrested in December, he was told that his execution was set for late February 1944. However he escaped during the raid and went on to survive the war.
Dr Robert Beaumont (*Bistouri*).	An agent for MI9's *Possum réseau d'évasion* from August 1942. Arrested and interned in the *Maison d'Arrêt* in Amiens on 15 February, he was killed during the attack. Married to Liliane.

The Enemy

Pierre Le Baube	Fifty-one-year-old Vichy-appointed *préfet* of the Somme, a notorious collaborator.

M. Pechon	Head of the Milice in Amiens.
Baumann	Head of the Gestapo in Amiens. His personal details remain unknown: German records suggest that he could have been one of three individuals, namely SS-Obersturmbannführer Dr Christian Baumann; SS officer (rank unknown) Wilhelm Baumann; or SS-Standartenführer Erwin Baumann.
Lucienne Den	Baumann's German interpreter, detested by the Resistance.
Lucien Pieri	A local Amiénois tailor and *collaborateur*, believed responsible for the arrest and execution of several FTPF *résistants* in Mers-les-Bains in 1943, and others. Assassinated by the FFI in 1944.

RAF

Air Chief Marshal Sir Trafford Leigh-Mallory RAF	C-in-C, AEAF. Died in air crash over France en route to the Far East, 14 November 1944.
Air Marshal Sir Arthur (Mary) Coningham RAF	AOC, 2 Tactical Air Force (2nd TAF). Born in Brisbane, he spent his formative years in New Zealand.
Air Vice Marshal Basil Embry RAF	AOC, No. 2 Group, 2nd TAF.
Air Commodore G. W. P. ('Tubby') Grant RAF	Deputy Director Intelligence, Air Ministry, and the man responsible for the coordination of plans with both MI6 and SOE.
Group Captain David Atcherley RAF	Senior Air Staff Officer (SASO), No. 2 Group.

Squadron Leader Ted Sismore, DFC and two Bars RAF	No. 2 Group. The chief planner for the raid.
Wing Commander Harry (Pat) Shallard RAF	Group Intelligence Officer, No. 2 Group.
Squadron Leader Edwin Houghton RAF	Second-in-command to Pat Shallard, and the man who visited Amiens in September 1944 to undertake a largely abortive investigation of the raid.

Mosquito Aircrews taking part in Ramrod 564

Wing Commander Irving Stanley ('Black') Smith, DFC RAF (Pilot) EG-R*	No. 487 Squadron RNZAF. Returned safely.
Flight Lieutenant Barnes, DFM (Navigator) EG-R	No. 487 Squadron RNZAF. Returned safely.
Flight Sergeant S. Jennings (Pilot) EG-H	No. 487 Squadron RNZAF. Returned safely.
Warrant Officer J. M. Nichols (Navigator) EG-H	No. 487 Squadron RNZAF. Returned safely.
Pilot Officer D. Robert (Bob) Fowler RNZAF (Pilot) EG-J	No. 487 Squadron RNZAF. Returned safely.
Warrant Officer Frank Wilkins (Navigator) EG-J	No. 487 Squadron RNZAF. Returned safely.
Pilot Officer Maxwell (Max) Sparks RNZAF (Pilot)	No. 487 Squadron RNZAF. Returned safely, although aircraft

---

* This sequence of letters as well as the following instances are the Aircraft Serial Numbers.

EG-T	damaged by flak.
Pilot Officer Arthur Dunlop RAF (Navigator) EG-T	New Zealander in the RAF. No. 487 Squadron RNZAF. Returned safely, although aircraft damaged by flak.
Flight Lieutenant Brian (Titch) Hanafin RAF (Pilot) EG-H	No. 487 Squadron RNZAF. Aborted mission. Returned safely, though badly injured by flak.
Pilot Officer C. Francis (Frank) Redgrave RAF (Navigator) EG-H	No. 487 Squadron RNZAF. Aborted mission. Returned safely.
Pilot Officer M. L. S. (Merv) Darrall RNZAF (Pilot) EG-C	No. 487 Squadron RNZAF. Returned safely.
Pilot Officer Fred (Steve) Stevenson RNZAF (Navigator) EG-C	No. 487 Squadron RNZAF. Returned safely.
Wing Commander Robert Wilson (Bob) Iredale DFC and Bar RAAF (Pilot) SB-F	No. 464 Squadron RAAF. Returned safely.
Flight Lieutenant John (Mac) McCaul, DFC RCAF (Navigator) SB-F	No. 464 Squadron RAAF. Returned safely.
Flying Officer Kingsley Lawrence Monaghan, DFM RAF (Pilot) SB-U	No. 464 Squadron RAAF. Returned safely.
Flying Officer Albert William (Dixie) Dean, DFM RAF (Navigator) SB-U	No. 464 Squadron RAAF. Returned safely.
Squadron Leader William	No. 464 Squadron RAAF.

Richard Craig (Dick) Sugden RAF (Pilot) SB-A	Returned safely.
Flying Officer Albert H. (Bunny) Bridger RAF (Navigator) SB-A	No. 464 Squadron RAAF. Returned safely.
Flight Lieutenant Tom McPhee, DFM RAF (Pilot) SB-T	No. 464 Squadron RAAF. Returned safely.
Flight Lieutenant G. W. Atkins RAF (Navigator) SB-T	No. 464 Squadron RAAF. Returned safely.
Group Captain Percy Charles ('Pick') Pickard, DSO, DFC RAF (Pilot) EG-F	Mission commander. Shot down and killed in action.
Flight Lieutenant J. A. (Bill) Broadley, DSO, DFC, DFM RAF (Navigator) EG-F	Shot down and killed in action.
Squadron Leader A. Ian McRitchie RAF (Pilot) SB-T	Australian in the RAF. Shot down and made prisoner of war.
Flight Lieutenant Richard (Dick) Webb (Sammy) Sampson RNZAF (Navigator) SB-T	Shot down and killed in action.
Wing Commander Ivor Gordon Easton (Daddy) Dale RAFVR (Pilot) H-U	No. 21 Squadron RAF. Did not attack. Returned safely.

Flying Officer E. W. P. Gabites RNZAF (Navigator) H-U	No. 21 Squadron RAF. Did not attack. Returned safely.
Flight Lieutenant A. E. C. Wheeler, DFC RAF (Pilot) H-C	No. 21 Squadron RAF. Did not attack. Returned safely.
Flying Officer Redington (Navigator) H-C	No. 21 Squadron RAF. Did not attack. Returned safely.
Flight Lieutenant M. J. W. Benn, DFC RAFVR (Pilot) YH-J	No. 21 Squadron RAF. Did not attack. Returned safely.
Flying Officer Roe (Navigator) YH-J	No. 21 Squadron RAF. Did not attack. Returned safely.
Flight Lieutenant D. A. Duncan Taylor, DFC RAF (Pilot) YH-D	No. 21 Squadron RAF. Did not attack. Returned safely.
Squadron Leader Philippe Level, DFC RAF (Navigator) YH-D	No. 21 Squadron RAF. Did not attack. Returned safely. Often called Livry or Livry-Level, his real name was Philippe Level.
Flight Lieutenant E. E. Hogan RAF (Pilot) YH-P	Abandoned task shortly after take-off owing to intercom failure, and VHS radio being unserviceable. Returned safely.
Flight Sergeant David Alan Stafford Crowfoot RAAF (Navigator) YH-P	Abandoned task shortly after take-off owing to intercom failure, and VHS radio being unserviceable. Returned safely.
Flight Sergeant A. J. Steadman RAF (Pilot) YH-F	Aborted in snowstorm over England after taking off late from Hunsdon due to engine trouble. Abandoned task over Littlehampton owing to

	failure to catch up with formation. Returned safely.
Pilot Officer E. J. Reynolds RCAF (Navigator) YH-F	Aborted in snowstorm over England after taking off late from Hunsdon due to magneto trouble. Abandoned task over Littlehampton owing to failure to catch up with formation. Returned safely.
Flight Lieutenant A. (Tony) Wickham, DFC RAF (Pilot) O	Film Production Unit (FPU). Filmed operation. Returned safely.
Pilot Officer Lee Howard RAF (Navigator/Cameraman) O	Film Production Unit (FPU). Filmed operation. Returned safely.

Preface

At 10 a.m. on 12 February 1944 Raymond Vivant, the *sous-préfet* of Abbeville, received a telephone call from the German authorities ordering him to attend the Kreiskommandantur in Amiens. He subsequently recorded the story of his arrest and incarceration for Gilbert Renault. What follows is in Raymond Vivant's own words.

Whereas [in the normal course of business] I was generally taken immediately into the Kreiskommandant's office, this time I was taken before the chief of police, a young man, with carroty hair, a paunch and a brutal-looking face. 'Would you be seated, *Monsieur le sous-préfet*? he said. 'The Amiens security officers are conducting a very important inquiry, and they would like to have your opinion on a certain matter.' Neither of us spoke until 11.25; by then my patience was exhausted, so I declared: 'I would like to remind you that as a *sous-préfet* I have many urgent things to attend to . . . If these security officers don't show up in five minutes, I shall go.'

Obsequious as ever, the German asked me to wait just a few more minutes, telling me that his colleagues would assuredly arrive before long. At half-past eleven two young men in civilian clothing came into the office and began a rapid conversation in German with the police chief. They were smartly dressed, and I remember thinking that it would be difficult to be sure of their nationality. One of them was wearing a bottle-green hat, but without the symbolic feather so dear to the smart set on the other side of the Rhine, and I thought idly that this green colour had been very fashionable at one time when I was a youngster. After they had talked at some length, the smaller of the newcomers turned to me, and asked drily:

'You are the *sous-préfet* of Abbeville?'

'Yes,' I answered.

'You are Monsieur Raymond Vivant?'

'Yes.'

Suddenly I felt something hard and metallic being poked into my side, and I realised then that these two men were from the Gestapo. 'Hands up!' said the second one. When he had made sure that I was not armed, he told me to sit down again.

'*Monsieur le sous-préfet,*' said the other, 'we must arrest you.'

'Here we go with another German judicial blunder,' I answered. 'By no means the first, by no means . . .'

'We'll talk about that later, Monsieur. For the moment, you must consider yourself our prisoner.'

'But what on earth am I being arrested for?'

'I cannot tell you,' came the response.

After a few more remarks to his henchman, he went out, leaving me to be guarded by the police chief. Later I learnt that they had gone to the *sous-préfecture*, had broken into my flat along with two other agents, and had rummaged about in every room – my office, the reception rooms, even the bedrooms, without finding any of the evidence necessary to their inquiry. They had questioned my wife, asking her how often I went out, if I stayed out long, if I received any strange visitors in my home . . . After an hour of this, the Gestapo had abandoned the search and left without finding any of the compromising documents, particularly a map of the coastal fortifications of Saint-Valéry which I had fortunately hidden among a lot of administrative files and papers.

Heavily escorted, in the usual iron-grey Citroën, I was taken to Amiens. On the way we drove through Ailly-le-Haut-Clocher, a little village that had been bombed the previous night. We had managed to get information through to London about some V1 launching platforms in the neighbourhood, and the Royal Air Force hadn't delayed in making the most of our directions. I was secretly jubilant as I watched the chagrin of my guards at the destruction of their precious 'secret' installations . . .

It was nearly two o'clock when we arrived at the prison in Amiens. I was interrogated in an office full of German soldiers, and a clerk wrote down all that was said. Standing silently at his side, watching me closely all the time, was a dark-haired young woman, about thirty years old, fairly well built and wearing a dark brown frock [Lucienne Den]. Then they took my wallet, my fountain pen, my propelling pencil and my belt, but left me with my watch, my tie and my braces, contrary to general prison practice. This done, I was taken to cell No. 16, on the ground floor.

At five o'clock the door opened to admit a German followed by a fellow carrying a pan of soup. The German said something to me in a very vehement voice. I made signs to him that not only could I not understand what he was saying, but that I could not take my serving of the soup as I had no bowl or plate. With a few more guttural grunts he went away, and I had to do without my soup. The rest of the night was uneventful, apart from the fact that the sentry on duty would come and look through the spyhole in my door to make sure that nothing unusual went on. I couldn't get to sleep. It was bitterly cold, and my paillasse, which was only about three feet long, was all I had – no blankets or covers at all. The next day at eleven o'clock two guards arrived, and one of them said to me in French: 'You are to go to the Sicherheitspolizei [Gestapo] for interrogation.'

At midday I was taken into an office where the young fellow who had arrested me the day before sat enthroned. He asked me what my clandestine activities were, to which group I belonged and so on . . . I had the uneasy impression that he knew altogether too much about too many things, and that he was just playing with me, watching my reactions. He decided to interrupt the interrogation at one o'clock. 'I must eat, you understand!' he told me. I wished him '*bon appétit*', which seemed to surprise him. Then I was put in the next room, a kind of cell with only a fixed bench as furniture. There I stayed until they let me out at three-thirty. After a little more desultory questioning, the young German said: 'We will go on with this interrogation later.' Doubtless, I thought to myself, he wants his siesta now. As for me, I was taken back to my cell. An hour later we had the 'soup' comedy all over again. Bulging-eyed, the German regarded my mime, shouted some more and went off – and still I had had no soup.

The next day at eleven in the morning I was taken once more before the Gestapo chief. This time he made no bones about it: 'We know that General de Gaulle has chosen you to be *préfet* of Amiens after the "liberation"; we know all your friends.' Then he described – very exactly – some of the Resistance members who had visited me at my office. In reply to my suggestion that a *sous-préfet* had to receive all callers, whatever their condition, he added: 'On such-and-such a day you received a certain person with whom you discussed such-and-such a subject.' In due course the soup-time performance was repeated, and once more my interrogation went on for only a short while, terminating with the 'We will continue this interrogation later' and then at five o'clock the soup farce again ... but this time I was really angry and created a tremendous fuss, with the result that a German guard brought me a kind of platter and – welcome sight – a suitcase from my wife full of spare clothing, toilet necessities and some food from my friends the Tenaillons, wholesale grocers in Abbeville. When the Tenaillon contributions came to light, the guard blustered for a while in German, and then obligingly trans-lated into French the fact that the two bottles would have to be confiscated. 'Alcohol, nix!' he announced, smiling broadly at me, and then took his departure.

The food seemed to me a gift from the gods by then, especially the sugar. I immediately put four or five lumps in each of my pockets, thinking that they would be some comfort for me during my next long interrogation, should I manage to eat them without being spotted by the guards. There was another pleasant surprise for me too: carefully wrapped in a tissue was a little chemist's bottle, labelled 'vitamin pills', which I could see had already been opened. I imagined that my wife had sent them to me, thinking that they would offset my undernourishment while in prison. As I felt well enough for the moment, I decided to keep them in hand for a time, and take only one each morning with breakfast.

Then came Friday 18 February, 1944.

On this day, just before 11 a.m., eighteen RAF Mosquito Mark VI fighter-bombers, accompanied by the only Mark IV Mosquito in the inventory of the RAF's Film Production Unit (FPU), lifted off from the airfield at Hunsdon in Hertfordshire to fly through snow blizzards and in zero visibility across the English Channel to launch a famous low-level precision raid against Amiens Prison on the Somme, well known to a previous generation as the epicentre of the British defence of Flanders in the Great War. It was one of a number of celebrated attacks by the extraordinarily fast Mosquito against Gestapo targets across occupied Europe, designed to counteract the deleterious effect of the highly successful German counter-espionage that threatened the survival of Resistance groups working to assist the Allies in the defeat of their common enemy. The RAF was told, through the Air Ministry, that the purpose of the raid, requested directly by the French Resistance, was to destroy the walls of the jail to allow incarcerated *résistants* to escape almost certain (and possibly imminent) execution.

In the traditional telling of this story, the primary component has been the famous Mosquito fighter-bombers of the RAF and Commonwealth air forces, the incredible 'Wooden Wonder', the fastest propeller-driven aircraft of the war, which could outfly

German fighters and deliver precision bombing attacks at the very nerve centres of enemy command and control in occupied Europe. The account is one of heroic, meticulous flying and bombing, and the sacrifice of one of its great heroes, Group Captain Percy Charles 'Pick' Pickard, who together with his navigator, Flight Lieutenant 'Bill' Broadley, was to die on the raid. But this is only a part – a small though significant part – of the whole story. What history slightly inaccurately recalls as Operation *Jericho** in fact boasts three parts, of which the raid itself is but one. It is, first of all, a narrative about the French Resistance – *La résistance intérieure française* – and the diverse networks of agents and supporters that made up what was until mid-1943 a slightly nebulous body, some-what stronger in concept than it was in hard reality.

Even in early 1944 *la résistance*, signifying a unified rather than a disparate venture, was an aspiration rather than actuality. The reality was a clutch of diverse organisations that existed to resist the Nazi occupation of their country and that kept alive the flames of a subdued but not subservient people. These groups worked more or less alongside each other, if not entirely hand in glove until the emergence of the Forces Françaises de l'Intérieur (FFI) in early 1944. In late 1943 and early 1944 the Resistance found itself hard pressed, following many months of German counter-espionage successes that ravaged its numbers and leadership.

The second part of the story concerns the relationship between some of these *réseaux* and the British Secret Intelligence Service, MI6, and the connection between the latter and General de

---

*   The raid had no operational codename. It was not referred to publicly as 'Jericho' until a French film based on the raid was produced with this title in 1946, although both Gilbert Renault and Philippe Level suggest that the phrase was in common use in RAF circles at the time of the raid. The correct RAF designation for the mission was 'Ramrod 564', as Ramrod was the code-name for this type of raid (see Glossary). The VHS radio call sign to identify aircraft on the operation for RAF Air Traffic Control was 'Renovate', which some have assumed to be the mission's codename. Indeed, an RAF training film of the mission was called *Operation Renovate*.

Gaulle's secret intelligence organisation, the Bureau Central de Renseignements et d'Action, or BCRA. The third part is, of course, the story of the courageous crews of 140 Wing, 2nd Tactical Air Force (2nd TAF), who flew their wooden Mosquito fighter-bombers on the mission to break down the walls of German-run Amiens Prison at noon on 18 February 1944.

In recent times doubt has been cast on the essential veracity of this three-part narrative, beginning with a surprisingly ill-informed *Panorama* documentary in 1982. Did the Resistance actually ask for the raid? Why are there so many apparent inconsistencies in the official account of it published for the media later in 1944? Why was there a long delay between the raid and its public announcement, and why do there appear to be so many gaps in the archival record? Do these not hint at an alternative truth behind this story, one that Britain wanted, for reasons of security, to keep hidden? Was not the role of MI6, revealed for the first time in 1982, in itself suspicious, a pointer to a more complex and less straight-forward rationale for the raid than merely the release of incarcer-ated *résistants*?

One such claim is that the raid was undertaken by Britain as part of the elaborate 'bodyguard of lies' to persuade the Germans that the Allied invasion of France, when it came, would be in the Pas-de-Calais (Operation *Fortitude South*) and that the traditional story – that the raid was undertaken to rescue French *résistants* facing almost certain death in German captivity – is a well-concealed lie. The implication of this revisionist argument is to suggest that the claims of French Resistance leaders to have asked for the attack were an invention, and that the sacrifice of the four RAF airmen lost on the raid was in vain. This book, however, will demonstrate that the original story is correct in all but the smallest detail, and that claims of an alternative narrative are simply not substantiated by the facts. There is not a scintilla of evidence, for instance, in the files of Operation *Fortitude South* to suggest that the raid was a part of a strategic deception against Germany. The truth is that there was no need for a relatively minor prison raid in Amiens in February to persuade the Germans of the *Fortitude South* deception: they already believed it, as did most French people in the region.

What follows is the story of the attempt by MI6 to assist one of its espionage operations in trouble, and perhaps also to rescue some of its own agents from certain death. It is an unashamedly heroic rescue story: of *résistants* (and possibly British agents also) incarcerated in the jail awaiting certain death or deportation to a concentration camp in the east (which meant the same thing); of a desperate request from their friends in MI6's resistance networks to their handlers in London to do something – anything – to effect their release; and of the talented and brave Mosquito crews of the RNZAF, RAAF and RAF who launched a devastating low-level attack on the prison to allow a significant proportion of the inmates to escape. The RAF report on the raid noted succinctly but accurately in September 1944: 'The attack on Amiens Prison will remain one of the RAF's epics.' This is the story of that attack and the reason for it, as well as a portrait of the men and women, in France and England, on land in occupied France and in the air above it, who made it happen.

ONE

Picardy in winter

Amiens is the capital of Picardy's three *départements* – Oise (capital Beauvais), Aisne (capital Laon) and the Somme. On Picardy's northern boundary lies the Pas-de-Calais *préfecture* and to its south lies Paris. In the extreme north-east its boundary, on the Aisne River, touches Belgium. It was administered, as was the case in all of France's 27 regions, through the prefecture system, established by Napoleon Bonaparte in 1800, which provided for a prefect (*préfet*) for each *département*. By this stage of the war, a *préfet* needed to be a loyal servant of Pétain's collaborationist government based in the otherwise tranquil Auvergne town of Vichy: those who had demonstrated less than full allegiance found themselves ejected from office as the first step to a concentration camp or life on the run, in the shadow of the law and on the margins of existence, as a *résistant*.

Préfets possessed executive powers. The prefecture was subdivided into districts, administered by a sub-prefect, or *sous-préfet*. The administrative heart of the prefecture of Picardy in 1944 was Amiens, with seven *sous-préfets* administering Abbeville, Beauvais, Compiègne, Creil, Laon, Saint-Quentin and Soissons. By January 1944 Émile Pelletier, the *préfet* of the Somme *département*, based in Amiens, who was secretly a leading member of the OCM (*Organisation Civile et Militaire*), was in hiding, and the post was now occupied by the notorious collaborator Pierre Le Baube.

*

Picardy was used to war. Indeed, its name, first coined in the thirteenth century, most probably derived from that of the pike (*pique*) that the locals used when fighting. It is possible that the name of the man who was to lead the RAF mission against the prison – Charles Pickard – had its origin in these parts. In the verdant hills of the Somme River valley north of Abbeville lies the battlefield of Crécy (1346). (Azincourt, location of the battle of 'Agincourt' as the English remember it, lies slightly to the north, in the Pas-de-Calais prefecture.)

It was in the First World War, however, that the names of the towns and villages of Picardy became firmly engraved in the psyche of subsequent generations of Britons, Canadians, Australians and New Zealanders by virtue of the great Battle of the Somme where, in one day in May 1916, over 60,000 British and Commonwealth troops became casualties at the start of an offensive designed to place pressure on the German death struggle against the French at Verdun. By 18 November 1916, when the long battle ended, more than a million men on both sides had become casualties. The British and French forces had secured a few square miles of mud for this sacrifice, but failed to capture the towns of Bapaume or Péronne. The bodies of hundreds of thousands of young men of many nationalities of that generation lie there still, remembered in the scores of Commonwealth cemeteries and memorials scattered across rich pastures that even today offer up an almost daily harvest of bones and unexploded bombs.

The beautifully manicured cemeteries of this war, both British and German, greeted the invaders in May 1940, the headstones standing row upon row, a dead army welcoming a new. The mute testimony of these cemeteries might have allowed the newcomers the opportunity to ask whether the sacrifice of their father's generation had achieved much, given that Europe was once again waking each morning to the sound of gunfire, and the sight of smoke rising over its towns and villages. If, that is, the speed of the German advance allowed its soldiers the opportunity to think. Moving so fast, they had little enough time to enjoy the beauty of the country they were once again introducing to the sights and sounds of war as their armoured columns clanked and rattled towards the Channel coast.

From the outset the German occupation of Picardy was harsh. Amiens endured three days of bombardment in May 1940 before the town fell, and full repairs to the devastation caused during this early bombardment did not take place until the war was over. Likewise, the town of Abbeville lay in ruins, half of its houses damaged to some degree by artillery fire. The Germans created a heavily guarded 'forbidden zone' north of the River Somme which they used extensively for armoured formation training, and live field-firing exercises. These activities were accompanied by severe movement restrictions for local people, and devastating consequences for the 1940 harvest. German military activity intensified significantly during the early months of 1941, a state of affairs the local populace ascribed to continuing German aspirations to invade Britain. Only when the troop trains were seen to roll east in May 1941 was there any suspicion that Hitler's eyes were focused not on England across the water, but on the Soviet Union.

The misery of the Picard population was compounded by a series of harsh winters, heavy and increasingly indiscriminate requisitioning of foodstuffs by members of the occupation forces, and severe shortages of heating fuel. Resistance against the invaders came in many forms, and showed early direction by the town's leaders: Doctor Antonin Mans, public health officer and head of the Civil Defence organisation (known as 'Passive Defence') for the Somme *département*; Émile Pelletier, *préfet* of the Somme; and M. Debouveric, the mayor of Amiens. By 1943 all three men were members of the *OCM*, a Resistance organisation mainly composed of right-leaning former army officers whose inclinations in the early years tended towards supporting General Henri Giraud's Resistance faction rather than that of General Charles de Gaulle.

'The whole of the intellectual elite of the Somme, particularly the medical corps,' recalled Gilbert Renault, 'was stiff with opposition in the face of the sufferings imposed on the people who, in their turn, were being galvanised into rebellion.' When Raymond Vivant was appointed *sous-préfet* of Abbeville in April 1943 he also quickly joined the ranks of the *OCM*, and was given responsibility for coordinating the gathering of intelligence for the entire coastal region of the Pas-de-Calais.

The Civil Defence organisation in the region, based on the fire stations of the *sapeurs-pompiers* located in every town, became a focal point for the early *résistants*. There does not appear to have been a single centralised decision to build up a Resistance organisation around the firemen: it just happened that way, most *pompiers* needing little encouragement to resist, coming together locally to do what they could to work against the occupiers. The *pompiers* proved an ideal organisation on which to build *réseaux*: most of the men had received military training and had been mobilised in 1939, were well organised and operated in self-contained units of friends and colleagues in every locality. Within the context of their local communities they all knew each other well, making it difficult for the Germans to infiltrate their ranks with agents provocateurs, a tactic deployed by the Gestapo and the Abwehr to devastating effect in those *réseaux* that did not take their security seriously enough. The organisation in Amiens was led by Captain André Tempez, an ex-army officer who was also secretly the local head of the *OCM*.

From 1942 the Luftwaffe developed several new airbases in the region, such as at Glisy, near Amiens, and at Poix and in the plains of Santerre. In due course these attracted the attention of the RAF: it was British attacks that allowed the French Civil Defence organisation to develop extensively across the region, as the Germans were forced to rely on the local *pompiers* to help clear up after air raids.

But resistance, in even its most benign forms, was met with a harsh response from the start. Mademoiselle Perdu, a girl of seventeen, was thrown into prison accused of insulting a German officer in the street, and the abbé Garbe, the curé of the hamlet of Boves, some five miles south-east of Amiens, was arrested, along with several others, on charges of sabotage. The charges did not need to be real to succeed in their ultimate purpose: to intimidate and cow the populace, unsubtle prompting not to step out of line. Those arrested in Amiens or the surrounding area found themselves jailed in one of two places. The first was the prison on the eastern outskirts of the town, sitting on the north side of the long, straight road to Albert, and the second was the Citadel in the centre, a stronghold since its construction at the beginning of the seventeenth century. Gilbert Renault described Amiens Prison as:

> built roughly in the shape of a cross, the shorter arms running
> north–south. In these were kept the 'political' prisoners taken by
> the Germans, who had their quarters in the other part of the
> building. Prisoners taken by the French police were kept in the
> base of the cross, except for the women, who were incarcerated at
> the top end. The tower, which is in the position of the nail that
> might hold the cross together, enabled the guards to keep watch
> over the whole building.

By early 1944 the Germans occupied whole parts of the building, especially those areas in which their terrorist suspects were kept.

During the occupation the prison in Amiens continued to be managed by French prison warders, supplemented by a small number of German guards. The real work of the German police and security services against incarcerated political prisoners was undertaken in the Citadel, a secure fortress in the heart of the town, a stone's throw from the Gestapo HQ on the corner of rue Jeanne d'Arc and rue Dhavernas, where interrogation, torture and execution could take place far from prying French eyes, and in which the guards were exclusively German.* Amiens Prison, by contrast, was much more of a holding centre for the processing of prisoners. M. Heannot, the Divisional Superintendent of Police at the time of the Amiens raid, reported on 23 February 1944 that the prison held 700 prisoners on the eve of the attack, with 520 men and women in the criminal (French) section (448 men and 72 women), together with 190 men and women in the German-run section for 'political' or 'terrorist' prisoners. A report three days later suggested that the number was actually substantially higher: according to the Chief Warden's tally, on Friday 18 February there were 832 people in the prison, including 180 in the area managed directly by the Gestapo. Twenty-nine of these, including three women, were due to be executed on 19 February.

By January 1944 the northern region of Picardy was labouring under nearly its fourth full year of German occupation, its people suffering extensive shortages of food, fuel and medicine. Much of the countryside was cordoned off for security reasons as the occupiers began to prepare defences for the inevitable Allied invasion. Indeed, ever since its capture in May 1940, Amiens had straddled what the Germans called the North-East Line, the demarcation between occupied France and their 'Military Administration of Belgium and Northern France', an area of especial security interest since it lay closest to the English coast. The entire region had a military government, strict movement controls and tight policing.

Since late 1942 men of working age had been conscripted and sent to undertake forced labour in Germany, under a bitterly resented law brought in by Pierre Laval's Vichy government, the Service du Travail Obligatoire (STO). Men of working age not in

---

* The building now bears a commemorative tablet inscribed: *'En Souvenir des Résistants Torturés dans cette maison par les Nazis 1942-1944'*.

reserved occupations now lived their lives with one eye constantly over their shoulder, for fear of the draft. Many had already slipped into the underground, not necessarily acting as *résistants* but lying low and surviving on the largesse of their families and friends. A bitter winter compounded the general misery. Now, too, German eyes had refocused on the region because it was here that Hitler expected the major battle of the impending Allied invasion to take place. On 3 November 1943 Hitler published his Directive No. 51, in which he made his concerns clear:

The hard and costly struggle against Bolshevism during the last two and a half years, which has involved the bulk of our military strength in the East, has demanded extreme exertions. The greatness of the danger and the general situation demanded it. But the situation has since changed. The danger in the East remains, but a greater danger now appears in the West: an Anglo-Saxon landing! In the East, the vast extent of the territory makes it possible for us to lose ground, even on a large scale, without a fatal blow being dealt to the nervous system of Germany.

It is very different in the West! Should the enemy succeed in breaching our defences on a wide front here, the immediate consequences would be unpredictable. Everything indicates that the enemy will launch an offensive against the Western front of Europe, at the latest in the spring, perhaps even earlier.

I can therefore no longer take responsibility for further weakening the West, in favour of other theatres of war. I have therefore decided to reinforce its defences, particularly those places from which the long-range bombardment of England will begin [a reference to the impending V1 and V2 rocket offensive]. For it is here [i.e. in the Pas-de-Calais, where most of the V-weapons would be launched] that the enemy must and will attack, and it is here – unless all indications are misleading – that the decisive battle against the landing forces will be fought.

Even before the massive Allied deception plan – Operation *Fortitude South*, designed to persuade the Germans that the invasion, when it came, would come through the Pas-de-Calais – was fully under way, it is clear that Hitler was convinced that the Pas-de-Calais would be the location for the next Battle of France.

TWO

La résistance intérieure française

The instinctive desire of many men and women in Picardy to resist, saw Picardy become a hotbed of rebellion from almost the very first moment of the German occupation. Formal, structured and organised resistance (as distinct from the instinctive and unorganised revolt undertaken by individuals of their own accord) evidenced itself in a number of ways. The first was gathering military intelligence for one of the three Allied powers in the West (Britain, Free France and, after 1942, the USA). The second was sabotage and the third was providing assistance to Allied servicemen escaping from or evading the clutches of the enemy as they tried to make their way back to Britain.

During the war in France there was only such a thing as *la résistance française* in the most general sense, at least until the formation of de Gaulle's Forces Françaises Combattantes in 1943 and the Conseil National de la Résistance (CNR) that same year, and then the Forces Françaises de l'Intérieur, or FFI, in 1944. Many in France who were naturally inclined towards resistance struggled at first to find an expression for their opposition to the enemy occupation, lost in a confusing world that had seen all of its certainties removed with the invasion of 1940 and the humiliating armistice that followed.

The first year of German occupation was one, according to Gilbert Renault, when 'those who intended to resist ... were still groping for each other, not knowing yet how best to harm the

invader'. The dramatic social and political divisions in France at
the time, exacerbated by the confusion of defeat, mean that resistance, when it emerged, had many parents, and struggled for several
years to find a united voice. Kenneth Cohen of MI6 described the
early resisters as 'a minute elite (who became known to us as
vintage 1940)'. De Gaulle's movement based in London provided
one rallying cry, but his voice took a long time to be accepted as the
genuine or primary expression of French liberation. For some
people, especially on the left in France, as well as policymakers in
Washington, he never succeeded. A relatively junior officer, de
Gaulle was virtually unknown in 1940: his greatest challenge was
to persuade a cowed and divided nation that he had the right to
speak on their behalf. In particular, in 1940 the people of France
needed to know that they could place their trust in something
more than a phantom, when their existing political leadership – of
all shades and hues – had so spectacularly failed them.

But by the end of 1940 six underground newspapers were being
printed in the *Zone Occupée*, the first sign of public challenge to
the occupation. An example of an early *réseau*, begun in Paris in
the late summer 1940, was based upon a group of friends who
worked at the Musée de l'Homme, housed in the massive Palais de
Chaillot on the rue du Trocadéro overlooking the Seine. The first
efforts of this group, led by Anatole Lewitsky (an anthropologist),
Boris Vildé (a linguist, who had escaped early German captivity)
and Yvonne Oddon (the museum's librarian), were to disseminate
anti-German literature, produced on a printing press in the basement of the museum. This became the newspaper *Résistance*. It
was in this *réseau* that Pierre Brossolette first laboured in the cause
of the Gaullist underground.

In May 1941, the first SOE agent, Georges Bégué, was dropped
into central France near Châteauroux to begin the work of establishing a local network of London-supported *résistants*. Bégué
arrived, in fact, at a time when the first embryonic and locally
inspired *réseaux* were establishing themselves and finding their

feet – *Combat, Franc-Tireur* and *Libération (Sud)* in the south, and in the north the *Organisation Civile et Militaire, Libération (Nord)*, and *Ceux de la Résistance*, for example, all bringing together people from a wide variety of backgrounds, professions, economic status and political views into the business of creating the authentic voice of anti-German and anti-Vichy resistance. Numbers, though, remained small. One estimate of the total number of *résistants* in 1942 across France puts it at no more than 4,000.

Very little of the resistance undertaken in occupied France in 1940 and 1941 could be described as organised or formal. The small amount that took place did so as spontaneous reactions by individuals humiliated by German occupation and angered by the collaboration of their political masters. The most common involved individual acts of protest such as anonymous graffiti, vandalism of German and Vichy posters, the cutting of telephone and electricity lines and the slashing of tyres on unguarded military vehicles. On 13 August 1940, barely two months after the occupation had begun, a German sentry was shot dead outside the Hôtel Golf in Royan in Charente-Maritime. In reprisal, the German authorities rounded up several prominent citizens and imprisoned them indefinitely as hostages against the threat of further 'terrorism'. On 22 August, in Bordeaux, a 32-year-old docker, Raoul Amat, allowed himself to be caught slashing the tyres of a German truck, and was sentenced by a military court to thirteen months' imprisonment. Others merely shook their fists – and lost their lives for it. On Saturday 24 August, Leizer Karp, a refugee Polish Jew, shouted abuse at German military musicians playing near the Saint-Jean railway station in Bordeaux. Taken into custody, he was transported to Sougez camp and sentenced to death. He was shot two days later.

It was the German invasion of the Soviet Union in June 1941 and their subsequent occupation of the *Zone Libre* in November 1942 that was responsible more than anything else for turning the tide of French popular support towards the idea of formal, active resistance. Operation *Barbarossa* was especially significant, in that it solidified communist opposition to the occupation, prevented until then, on Moscow's explicit instructions, as a result of the Molotov–Ribbentrop pact. With this restriction lifted, direct action quickly grew, but mass protest failed miserably. The industrial region in the north was the centre of communist-inspired resistance after mid-1941, with a strike by coal miners in the Nord and Pas-de-Calais region between 27 May and 6 June. But the communists had badly misjudged the tenor of the German response: this was no benign occupation, as 250 miners discovered to their cost when they were forced at gunpoint into cattle trucks and transported to Sachsenhausen. Equally, the process of amalgamation or consolidation of the various resistance factions moved a lot faster after the German occupation of the *Zone Libre* in November 1942, which turned many towards active resistance, as people found solid, rational grounds for rejecting the collaborationist imperatives of the Vichy regime as well as the aggressively right-wing policies established by the dictatorship of Pétain's 'Etat Français'.

A number of assassinations of prominent Germans took place, which triggered vicious reprisals authorised from Berlin, Hitler insisting that a hundred Frenchmen be executed for every German killed by the Resistance. On 21 August 1941, Pierre-Georges Fabien of the French Communist Party's Francs-Tireurs et Partisans Français (FTPF) assassinated a German officer on the Paris Métro, and Colonel Karl Hotz, the Feldkommandant of Nantes, was shot dead on 20 October by a three-man FTPF hit squad. Dr Hans-Gottfried Reimers, a senior member of the Wehrmacht's civilian staff in Bordeaux, was shot dead on 21 October 1941 by a team of young communists who had travelled to Bordeaux by train from Paris for this purpose. The German response was savage: forty-eight hostages were shot on 22 October in reprisal for both attacks.

Most of the attacks and acts of sabotage carried out in France by the Resistance during 1941 and 1942 took place in north-eastern France. Between 1940 and 1944, the Germans shot 1,143 Frenchmen in Lille and the Arras Citadel alone. In the course of time it is estimated that some 30,000 *résistants* in France lost their lives, executed in France or deported to concentration camps in Germany, there to disappear without trace under the deliberate policy (*'Nacht und Nebel'*) of secret execution and the disposal of evidence (usually by cremation) ordered by Hitler on 7 December 1941 and carried out with alacrity and efficiency by the German state.*

Throughout 1943 the growing harshness of the occupation across France, together with the fear of the hated STO, drove large numbers of men and women into the arms of one sort or another of rebellion, some organised, some not, to resist forced deportation to Germany. These attitudes were reinforced by the rapid onset of economic penury in 1941 and 1942, caused in part by Germany's systematic pillaging of France's economy. The Abwehr's Sergeant Hugo Bleicher, the nemesis of many Resistance networks between 1942 and 1944, observed during 1941 the 'strong and instinctive opposition of the inhabitants to the invader'. He should not have been surprised. In 1942 he commented on the obvious strengthening of the resistance movements, as organisations that were previously disparate joined together, supported by drops of arms and the arrival of leaders, radio transmitters and equipment from Britain. The challenge for French people was to decide when to move from passive acceptance of the status quo in their country to active resistance. In 1942, with the Germans strongly in the ascendant even after two years of war, it remained uncertain to any but the most committed *résistant* whether anything other than resigned acquiescence to the new rulers of France was worthwhile. The Allies remained too weak for the prospect of liberation to be anything other than a pipe dream.

---

* See Appendix 2.

In 1941 and 1942 three London-based organisations sought to develop resistance networks in France: SOE, MI6 and the Free French BCRA. These three were joined in 1943 by the American Office of Strategic Services (OSS), the forerunner of the CIA. Each organisation had its own purpose for engaging in underground activity in France, the two primary activities undertaken being the securing of intelligence, and sabotage. From the outset degrees of friction existed between each of these organisations, although by far and away the most fractious relationship was between SOE and MI6. SOE had been established not to compete with MI6 but to undertake tasks that were not part of the latter's mandate (which was to acquire and interpret secret intelligence), especially acts of sabotage. The purpose of SOE was to fight an irregular or partisan-type war from inside enemy territory. It aimed to sow discord amongst subject peoples abroad, to commit sabotage and acts of murder against the Nazi armies of occupation across Europe.

According to Major Maurice Buckmaster, who joined SOE in March 1941 and who went on in September to become head of F Section, the objective of SOE was to do the Germans harm:

> Our role at Special Operations Headquarters was not that of spy-masters, but of active and belligerent planners of operations to be carried out in advance of the Allied landings. The usual picture of an agent is of a man lying up and watching enemy movements and reporting them back to his home base, in short an essentially passive under-cover man. The agents of SOE were essentially active.

SOE had a number of separate parts. Those relating to France comprised Buckmaster's F Section, an all-British operation working from offices in Baker Street, while RF Section, operating out of offices in Dorset Square, worked exclusively with the BCRA. The latter in consequence enjoyed an indirect relationship with MI6, something that could not be said for F Section. These two sections of SOE enjoyed limited operational crossover.*

SOE had been deliberately kept apart from the Foreign Office (and thus MI6) by Winston Churchill, who had recognised perhaps that his idea of 'setting Europe ablaze' by means of guerrilla activity and sabotage, a very un-British approach to war, might not survive long in the hands of a traditionally minded Foreign Office. Although the SOE had fortnightly meetings with MI6 in an attempt to coordinate the affairs of both organisations, the Foreign Office (under the leadership of Anthony Eden, the Foreign Secretary) had always opposed Churchill's move to establish an organisation designed to prosecute clandestine sabotage and subversion behind enemy lines and to operate outside the direct control of the Secret Intelligence Service. Part of MI6's fundamental conceit was to imagine that intelligence was the only valid product of underground activity, and to refuse to cooperate as fully as the military situation demanded with the necessary existence – at least so long as the war continued – of both organisations. Nevertheless, the reverse accusation can be made, which was that SOE paid too little heed to the necessary requirement to secure military intelligence through use of the underground, only paying apparent interest in blowing things up. These mindsets do not sit easily together.

The communist hit-and-run type actions of 1941 were not typical of formalised resistance, and although sabotage played an important role in many *réseau* operations, particularly those supported by the SOE, and especially against railways, by far the most significant activity from 1941 until Operation *Overlord* in June 1944 was the gathering of intelligence. It was this activity that principally concerned MI6, and the BCRA was involved in both, with inevitable tensions arising out of these widely different roles. Despite the agreement between MI6 and SOE in September 1941

---

* There were in fact six French sections in SOE by 1944. In addition to F and RF, there were also EU/P (Poles), DF (escape lines), AL (air liaison) and AMF (Algiers).

that, in Keith Jeffery's words, 'all of SOE's cypher communications would run through SIS, that intelligence collected by SOE would be passed on to SIS and that SIS's approval would be sought when engaging agents', it was precisely these areas that provided the basis for friction. Jealousy undoubtedly played a part. The fact that the 'amateurs' in SOE proved to be as successful as MI6 in mounting operations could not have helped. Indeed, the overall success of SOE strengthened the general argument that the Resistance networks across France needed support, protection and encouragement, despite their origin or the nature of their London-based sponsor and their specific rationale and mode of operations.

SOE achievements were indeed impressive. In Sir Charles Hambro's quarterly report to the Prime Minister in October 1942 relating to the period between July and September of that year, the Director of SOE reported that occupied Europe was 'seething with the spirit of revolt and revolution'.* In his next report, in January 1943, he described the spirit of resistance as growing daily stronger, and SOE as continuing 'to stoke the furnace'. In the anti-German turmoil across occupied Europe, in which he listed 226 attacks on Axis or collaborationist premises and personnel, 104 train derailments and acts of railways sabotage, 155 general acts of incendiarism, and 53 acts of sabotage in factories or against public services, he claimed that 'S.O.E. have been the moving spirit'. This was clearly hyperbole (much of his information was gleaned from reading newspapers published in the occupied territories), but SOE's capacity to strike was developing fast. Sabotage attacks on the railways became a hallmark of resistance operations, the number of such operations reaching an average of twenty per day by the end of 1943.

In the earlier quarter Hambro recorded that 52 agents had been dropped into enemy territory, along with 298 containers carrying 300 pounds each of arms and explosive, together with six 50-pound

---

* Hambro had replaced Sir Frank Nelson as executive head of SOE earlier in 1942.

packages of stores and 137 radio transmitter sets. By the start of October 1942 SOE had sent into the field 458 agents; 643 were fully trained and awaiting assignment, and a further 734 men and women were undergoing training. By January 1943 Hambro was able to report that the number of agents in the field had risen threefold (to 150), and 347 containers of arms and explosives had been dropped, together with a further 187 radio transmitters. Between January and June 1943, there were 130 acts of sabotage against rail lines each month across France, many of them undertaken or supported by SOE manpower, training and explosives. By September 1943 the number of attacks had increased to 530, and between April and May, as D-Day approached, the Resistance destroyed 1,800 railway engines.

It is no surprise therefore that the agreement reached between the Allies in late 1943 was that the French Resistance, controlled by what later became the FFI, was to play a significant role in sabotage operations against the German lines of communication across northern France in support of Operation *Overlord* the following year. These plans ultimately entailed a series of comprehensive and coordinated attacks against railways, power and telecommunication installations, ammunition depots, command posts, fuel depots and vehicle traffic. It was critical therefore to ensure that the Resistance movement was in as fine fettle as was possible before D-Day. In the event, the effect of Resistance attacks on the Germans was, by every account, significant. Churchill considered that, in Brittany at least: 'The French Resistance Movement, which here numbered 30,000 men, played a notable part, and the peninsula was quickly overrun.' General Dwight D. Eisenhower observed at the end of the war:

Throughout France, the Free French had been of inestimable value in the campaign. They were particularly active in Brittany, but on every portion of the front we secured help from them in a multitude of ways. Without their great assistance, the liberation of

France and the defeat of the enemy in Western Europe would
have consumed a much longer time and meant greater losses to
ourselves.

Both the SOE and the BCRA undertook the construction of new
resistance networks, as well as supporting those that were home-
grown, while MI6 worked successfully to replace the intelligence
contacts that had been lost as a result of the German invasion in
1940, although this took time. In this process an important source
remained the old Deuxième Bureau, the military intelligence
branch of the French General Staff, resurrected to serve Vichy, and
populated in the main by men who, although invariably right-
wing, were strongly opposed to Germany. Consequently, for the
most part the revived Deuxième Bureau worked assiduously
against German interests in the *Zone Libre* until the French occupation of this remaining part of France following Operation *Torch*
on 11 November 1942.

Consequently the support of Vichy's secret service proved of
incalculable benefit to the Allies. It did so not primarily on behalf
of the Allies, but to assert the autonomy and authority of Vichy.
The man in MI6 responsible for maintaining these relationships
was Commander Wilfred ('Biffy') Dunderdale, a career SIS agent
and talented mid-European linguist who until 1940 had been SIS's
station chief in Paris. Through Dunderdale, MI6 remained in close
touch with what remained of the French intelligence service in
what is still an almost entirely forgotten aspect of MI6 operations
in France, especially with men who played a role in the Amiens
affair, such as Colonel Georges-André Groussard, Major Gustave
Bertrand and Captain Paul Paillole.

The issue of Vichy's collaboration with Germany was much
more complicated than a simple matter of 'de Gaulle good, Vichy
bad': a number of significant *résistants* in the period through to the
end of 1942 were also anti-Nazi members of the Vichy regime. The
Germans established a considerable espionage operation against

Vichy following the armistice, primarily to maintain control of their defeated foe, and the French had their work cut out to keep on top of this activity. Colonel Louis Rivet, head of the Deuxième Bureau since 1936, together with Captain Paillole, Colonel Groussard and other members of the counter-intelligence service, met at the Seminary of Bon-Encontre near Agen after the fall of France in 1940, with the purpose of reviving French counter-intelligence to resist German domination. The organisation they created – the Bureau des Menées Antinationales (Bureau of Anti-national Activities, BMA), disguised as the Entreprise des Travaux Ruraux – was accepted by the Germans under the terms of the armistice, but was in fact a cover for the pursuit of those actively collaborating with the Germans. Paillole was placed in charge of this organisation, and when it was dissolved in November 1942, remained in command of its (secret) replacement.

The BMA proved to be remarkably successful. It has been estimated that over 2,000 individuals were arrested by Vichy for pro-German intelligence activity between 1940 and 1942. An example of the continued independence of Vichy in matters of state security during this period was the execution of Henri Devillers. He had been arrested in February 1942 by Vichy police on the charge of having infiltrated a Gaullist *réseau* (*Combat*) on behalf of the Abwehr. His plea for clemency was turned down by Pétain himself, and he was executed on 19 June. Most of the leading Vichy-employed officers associated with the BMA were simultaneously working for MI6 through Biffy Dunderdale. When the American Allen Dulles began espionage operations in earnest in Berne in 1942, as OSS station chief, it was to members of the Deuxième Bureau that he first turned, the introductions having been made by MI6. In 1963, he acknowledged the importance of MI6, the BCRA and the BMA, commenting guardedly:

I had the privilege of working with the British service [i.e. MI6] and developed close personal and service relationships which remained intact after the war. In Switzerland I made contact with a group of French officers who had maintained the tradition of the French Deuxième Bureau and who helped to build up the intelligence service of General de Gaulle and the Free French.

The birth of de Gaulle's Free French intelligence agency, the BCRA, began with the arrival in London in June 1940 of a young army officer, André Dewavrin (codenamed *Passy*), who presented himself in front of de Gaulle asking for a job.* With no intelligence background, he was nevertheless put straight to work to create de Gaulle's eyes and ears across occupied France. Cunning and sharp-witted, yet pragmatic and approachable, he was the perfect appointment.

The first place Dewavrin turned for assistance was MI6: he had no resources or experience of his own. As with the espionage organisations of other refugee states that turned to him for help, Claude Dansey, assistant chief of MI6, recognised the benefits to both parties of an arrangement that gave British financial and logistical support to a Free French espionage network, in exchange for access to the intelligence thus provided. He nevertheless recognised that results would take time to appear, not least because of de Gaulle's low standing in France (a fact that the Foreign and Commonwealth Office were eager to emphasise), and took the energetic young Dewavrin under his wing. In fact, the older Englishman struck up an unusual rapport with the younger Frenchman, and the two men worked in close alignment for the remainder of the war, operating successfully at the level of planning and delivery of espionage and, in the BCRA's case also of sabotage operations. Churchill and de Gaulle signed the agreement to work together in this way on 7 August 1940.

* Initially called the Service de Renseignements (SR) when it was exclusively an intelligence-gathering organisation, it changed its name to Bureau Central de Renseignements et d'Action Militaire (BCRAM) on 15 April 1941 when it added sabotage to its repertoire, shortening it to BCRA on 17 January 1942.

Dewavrin appointed Captain André Manuel (*Pallas*) in command of the intelligence branch (Renseignements [R]), which was to be the link with Dansey's organisation.* Thus began a close and mutually profitable association between the Free French and MI6 which survived the various storms that swept the relationship between de Gaulle and Churchill, through the strength of the rapport created between the aging British spymaster and his young French protégé. In his memoirs Dewavrin expressed his debt to Dansey in fulsome terms:

I was fortunate to have a teacher who saved me from many a pitfall and trap . . . He was one of the pillars of that famous organisation for almost thirty years. He saw everything, he knows everything. To me, at first, he was a master beyond compare; he soon became a friend. He had a shrewd and sceptical intellect, he was admired for his merit and feared by his subordinates for his stinging or scornful comments . . .

Good old 'Uncle Claude', how can I thank you enough? You were always there to curb the ventures that were too risky. You always pointed out the snags and dangers along the way – spotted immediately by your greatly experienced eye.

Within MI6 the staff officer given responsibility for managing the new relationship was Kenneth Cohen, who had worked for Dansey in MI6 since retiring from the Royal Navy as a Lieutenant Commander in 1935. Dansey introduced Dewavrin to SOE,

* Four subsequent sections were added as follows: (1) 'Military Action' in April 1941, commanded by Captain Raymond Lagier (*Bienvenue*) and Fred Scamaroni, which worked alongside the RF Section of SOE; (2) 'Counter-espionage' in December 1941, commanded by Roger Warin (*Roger Wybot*) and Stanislas Mangin, working with MI5; (3) 'Evasion' in February 1942, commanded by Lieutenant Roger Mitchell, a French officer of Scottish descent, working with MI9; and (4) 'Political' in August 1942, commanded by Jacques Bingen, Jean-Pierre Bloch and Louis Vallon.

through the medium of its Executive Director, Frank Nelson, in 1941, and it was this relationship that created the RF Section of SOE, especially dedicated to the work of the Free French, and entirely separate from Buckmaster's F Section. It meant that MI6's influence in general, and Dansey's hand in particular, could be felt deeply across the BCRA and SOE; Dansey was effectively in operational control of the BCRA across the whole of its intelligence operations in France.

The BCRA probably grew faster and delivered better results than even Dansey could have expected. By late 1943 the relationship between the BCRA and MI6 was viewed by London as essential to the future success of the invasion of Europe. This was demonstrated strongly by a message sent by 'C' to Harold Macmillan, then the British Minister of State in Algiers, concerned lest the political developments that were then leading towards closer relations between the two great factions of French resistance to German occupation, General Henri Giraud and General Charles de Gaulle (seen in the establishment of the newly formed French Committee of National Liberation in Algiers), might in fact lead to a perverse consequence for London in that it could turn off the BCRA tap that had poured intelligence to MI6 since 1940. In his note to Macmillan 'C' quoted a letter he had received from the Director of Military Intelligence at the War Office 'saying that the intelligence supplied by this joint French–British service has been of greatest value to General Staff particularly during last month' and added that the War Office 'would view with great misgiving any action which might interfere with our relations with BCRA and perhaps decrease the flow of military information'.

One of the first of his countrymen across the threshold of Dewavrin's office in London, within weeks of his own arrival, was a middle-aged patriot desperate to contribute in an active way to the war effort, Gilbert Renault. A father of five, Renault had been working in the French film business when the outbreak of war put paid to his plans, and he made his way to London to continue the fight when France fell. On the face of it he had little to offer Dewavrin, although he had the advantage of having a Spanish visa in his passport, and it was this that resulted in his immediate dispatch to France via Spain in mid-August 1940. He was, to Dewavrin, an unknown quantity.

For several months there was silence from the first Free French secret agent sent back to France, and it is fair to assume that this caused a certain despondency in the BCRA's headquarters in St Stephen's House, just behind MI6's offices in Broadway.* Then, on 1 December 1940, a heavy parcel landed on Dewavrin's desk. It was *Rémy*'s (Renault's codename) first dispatch, reconstituted from the microfilm in which it had travelled out of France and quickly labelled RZ1 – 'R' for Renault, 'Z' for Correspondence. It was a gold mine, but it didn't stop there. It was the start of an extraordinary mass of intelligence that flowed back to London over the next fourteen months, a hoard that included a full set of 'General Staff' maps from the official cartography office in Paris.

During this time Renault sent a total of thirty-nine bulky consignments. Much of the information it contained still sits in the National Archives in Kew, filling out thick manila envelopes in a wide range of different files, providing information about a variety of targets, from German battleships in Brest to the radar station at Bruneval and the massive dry dock at Saint-Nazaire. In the months since he returned to France, Renault had been busy recruiting and establishing agents along the length and breadth of the French Atlantic coast, with watchers in Bordeaux, Brest, Quiberon, Lorient, La Pallice and Mérignac (Bordeaux's airport), which already boasted a sizeable Luftwaffe bomber force.

What he didn't have, however, was a means of communicating quickly with London. This was a real problem in 1941, when information had to be transported by sea, using fishing vessels

---

* This was also originally de Gaulle's' HQ. In May 1943 the BCRA moved to 10 Duke Street, in the West End.

setting out from Breton ports under German noses. It was a further nine months before six bulky radio transmitters, provided by Claude Dansey, were in operation to support Renault's *réseau Confrérie Notre-Dame (CND)*, which by the end of 1941 stretched from Bayonne to the Pas-de-Calais.* All of the six MI6-provided transmitters were hidden in Paris. Messages for collecting supplies were made after March 1943 by radio to a BCRA collecting unit, the Bureau des Opérations Aériennes (BOA). Following approval by MI6 the requests were sent to the Air Ministry, who would then task one of the Special Duties squadrons. By 1943 these were 138 and 161 Squadron, flying out of the newly built RAF Tempsford in Bedfordshire and RAF Tangmere in Sussex. They also sent coded messages to the BBC's French-language service for broadcast.

In some cases, transmitters were built in France. One such became operational from the Château La Roque, north-east of Bordeaux, overlooking the Dordogne, where it was hidden, in February 1941. One of the originators of this branch of the *réseau CND* was Louis de la Bardonnie, who recalled: 'When our radio links were established with London, I went every week to Bordeaux and returned each time with a richer harvest.' From the outset of the occupation, two experienced river pilots working for the Port of Bordeaux, Jean Fleuret and Marie-Ange Gaudin, provided information to London about shipping activity in the Gironde through letters that were smuggled to Spain or into the unoccupied zone. The men knew the tiniest movement along the river:

Not only did they serve as pilots for many cargo ships, submarines and submarine support vessels, but they kept London fully informed of troop movements, the establishment of fortifications on the coast, the activities of aerodromes, those factories and

---

* Radio traffic was collected at MI6's listening station at Whaddon Hall, and the material sent to Bletchley Park for analysis.

construction sites working for the enemy: nothing escaped their vigilance.

It is absolutely no exaggeration to say that nothing worthwhile remained unreported to the Allies. To achieve these results, Gaudin had recruited his son, Mark, together with a number of local agents, particularly young people, mad with audacity, who penetrated everywhere, saw everything and found out everything.

This radio was able to replace the need for a courier, the 27-year-old Laure Gatet, to carry sensitive information across the frontier into Spain.* She was strip-searched each time she travelled from Perpignan across the demarcation line at Sainte-Foy-la-Grande, hiding the letters she carried in bottles of caustic soda. However, the antenna of Gaudin's radio was betrayed to the Germans in June 1942. He and his son escaped arrest, but Fleuret was caught and deported to Buchenwald.† Louis de la Bardonnie had been arrested in December 1941 and held at a camp near Mérignac, but was released in early 1942 for lack of evidence.

Renault based himself in Paris, hiding in the anonymity of the city, where he was able to coordinate, after a fashion, the activities of the hundred or so agents he had in place by the autumn of 1941. At its peak *CND* grew to around 2,000 agents. Renault was the stand-out BCRA agent of the war in terms of the extent and usefulness of the intelligence-gathering network he was able to establish under his *réseau Confrérie Notre-Dame*. Such was his success that Claude Dansey described him as 'the greatest spy I have ever known', praise indeed from one of Britain's least known but most successful spymasters. When MI6 required intelligence to prepare for the parachute raid on Bruneval in February 1942, for instance,

---

* Laure Gatet was betrayed to the Germans, and died at Auschwitz on 25 February 1943.
† He survived the war.

it was Renault's men who undertook the close reconnaissance of the target. Although Renault had not yet met Dansey at this point they did so shortly after the raid, both men getting on extremely well, their relationship setting the seal on the growing link between the BCRA and MI6. From 1942 Passy gave *Rémy* responsibility for building intelligence-gathering networks across the whole of France, a task he undertook as Operation *Overlord* approached. Captain Pierre Julitte (*Robin*) arrived in France by Lysander on 10 May 1941 and supervised the work of the radio operators – *pianistes* in espionage parlance – for three BCRA/MI6 *réseaux*, including Renault's *CND*, Pierre Fourcaud's (*Bombshell*) *Lucas* network, and Maurice Duclos's (*Saint-Jacques*) network.

The initially disparate self-generated resistance networks across France began the slow process of unification as early as 1941, with three powerful groups in the *Zone Libre* – *Combat* (under Henri Frenay), *Libération-Sud* (Emmanuel d'Astier de la Vigerie), and *Liberté* (François de Menthon) – coming together that year. There were political and indeed organisational advantages to these moves, but they were undertaken often at the expense of security, a factor that the Germans were quick to exploit. By 1943, through the work of men such as Jean Moulin, Christian Pineau and Pierre Brossolette, most of these organisations had agreed to work more or less together under the aegis of de Gaulle's Conseil National de la Résistance (CNR). The communist networks remained unaffiliated, but this did not seem to detract from their energy or effectiveness in the field.

The CNR had in fact come about as a result of the far-sightedness and advocacy of Jean Moulin, a remarkable political leader and *résistant* and originator of *Combat*, who made his way to London via Lisbon in September 1941. De Gaulle was initially nervous about agreeing to an operational or war-fighting role for a unified Resistance in France (beyond the gathering of intelligence) because of the political threat to his developing 'Gaullist' movement posed by strong communist representation. He was persuaded to change

his mind by Jean Moulin. Previously a *préfet* of the Eure-et-Loir
department, the Germans ejected him from office in November
1940, after which he – having never previously met de Gaulle –
preached the notion of active (i.e. both political and military)
resistance to Pétain and Vichy to each and every clandestine
network he could find across the *Zone Libre*. To Moulin the concept
of 'political' resistance meant unified resistance, built around the
twin imperatives of political *and* military action.

In London, even de Gaulle was impressed with Moulin's clear-
sightedness, although critics would always aver that unity was a
policy intended to facilitate de Gaulle's seizure of power when
France was liberated. Active resistance would take time, was potentially dangerous and even counter-productive in the short term
(because of the potential for German reprisals against innocent
civilians and because of the weakening of small, self-contained
réseaux when they began to work together), but it was only through
an armed struggle that the authentic voice of French resistance to
Nazi occupation could be articulated. Equally, the armed struggle
needed to be the physical arm of a unified Resistance, or else it
would be mere brigandry, and a unified Resistance movement
entailed a political idea and political control. If de Gaulle did not
provide this political idea and exercise this control, the communists would, and the underground war in France would be won –
and the post-war political future dominated – by the organisation
best able to provide the leadership and discipline required.

Moulin argued convincingly that a failure to act across both
spheres – through politics and by military action – would create a
dangerous vacuum that only the fantastically well organised and
ruthlessly efficient Communist Party would be able to exploit, and
which, once the Germans had been ejected from France, only civil
war would resolve. Accordingly, the Free French leader agreed to
Moulin's suggestion to form the CNR. It would have a political
structure, led in France by Moulin himself, while the military
structure – the so-called Secret Army – would be commanded by

General Charles Delestraint (*Vidal*), a retired officer called back to the ranks, to prepare the newly unified Resistance to take up arms when the time came.

The process of persuading these groups to cooperate and then welding the disparate networks together was undertaken by Moulin, Pierre Brossolette and the remarkable SOE (RF Section) agent Wing Commander Tommy Yeo-Thomas (*Shelley*, but known to the Germans by his other codename, 'White Rabbit'). It took place during the spring of 1943. Initially all went well. On 2 March Dewavrin and Brossolette met with Colonel Alfred Touny (*Lacroix*) of the *OCM* in Paris, the former head of the military intelligence branch of the French Fourth Army, who agreed to coordinate forty or so of the disparate networks across northern France. A separate *réseau* was established to do this, *Century*, run by Touny's deputy, Marcel Berthelot.

In the months that followed Moulin wooed the leaders of four other movements similar to Touny's *OCM* – Jacques Lecompte-Boinet of *Ceux de la Résistance*, Roger Coquoin of *Ceux de la Libération*, Jacques Brunschwig (*Périgny*) of *Libération*, and the Communist Roger Ginsberger (*Pierre Villon*) of *Front National*. During these discussions Brossolette visited Normandy, Yeo-Thomas went south and André Dewavrin visited the *réseaux* in the Somme area, meeting the *résistants* in a number of organisations in and around the town of Amiens, some of whom eight months later would play a leading role in requesting, and then planning for, the attack on Amiens Prison. Once the initial plans had been made, Dewavrin, Yeo-Thomas and Brossolette returned to London by Lysander on 16 April from a field near Lyons-la-Forêt, 80 miles south-west of Amiens.

THREE

MI6 offensive intelligence
operations in France

Offensive intelligence operations by the Allies (as opposed to counter-espionage, the business of tracking down enemy spies) in France in 1941 and 1942 using French-based *réseaux*, like the resistance movement as a whole during this period, can best be described as nascent. Most formal resistance organisations did not reach their apogee until 1944, while many that flowered in 1943 did so briefly, cut down in their eager prime by a ruthless and brutally efficient German counter-espionage machine that made the most of the youthful naivety of many *résistants* and the disparate and disorganised nature of their resistance. The imperative to come together in a single movement, whilst good for political and military unity, had the unfortunate result of destroying the very secrecy that was the only real guarantor of a network's security.

However, there were early flowerings of resistance, and dramatic successes for some of these organisations in the relatively early days of the war. The comprehensive material that was secured by subterfuge from under German noses about the French Atlantic ports in 1940 and 1941, for example, provides astonishing evidence of the complexity of early resistance capabilities at what is generally considered to have been a relatively unfruitful period in the history of resistance in France. At this early stage intelligence was secured by courageous individual men and women, some of whom were in the pay of British, Polish and Free French intelligence services, but many of whom were not, and who did what they did for private motives, or simply for no other reason than for *la gloire de la France* at a time when the omens for eventual victory, given the seemingly superhuman powers of both the Nazi state and its war machine, were so few as to seem to many non-existent.

Some of the earliest, most energetic and most successful intelligence-gatherers on the Allied side were the Poles, the residue of the close links between Poland and France in the inter-war years; some were sponsored by MI6, some by de Gaulle's BCRA and some by SOE. Others were entirely self-made, the spontaneous eruption of resistance to the occupiers by men and women outraged at their sudden loss of liberty, and the violent repression of their freedoms by a wholly assertive and sometimes (but increasingly) violent Germanic totalitarianism. Whatever its view of perfidious Albion or of pre-war political differences between Left and Right, Church and State, Gallic pride needed very little patriotic motivation when confronted by the sight of polished jackboots strutting over ancient French cobbles.

By early 1944, however, the situation had changed dramatically. Despite savage German counter-measures during 1943 in which thousands of *résistants* were rounded up and imprisoned, deported to an uncertain fate in Germany or put to death*, a range of intelligence-gathering *réseaux* working for MI6 provided critical eyes and ears on the ground in France during the preparations for D-Day, as well as countering the threat to London from Hitler's V-weapons. There is a very strong case for arguing that what we know loosely as 'the French Resistance', but especially that part interested in the gathering of intelligence (as opposed to those intent merely on murder and mayhem), can be described as the 'fourth arm' of the Allied military effort alongside more traditional forms of endeavour on land, in the sea and in the air, and had an especial impact during the first six months of 1944.

---

* See Chapter Six.

Since 1940 the Germans had relied for their regular transmissions not on wireless traffic but on the fixed lines of the French pre-war telephone network, which meant that *Ultra*, the Allies' secret signals intelligence decryption service, had limited utility in France at the time. Although Allied bombing included attacks on these networks in order to force the Germans to communicate by radio, very little fruitful material had been secured as a consequence. The role of secret intelligence, using agents on the ground reporting back to London by radio, therefore remained crucial in the France of late 1943 and early 1944. Indeed, if it were not for MI6's active *réseaux* in northern France in early 1944, British operational planners would have been virtually blind to German intentions and activity in the run-up to Operation *Overlord*, reliant only on aerial reconnaissance which, for all the advances of photography, techniques and interpretation, still remained at the mercy of the clouds.

The man responsible for running MI6 operations in France was a professional spymaster, the Assistant Chief of SIS – Lieutenant Colonel Claude Edward Marjoribanks Dansey. For obvious reasons he was considerably less well known in public (and to history) than his colleagues in arguably the more glamorous side of the business, Major General Colin Gubbins and Colonel Maurice Buckmaster of SOE. Dansey, a short, balding bespectacled friend of Winston Churchill, deliberately spent his life in the shadows, hiding behind the extensive variety of networks he and his team built up across Europe almost from scratch following the devastation caused to the traditional SIS structures after the declaration of war and the Venlo Incident in 1939. 'Uncle Claude', as Dansey was known to those who worked for him, was sixty-eight in 1944. He spent most of his life as a bachelor. A tough, hard exterior concealed a man of extensive experience in spy-craft and of surprising personal tenderness, sentimentality perhaps, for women. His reputation as a sociopath, a blunt and unforgiving taskmaster, a misogynist bully even, was in part the external but shallow armour that shrouded a man of otherwise well-hidden sensitivity who detested the bureaucratic incompetence and rank amateurism that he believed characterised organised British espionage in the years before the war.

Not everyone saw through the hard shell with which Dansey armoured himself, and in several quarters his legendary toughness, which some have equated to brutality, is all that remains. The historian Hugh Trevor-Roper (later Lord Dacre), who worked for MI6 during the war, famously described him, for example, as 'an utter shit; corrupt, incompetent, but with a certain low cunning', although Malcolm Muggeridge defended him as being the 'only real professional in MI6'. The traitor Kim Philby touched closely on the truth when he acknowledged Dansey's single-minded focus during the war on the application of intelligence to defeat the German armies in the field: 'He was an elderly gentleman of austerely limited outlook who regarded counter-espionage as a waste of effort in wartime, and lost no opportunity in saying so.' Guy Liddell, head of MI5's counter-espionage (B) division, held similar views with regard to the relative importance of 'counter-' as opposed to 'offensive' espionage and Dansey's interest only in the latter.* Keith Jeffery quotes Kenneth Cohen describing Dansey in a more balanced way perhaps as 'a "copybook" secret service man. Dapper, establishment, Boodles, poker-playing expression, bitterly cynical, but with unlimited and illogical charm available, especially for women.'

Anthony Read and David Fisher demonstrate in their biography of Dansey just why it is an error to dismiss him simply because of his marked sociopathology, and quote Dewavrin, who told them that Dansey was 'the most professional intelligence officer I ever met'. His motivations and behaviour were complex, but rooted in a determination to ensure that his part of MI6 at least conducted itself with the utmost professionalism. Determined to protect the prerogatives of intelligence against the brash usurpers in SOE, he

---

* TNA, KV 4/189, 16 January 1942. Volume five of the diary kept by Guy Liddell.

was certainly a hardened pragmatist in his approach to questions both of policy and of operations. He considered that allowing SOE to operate in parallel to MI6, and to carry out acts of sabotage, put at risk the work of the latter, especially if the two were not jointly orchestrated. This antipathy to SOE's rationale and its methods was the source of Dansey's reputation for being at best anti-SOE and at worst (and more fancifully) a deliberate saboteur of SOE operations. His influence reached far, not least to the USA, where during the pre-war years he proved to be a formative influence on Colonel Bill Donovan, the architect of the OSS.

Read and Fisher quote Dewavrin's memoirs to illustrate Dansey's fabled harshness. In early 1943, when Dewavrin was visiting France:

> . . . he found the whole Paris network in a state of uproar. The Germans had clamped down in the city; travel had become extremely difficult. This meant that some ninety Allied evaders and escapers were trapped in the city, unable to move south along the usual escape lines. They were young, high-spirited, and bored with the discomfort of hiding out in attics and cellars. Many of them grew careless; some left their hiding places and went for walks and even visited cafés and clubs, while waiting to be moved. Their Resistance hosts were horrified. It only needed one man to be stopped by the police and questioned and the whole network could be in jeopardy. The Resistance workers turned to Dewavrin for advice: what could they do? They had no authority over the men. Dewavrin radioed Dansey. After all, most of the men were British and American, and M19 was his responsibility. Dansey's reply was short and to the point. It consisted only of two words: 'Kill them'. Fortunately the Germans relaxed their grip on the city before Dewavrin had to decide whether to follow Dansey's advice.

Whatever one thinks of him as a person – and he certainly divided opinion – the dramatic success that Dansey was able to achieve in terms of the creation and maintenance of a multitude of intelligence networks across France during the toughest days of the war is not in doubt. Major General Sir Stewart Menzies has often been assigned the glory for these achievements, but in the breadth of their conception (full integration with the Free French secret service especially, and the pragmatic exploitation of secret relationships with anti-Nazi officers working for the Vichy regime) and the detail of their management in the face of continuous attack by the Gestapo, Abwehr and others, it was Dansey, the man in the shadows, who deserves the laurels for most if not all that MI6 achieved in wartime France.

What he and MI6 accomplished came as a result of a remarkable connection between the Secret Intelligence Service and the Free French. Indeed, the interaction between both organisations, and between the men who ran both, unlike those between their respective political leaders, remained close and harmonious, even intimate, throughout the war. In particular, André Dewavrin, head of the BCRA, the Free French equivalent of both SIS and SOE, and his primary subordinate from 1942, Colonel Gilbert Renault (*Rémy*), could be described as close friends, as well as trusted colleagues, of Dansey, Cohen, and what became the 'P1' team (which dealt exclusively with secret intelligence networks in France) within MI6. Evidence of this closeness can be seen in the fact that at the war's end Renault was awarded both the DSO and the OBE by the British government, recommended by MI6, and Dominique Ponchardier – the leader of an important MI6-managed *réseau* in northern France, and the man principally responsible for urging MI6 to launch an attack on Amiens Prison – the MBE. In an interview in 1946 Ponchardier observed that 'everyone more or less directly worked for MI6 for the duration of the war' and that 'Passy's attempt to organise an independent BCRA was "a joke" [as] all of the information, the messages given to its agents by Passy passed obligatorily through MI6.'

*

Dansey was supported by a small number of men who had responsibility for discrete groups of *réseaux* across France. His pre-war organisation had been in two parts, the first based on agents working as Passport Control Officers within the diplomatic service, the second built around what was known as the Z organisation, agents operating under the cover of commercial interests, some of them genuine – a modus operandi Dansey always believed to be more secure than the old diplomatic cover, which had been blown long ago. In the years immediately preceding the war Kenneth Cohen had been responsible for the Z organisation in Europe. With the codename of Z1 (Dansey was 'Z') and the *nom de guerre* of Keith Crane, Cohen built up a network of businessmen and journalists who had reason to travel extensively across Europe, including the film director Alexander Korda, Frederick Voight, the Central European correspondent of the *Manchester Guardian*, and Sigismund Best, a businessman living in The Hague who was married to the daughter of a Dutch admiral.

At the onset of the German invasion of France and the Low Countries in 1940 and the destruction of the pre-war MI6 organisation, Dansey's distributed espionage network across Europe was the only part that survived, regrouping in the first instance in Switzerland. Its members included Major Frederick ('Fanny') van den Heuvel, Victor Farrell, an experienced MI6 officer who had been previously based in Budapest, and Andrew King (Z2), whose cover involved working for Alexander Korda. Van den Heuvel was appointed station chief in Geneva, while Victor Farrell was given the cover of press attaché at the British Embassy in Berne, where he joined the air attaché, Air Commodore Freddie West, VC, MC, and the military attaché, Colonel H. A. Cartwright, MC. Lancelot de Garston was vice-consul in Lugarno while Tim Frenken was based in Basle.

The team in Berne led by Farrell was to have much to do with the French-based intelligence *réseaux* of MI6 and the growing number of escape lines (*réseaux d'évasion*) coordinated by MI9, a branch of MI6, considered in more detail in chapter 4. Neville

Wylie suggests that 'there were probably a dozen SIS regulars working in Switzerland during the war, the majority masquerading either as press attachés or vice consuls.' It was MI6's intimate involvement in the development of several phenomenally successful *réseaux* in north-eastern France in late 1943 and early 1944, supported from both London and Switzerland, that was to play an important role in supporting the request by MI6 for the raid on Amiens Prison.

In terms of specifically offensive intelligence, Dansey ran a series of complex networks across occupied France that proved in due course to be of incalculable value to the security of Britain during the war and to the undoing of German plans, and which are still little known or appreciated today. The discovery of the real purpose of Peenemünde, the location and identification of the V-weapon launch sites in northern France, the building up of intelligence agents in an offensive capacity to work alongside conventional forces in preparation for D-Day, not to mention the sponsorship of many different *réseaux d'évasion* that together assisted in the recovery of many hundreds of precious (and expensive) aircrew back to Britain – all these were products of Dansey's genius for active, aggressive, operational espionage.

It seems certain that it was Dansey's desire to protect and nurture the various strands he had created within the Resistance movement that led him to consider and authorise the Amiens raid. It is true that he would have been against it at one level: agents once dispatched were on their own; trusting London to rescue them when *in extremis* was a fool's notion, and something he specifically warned agents not to countenance. Nor did he have any time for sentimentality: he was not interested in rescuing agents or *résistants* just because they were in trouble or in some way believed that they deserved London's special attention. All agents on operations were on their own, dependent solely on their wits, and the expensive and lengthy training they had undergone. Of course, for those foreign agents and *passeurs* who had been recruited through local networks, and who had only a hazy notion of their ultimate employer, such moral obligations on MI6 simply did not exist. Sentimentality was the criticism he made repeatedly of Jimmy Langley, the liaision officer between MI6 and MI9 who was intimately involved in support the escape and evasion lines in occupied Europe, telling him on one occasion that his problem was that 'he loved his agents' too much, a characteristic Dansey regarded as a fatal flaw in the dangerous world of the intelligence war. But at the same time he was able to recognise the virtues of protecting the extraordinary espionage capability that he and his small team had created in France in the midst of one of the most brutal military occupations of modern times. For this reason, the arguments for and against a low-level attack by the RAF against the walls of Amiens Prison, to allow jailed *résistants* to escape and to rejoin the ranks of the secret army that MI6 had been instrumental in creating, favoured action rather than benign neglect.

Dansey benefited considerably from the initiative of others in the construction of an intelligence picture of occupied France. Vichy's Deuxième Bureau was one such source, the pre-war Polish secret service that rebuilt a number of its networks after the occupation another. A third was the series of *réseaux* set up by French patriots in partnership with MI6, operating exclusively with them during the war, some to acquire offensive intelligence, others to help evading and escaping Allied servicemen on the run behind enemy lines. The latter was the work of MI9. The close working relationship between MI6 and the BCRA has already been noted.

The Poles were tenacious and effective spymasters. By the end of 1940 four separate Polish cells had been established covering all of occupied and Vichy France (*Tudor* in Marseille, *Panhard* in Lyon, *Rab* in Toulouse and *Interallié* in Paris). Within the *Tudor* network (run by Colonel Wincenty Zarembski, who had been head of Polish intelligence in Paris at the outbreak of war), but working directly to MI6 in London, was an agent working under the codename of *Doctor*. A former Polish naval officer, Lieutenant Tadeusz Witold

Jekiel had escaped to Britain, and now operated out of Bordeaux, but specialised in securing intelligence about shipping movements from all five of the French Atlantic ports, eventually leading what became known as the Marine cell. Not much escaped the gaze of this group. Information gathered by these men made its way back to London either by radio or by ship-borne courier and, after 1941, by Lysander. Gilbert Renault managed to get three sacks of material back to London on one of these flights (Operation *Julie*) on the night of 27 February 1942, from a snow-covered field at Saint-Saëns.*

Zarembski ran a primitive transmitter from Toulouse, and in July 1941 *Armand* (Captain Roman Garby-Czerniawski, later to play a crucial role in the success of the Allied 'Double Cross' system, where his codename was *Brutus*) had established his own radio link with London from Paris as part of his *réseau Interallié*.† In the French capital information would arrive courtesy of a wagon-lit attendant on the Paris–Marseille express, which was then transmitted to MI6 via agents working for Biffy Dunderdale, using a radio set that had arrived from London in August 1940. The men of the French state railway company, SNCF, proved to be overwhelmingly supportive of resistance: many were themselves *résistants*. In Picardy the *réseau Zéro*, which was to play a role in the unfolding of the drama at Amiens in February 1944, was based very substantially on employees of the SNCF reporting intelligence about German railway troop movements back to London. Indeed, the station master at Amiens, Germain Bleuet, was the linchpin of this network, and was executed for his activities in the Citadel at Arras a few short months after the Amiens raid. One of the members of *Zéro*, Gendarme Lieutenant Marceau Laverdure, was instrumental in transmitting information to London about the prisoners in Amiens's *Maison d'Arrêt*. It was his file of information, which Dominique Ponchardier carried to

---

* This was consignment RZ39.
† This *réseau* ultimately collapsed through the treachery of Mathilde Carré ('the Cat'), whom Roman Garby-Czerniawski had persuaded to join in 1940.

Geneva in late November 1943, that first revealed the scale of the
Gestapo successes against the *OCM* in the region.

Because of the political gulf that separated the Free France of
General Charles de Gaulle from that of Vichy, MI6 was forced to
operate two almost entirely separate sections supporting the two
principal sources of intelligence coming from France. The first, A5,
specifically for Free France (i.e. the BCRA), was led by Kenneth
Cohen (and therefore had much in common with the RF Section
of SOE), and the second – A4 – recruiting from anti-German
sources within Vichy, was under Biffy Dunderdale.* Both were run
out of the SIS offices at Broadway House, opposite the entrance to
St James's Park tube station. Several members of the Vichy intelligence apparatus worked for MI6, including Colonel Louis Barel,
head of the reconstituted Deuxième Bureau in Vichy, Colonel
Louis Rivet, and Captain Paul Paillole, who was responsible for
counter-espionage. Colonel Georges-André Groussard ran the
small Vichy internal security office, and from the earliest days of
the war (he visited London three times in 1940 and 1941) provided
MI6 with secret intelligence from within the heart of the Vichy
establishment. His MI6 codename was *Eric*, and from early 1942,
accompanied by Paillole, he operated from Geneva. It was here
that he first encountered the man who would initiate the call for
London to organise the attack on Amiens Prison, Dominique
Ponchardier, joint head – with his brother – of the *réseau Sosies*.

MI6 created a wide range of networks across France in the years
after 1940, building an important pattern of intelligence that
became an integral, even vital, component of Allied planning and
operations during 1944. For example, in 1940 Christian Pineau
(later leader of *Libération-Nord*), founded two *réseaux*,

* In due course A4 and A5 were combined into a section called P1, and the
early distinctions between Free France and Vichy in terms of MI6's management of its various networks in France were dissolved, although Dunderdale
worked directly to 'C' rather than to Dansey.

Phalanx-Phidias and *Cohors*, both in support of the BCRA and MI6. Likewise, Captain Claude Arnould, an officer in Vichy's Deuxième Bureau (whose *noms de guerre* included *Colonel Olivier*, *Désiré* and *Amand*), together with Father Anthony Dieuzayde, the Jesuit chaplain general of the Catholic Association of French Youth, founded *Jade-Amicol* in October in support of A4. *Jade-Amicol* was led by Philippe Keun (codenamed variously *Admiral*, *Friend* and *Deux*).* The son of a Sephardic Jew with a Danish passport who was a good friend of Biffy Dunderdale before the war, Keun had been educated in Britain (at Downside School) and was thus able convincingly to pass himself off as an Englishman.

By 1943, *Jade-Amicol*, run for MI6 by Dunderdale, was to become one of Dansey's most significant networks in northern France, with over 1,500 agents. Although they brutally hunted down its agents, the Germans never located its headquarters, the convent of the Nuns of the Passion of our Blessed Lord at 127 rue de la Santé, where one of its radio transmitters was also hidden and from whence the convent's nine sisters and the Mother Superior, Madame Henriette Frede, daily sallied out onto the Parisian streets acting as couriers for Keun.† *Jade-Amicol* was to prove extraordinarily successful in providing critical intelligence to London about the Atlantic coast in preparation for D-Day. It is not as well understood as it should be just how critical were MI6 operations in France to the survival of Britain at this time. From as early as 1941, when networks from both A4 and A5 were established to help in the Battle of the Atlantic, to late 1943, when they were critical observers of the deployment of Hitler's V weapons and of the state of the Atlantic Wall defences along the coast through to Operation

---

* Several MI6 *réseaux* were named after precious stones. *Jade-Amicol*'s second name was formed from mixing the codenames of their leaders: Olivier (*Le Colonel*) and Keun (*L'Amiral*) form *Amicol*.

† Philippe Keun was captured in June 1944 and transported to Buchenwald, where he was executed three months later. Claude Arnould survived the war despite being imprisoned at Dachau.

Overlord itself in June 1944, the Resistance was an element of critical importance in both the defence of London and the preparation for the invasion of continental Europe. It was the singular importance of these diverse *réseaux* that formed the basis of the deliberation in London in early February 1944 about the need to attack one of the places where captured *résistants* were incarcerated, Amiens's *Maison d'Arrêt*.

Gilbert Renault's *CND* was one *réseau* engaged in this work for the BCRA and MI6 from late 1940. On 20 December 1941 Renault was in his apartment in Paris, together with his wife Edith, when one of his agents, Alex, arrived with 'an enormous parcel' that he placed on the kitchen table. He undid the string. Renault was astonished at what he saw:

I could hardly believe my eyes. It contained the original German plans of the submarine bases, not only at Lorient, but also at Brest, Saint-Nazaire, La Pallice, and Bordeaux . . .

My wife and I exchanged anxious looks. The value of the dossier was beyond imagination. Almost too good to be true . . .

'It was the six bottles of Sauterne that did the trick,' said Alex with a smile. 'My German boss was very pleased. He went on leave to Berlin three days ago.'

We looked at him, awaiting the sequel.

'I had taken a wax impression of the key of the steel cabinet in which he kept the plans and also of the key to his office, which he locked up when he went away. It was no trouble at all to get into the office during lunch hour. And here we are.'

'But when he comes back, he will notice that the plans have gone?'

'Not immediately. There are twelve copies of each plan. I have taken one of each, so it won't be noticed. And then if he did notice, he's not likely to publish the fact. He'll be too worried about his own position.'

So it was that a matter of days later, this priceless intelligence made its way to London via a courier route Renault had set up through Spain. It very nearly did not get there. On arrival at Montparnasse station in Paris, Alex was fearful that his prominent package would be examined by the ever-vigilant guards at the exits. Seeing an elderly lady struggling with her suitcase, he offered to help. Gratefully accepting, she carried the smaller package in exchange. 'His' suitcase was carefully examined; the old lady with 'her' package was waved through with a nod.

Earlier in 1941 *Alliance* also managed to send material about the French Atlantic ports to London. Marie-Madeleine Fourcade (*Poz55*, *Hedgehog*), the audacious leader of this Resistance group, recalled in *Noah's Ark* how one of her agents, Antoine Hugon, arrived one day in the late summer of 1941 at her secret HQ in Pau, in the foothills of the Pyrenees:

> He was a garage owner and had the unusual distinction of having been awarded the Iron Cross for having saved the life of a drowning German soldier in the First World War. He made a point of wearing it openly, which presumably made his missions into the less accessible zones that much easier. He proudly unfolded a huge plan that he had wrapped round his body and smuggled across the demarcation line. It showed all the U-boat pens recently built at Saint-Nazaire, reproduced to scale, down to the last inch, by the engineer Henri Mouren.*

Alliance was an integral and increasingly important part of MI6's orbit in the *Zone Libre* from early 1941 all the way through to the liberation in 1944. Kenneth Cohen initially came to an arrangement with its then leader, the right-wing Georges Loustaunau-Lacau (code named *Navarre*, or N1), for intelligence in exchange for money, radios and logistics support by airdrop. Loustaunau-Lacau,

---

*   Hugon was executed at Mont-Valérien Prison on 30 November 1942.

who after the armistice with Germany had been appointed by Vichy to lead the *Légion française des combattants*, a veterans' organisation created by the regime, was only too happy to commit to providing intelligence to London (but not to be subordinate to de Gaulle), and to use his position to recruit agents in *Alliance*, as well as to establish *réseaux d'évasion* routes to Spain, for which he received money from London. He also helped establish links between London and other anti-German Vichy intelligence officers, such as Georges-André Groussard, with whom he had worked in the right-wing Cagoule organisation during the mid-1930s.*

The radio provided by Cohen (together with its operator, Lucien Vallet) was first placed in Pau. The original link between anti-German intelligence officers in Vichy and London was established by Jacques Bridou, one of Loustaunau's most trusted lieutenants, who made his way to London via Tangier and Gibraltar in November 1940 to make contact with MI6. Cohen had him para-chuted back into France in March 1941 to help Loustaunau-Lacau establish the *réseau*. Bridou's sister, Marie-Madeleine Méric (later Fourcade), had worked alongside Loustaunau-Lacau since 1937, and when the latter was arrested by Vichy in May 1941 she stepped seamlessly into his shoes. Dansey was happy (indeed, he had little choice) to allow the leadership of *Alliance* to transfer to an agent in France who he was told went under the codename of *Hedgehog* – all *Alliance* agents were named after animals: the Germans called the organisation 'Noah's Ark' – but he was shocked when he discovered at the end of that year that the new leader of one of MI6's most important networks was a woman.

Kenneth Cohen records *Alliance* as having 3,000 agents by 1943, although the number of those in direct intelligence-gathering roles would have been much fewer – Keith Jeffery estimates as few as 145. *Alliance* was important because it provided a direct channel between the anti-German officers in Vichy's Deuxième Bureau and

* He ended up in Mauthausen concentration camp, but survived the war.

MI6, information from this source also being provided to the BCRA in line with Dansey and Dewavrin's agreement. The relationship would have been anathema to de Gaulle, but the more pragmatic Dewavrin used it to his advantage. So far as he was concerned, political considerations were secondary to the need to defeat the Germans. By late 1943 *Alliance* played a significant role in the exposure and destruction of the threat to London from the first of Hitler's V-weapons, the 'doodlebug' (V1) and, in mid-1944, the V2 rocket (see Chapter Five). So significant was it that it had more radio transmitters than all other MI6-sponsored *réseaux* combined. Cohen observed that no 'single French network can claim the monopoly of intelligence-gathering from occupied territory (soon to include the whole of France), but . . . the *Alliance* survivors and their 500 dead had particularly well served the allied services with their emphasis on information concerning German submarine bases and, in 1944, rocket sites.'

By early 1944 there were as many as sixty *réseaux* across France feeding information to MI6, and the volume of radio and written reports increased significantly in the years after 1941. In 1941 700 telegrams had been received by London; during the first eight months of 1944 this number had risen to 8,025. But volume alone says little. Estimates of the value of BCRA vary, but all sources agree that without it MI6's contribution from inside France would have been substantially diminished. Dewavrin estimated that between 75 and 95 per cent of MI6's information on the Wehrmacht in France came from his networks, although MI6's own assessment was lower, at 40 per cent. What is indisputable is that MI6 under Dansey's leadership enjoyed many relationships with separate intelligence networks in France. In north-eastern France it sourced intelligence from a variety of networks, some of which would play key roles in the plans to attack Amiens Prison.

One of these networks was the *réseau Sosies* ('Lookalikes'). The fact that *Sosies* was an MI6-managed *réseau* (rather than an SOE one) was formally revealed by Professor Keith Jeffery in 2010.

From evidence provided by the brothers Dominique and Pierre Ponchardier, *Sosies* began life in 1942 as a small group of ex-military officers of their previous acquaintance, with whom they had served in the pre-war French army and navy. When war was declared in 1939 the 22-year-old Dominique was practising as an estate agent in Paris. Born in Saint-Étienne on the Loire, he was conscripted at the outbreak of war. After recovering from wounds sustained during the final days of the Battle of France he established with his wife Simone a *réseau d'évasion* for British soldiers left in France, working in a triangle linking Dijon, Besançon and Vesoul.

With no connection at all with any formal intelligence organisation, Ponchardier took it upon himself to run an almost single-handed resistance operation, with the assistance of his brother Pierre. From small beginnings finding secret accommodation for evaders, it wasn't long before he moved into the production and distribution of leaflets, posters and underground newspapers, drawing his own anti-German and anti-collaborationist cartoons to provide the artwork for such publications as *La France combat*, *IVème République* and *Le Prix du Sang*. From there it was a short step into sabotage and intelligence gathering. In the Archives Nationales housed in the Hôtel de Soubise in Paris sits a report written by Pierre Ponchardier (*Geneviève*) on 28 September 1944 about the activities of the *réseau Sosies*, written within days of the German expulsion from France and before his memory faded; he noted that for security reasons little had been consigned to paper during the occupation. The purpose of the *réseau* was to secure intelligence for MI6 about the Atlantic coast and German military activities in the rest of France.

Ponchardier records that the *réseau Sosies* undertook three sets of activities, each one separate from the other for security reasons: intelligence gathering, one group in the North and the other in the South; the regional consolidation of this intelligence to avoid duplication with other networks (undertaken by the *réseau*

Century); and what was described as 'Special Liaison', which included the couriering of messages and intelligence to safety in Britain via Switzerland or MGB from Brittany. Dominique (*Elizabeth*), his brother, was responsible for the Northern Zone, which comprised Section MA1 (the Atlantic Wall between Dunkirk and Lorient); MA2 (the coast between Lorient and St Jean-de-Luz); MA3, led after 1942 by Edouard Rivière; *réseau 1342* (north-eastern France); the *réseau Michele* (the north-western part of the south-west led by Philippe Quenouelle); the *réseau Hector* (between the Loire and the Seine); Paris and the SNCF, also known as the *réseau Oscar*, after its leader's *nom de guerre*.

By 1944 *Sosies* boasted 390 agents, 300 under Dominique in the north-east and 90 under Pierre in the south and the Atlantic coast. Dominique's right-hand man, René Chapelle, is known to history through his alias, *Pépé*. Chapelle, who had fought in the International Brigade in Spain, where he met his future wife, Maria Benitez Luqua, had escaped from a German POW camp in 1941. He had returned home to Ponts-et-Marais, where he owned a bicycle-repair business. Because of his strong communist credentials he led the local FTPF network, but he also doubled as a *Sosies* agent, controlling the entire northern zone, dealing both in intelligence (for *Sosies*) and sabotage (for the FTPF). Maria acted as a courier, taking material from Amiens to Paris by train, hidden in the clothes of her young son Jean. In Paris they gave the information to their fellow *résistant* Vice Admiral Edouard Rivière, who worked in the office of the French Naval Hydrographer.

The demarcation line between the various *réseaux* at a local level was often blurred, and organisations such as the right-leaning *OCM* and the communist FTPF worked well together, as did the FTPF and the *Sosies*. It suited both men to cooperate, Ponchardier on issues associated with intelligence, and René Chapelle with blowing things up. In the list Dominique Ponchardier provided at the end of the war he proudly listed both René and Maria Chapelle from Ponts-et-Marais as members of the *Sosies*.

Dominique Ponchardier, Edouard Rivière and René Chapelle were known personally to Renault. Ponchardier first came to the attention of MI6 either through Gilbert Renault and the BCRA, or because of Ponchardier's connection with Colonel Georges-André Groussard in Geneva. In London Renault effectively acted as *Sosies*'s BCRA case officer, while MI6's case officer was known to Dominique Ponchardier only as 'Captain Thomas' (see Appendix 3). Renault knew the network and its operators, well. He wrote in 1955:

> As soon as the Third Reich declared war on Russia, Pépé became the leader of an armed group composed of communists, which operated in the Somme and Seine-Inférieure, and called itself the FTPF. I first came to know the FTPF in 1942, and although I could never have shared all their convictions, I could not fail to acknowledge their courage. With Pépé acting as go-between, they willingly carried out all Ponchardier's dangerous orders, for, like Pépé, they were devoted to him. Eleven members of the FTPF, who had been working in the Mers-les-Bains region, were shot in Amiens in December 1943, along with Le Sec, their leader.

The role played by René Chapelle demonstrated the porous nature of the boundaries drawn around different *réseaux*: many *résistants* in and around Picardy supported more than one local network. There were many instances where those involved in escape lines for MI9 were also involved in either intelligence-gathering or sabotage operations for MI6 and the BCRA, and sometimes the RF section of SOE or any other one of the networks that worked in their various ways to undermine the authority of the occupiers. By late 1943 the hunt was on for anyone associated with the members of Chapelle's group. His friends in Mers-les-Bains had, the Resistance believed, been betrayed by Lucien Pieri, a tailor in Amiens, who worked closely with the Abwehr to infiltrate and then betray local *réseaux*.

The *Sosies* HQ was located in Paris but was moved every month to avoid detection. The post box for couriers to send messages and intelligence was likewise moved regularly. Information was posted into the letter box every week from across the *Sosies* network. This information was then sent to London through Geneva, through routes managed by Lieutenant André Devigny (*Valentin*), organiser of Groussard's *Gilbert* network, of which Ponchardier was also a member. The so-called 'Eastern Route' carried information through the border town of Annemasse (the border between France and Switzerland runs through the town). Pierre Ponchardier recorded a 'Northern Route' to London, but does not provide any details. It is possible that this was the sea route through Brittany. In addition, emergency messages were sent directly by radio to London using the radio transmitters of other networks, such as that of the *réseau Alibi* run by Georges Charraudeau, and although Ponchardier never mentioned it there is a possibility that his second-in-command in Paris, Edouard Rivière, also had access to a *pianiste* for radio transmissions.

The primary route into Switzerland was, however, via Groussard, who also provided direct liaison with MI6's operatives in Berne and Geneva. Pierre noted that either he or Dominique travelled to Geneva to hand over information to Groussard at least once every month. The Ponchardier brothers had worked from the early days of their network with Admiral Henry Nomy and André Devigny, whose remarkable exploits in escaping from Gestapo captivity can be found in his biography. Devigny was one of Groussard's closest helpers, one of the early members of MI6's *réseau Gilbert*, and the man who constructed and managed the 'Eastern Route' through Annemasse.*

Pierre Ponchardier recorded that 1944 began badly for the Resistance. The Milice (established at the start of 1943 as a direct

---

* It was here that he was arrested by the Gestapo on 17 April 1943. Tortured by Klaus Barbie, he managed to escape from Montluc Prison, thus avoiding execution, and returned to France with the Allied armies in August 1944.

counter by Vichy to the growing threat posed by the Resistance) and the Gestapo had stepped up the reach and the aggressiveness of their attacks on the underground. Moving across France had grown more and more difficult because of travel restrictions, and the Germans managed to capture one of the couriers that *Sosies* used for its Southern Route into Geneva, and then arrested other members of the Southern Network. Several other parts of *Sosies* were hit hard, and then in February 1944 'two agents of the MA1 Network were arrested and put away in Amiens prison by the Gestapo'. These two arrests encouraged, he suggested, the work that his brother and Edouard Rivière then undertook to persuade MI6 to sanction the raid on the prison by the RAF. He adds that the raid was successful in 'freeing not only one of these agents but several hundred prisoners, of which the majority would have been shot in the following days (of which 12 would have occurred on the 19th February).'

The *Alibi* network run by Georges Charraudeau (alias *Chambon* and *Chobière*) also provided intelligence exclusively to MI6. Gilbert Renault described the primary role of this *réseau* as 'liaison work – wireless messages, organising landing or parachuting operations, helping Allied airmen to escape etc.' *Alibi* had many similarities to *Alliance*. On the political right in pre-war France, Charraudeau had worked for French intelligence in Spain, providing information about the Civil War through a fashion house front in Madrid. In June 1940, fleeing to Britain through Spain with his family, he bumped into an MI6 agent in San Sebastian – possibly Michael Creswell (*Monday*), who would have been known to him from espionage circles from before the war – and was persuaded to stay in Madrid and operate an intelligence line into France. Charraudeau was comfortable in Spain, where he was protected by powerful members of Franco's administration, and he understood espionage. He accepted MI6's proposal.

Charraudeau re-entered France on 10 July in the boot of a Spanish car carrying diplomatic number plates, reconnoitring the

Zone Libre and recruiting agents where he thought they might prove useful. He successfully recruited a range of well-placed agents, but for various reasons, mostly to do with lax security, the Germans eventually rolled up the first group he established in 1941 (*Phill*) by using thugs of the so-called 'French Gestapo' – the *Corps d'Autoprotection Française*. Over four years the *réseau*, which had 423 agents by 1945, had lost 28 to deportation to Germany (of whom only three survived) and 15 killed. These were in fact relatively low figures, mainly because intelligence networks suffered proportionately fewer casualties than those networks engaged directly in sabotage. But the Germans did not differentiate between these different types of network, treating all with equal, easy brutality. Five of the seven men of an *Alibi* subgroup caught by the Abwehr in 1941 (Jacques Kellner, Auguste Paulin, Robert Etienne, Fernand Fenzi and Roger Raven), for instance, were executed in a ditch at Mont-Valérien on the night of 21 March 1942 and their bodies thrown into anonymous graves. Two others were sentenced to five years' imprisonment.

Despite these setbacks *Alibi* flourished as an exclusively MI6-managed intelligence organisation, taking under its wing a number of smaller *réseaux*, such as *Klan* (François de La Rocque) from September 1942 and in April 1944 *Maurice*. It was divided into twenty subgroups and communicated with its MI6 handlers in London through fifteen radio transmitters. Its tasks were to secure the broadest possible spread of intelligence about every aspect of the German war effort in France. For example, the network organised the first bombing of the Renault factory, in the town of Boulogne-Billancourt just west of the centre of Paris, by 235 aircraft of the RAF on 3 March 1942, having sent London intelligence about the construction there of parts of the revolutionary Messerschmitt 262 jet aircraft. Pierre Brossolette played a role in this operation. Following the Armistice, Brossolette and his wife had taken over a bookstore specialising in Russian literature in the rue de la Pompe, the shop soon becoming a hub of the Paris

Resistance where documents such as those supporting the attack on the Renault factory were organised.

Likewise Lieutenant Pierre Lallart recruited two French test pilots at the Francazal aircraft factory in Toulouse, and all the details of the Heinkel 111 bomber were sent to London. Lallart also recruited the contractor who provided the Germans with fruit and vegetables. According to Paul Cousseran, a member of *Alibi*, from this information they were able to deduce most of the German order of battle in southern France. For his part, Cousseran in 1943 organised a system of eavesdropping on long-distance telephone lines, on which the Germans, believing the network to be secure, habitually did not use code. George Charraudeau claims that he was able to use his contacts within Vichy to send to London copies of correspondence between Pétain and Hitler, and between the German Otto Abetz (the German ambassador to Vichy) and Pierre Laval (the Vichy head of government between April 1942 and August 1944).

Until the closure of the US consulate in Lyon in November 1942, one of the channels by which intelligence reports reached London from across France was via the US diplomatic bag, arranged through the auspices of the librarian, Miss Penelope Royall, and Constance Ray Harvey, the vice consul, who regularly drove back to Berne, under the protection of her diplomatic status, where she gave the material to the US military attaché in Switzerland, Barnwell Legge. In addition to this route via Lyon, Charraudeau organised the smuggling of information over the Pyrenees into Spain. A small boat ran each month from the seaside village of Saint-Raphaël, midway between Cannes and Saint-Tropez, making for Gibraltar, carrying contraband, evaders and escapers as well as packages destined for London. Landings with Lysanders followed from 1942, and in 1943 and 1944 Charraudeau was closely associated with the successful operations by MGBs between Dartmouth and Brittany. In November 1943 he spent a month in England planning the establishment of sea routes into Brittany, which

would be able to transfer far larger quantities of supplies and equipment than was possible by aircraft. Nine mail runs were successfully undertaken by sea in early 1944 by the 15th MGB Flotilla.
Charraudeau returned from London by Lysander on the night of
16 December 1943.

From the spring of 1943 Dansey worked hard to build a series of
réseaux in northern France that could be useful for D-Day.
Understanding every nuance of the Atlantic Wall was now MI6's
paramount responsibility, one that was extended as the year
progressed to the hunting down of V-weapon sites. Both were the
focus of all MI6 *réseaux* in northern France by early 1944. In
early 1942 Hitler had initiated a defensive strategy that was to
evidence itself in the construction of a massive German coastal
version of the Maginot Line, called by them for propaganda
purposes the Atlantic Wall, stretching some 6,000 miles from the
Spanish border to Norway. Hitler's long, rambling speech to the
Reichstag on 11 December 1941, in which he declared war on the
United States, also announced the implementation of this defensive strategy:

> From Kirkenes [in Norway] to the Spanish frontier stretches the
> most extensive belt of great defence installations and fortresses.
> Countless airfields have been built, including some in the far
> north that were blasted out of granite. The number and strength
> of the protected submarine shelters that defend naval bases are
> such that they are practically impregnable from both the sea and
> the air. They are defended by more than one and a half thousand
> gun battery emplacements, which had to be surveyed, planned
> and built. A network of roads and rail lines has been laid out so
> that the connections [to the installations] between the Spanish
> frontier and Petsamo [in northern Norway] can be defended
> independently from the sea. The installations built by the Pioneer
> and construction battalions of the navy, army and air force in

cooperation with the Todt Organisation are not at all inferior to those of the Westwall [along the German frontier with France]. The work to further strengthen all this continues without pause. I am determined to make this European front impregnable against any enemy attack.

The operation by the Resistance the following year to secure the secrets of the fortifications along the French coast began through a stroke of good fortune. Early in May 1943, outside Caen town hall, a notice appeared inviting tenders for some minor housekeeping tasks at the headquarters of the Todt Organisation, which was responsible for designing and building the fortifications for the Atlantic Wall, work that had begun in the late spring of 1942. René Duchez, a painter who was a member of *Century* (whose links to *Jade-Amicol* were through a connection with the *réseau Sosies*), was awarded the contract. During these works, in mid-May 1943, he managed to get hold of a copy of a map containing the printed plans for the defensive works being prepared for the entire region between Le Havre to Cherbourg. He rolled it up between some wallpaper and simply walked out of the building with it at the end of the week. Within a few days it was in the hands of Vice Admiral Edouard Rivière in the *Sosies* headquarters in Paris, where it was copied. Philippe Keun then arranged for it to be flown by Lysander to London. It was through feats of intelligence-gathering like this that by December 1943 the extent of the Allies' knowledge about the Atlantic Wall and of the Wehrmacht order of battle facing them in Normandy was unsurpassed.

The importance to London during late 1943 and early 1944 therefore of *Jade-Amicol*, *Century*, *CND*, *Alliance*, *Alibi*, *OCM*, *Agir* and *Sosies*, among others, cannot be overstated. It is important, however, to be clear about this argument: it is not that the Resistance per se was indispensable to Allied victory. That argument can be overstated. Rather, it is that without Dansey's intelligence networks, listed and described above, the Allies would have been blind to the

V-weapons threat from Picardy*, and ignorant of the detail of the Atlantic Wall, intelligence that was not immediately available through other means such as aerial photography or secret signals intelligence through the *Ultra* project at Bletchley Park. It was these Resistance networks in their various forms that provided order to the jigsaw puzzle, and allowed Allied planners to make sense of what lay beyond the grey moat of the English Channel prior to the greatest amphibious invasion in history.

Likewise, it is important to recognise the role that MI6 would play in D-Day itself, when it came. As early as mid-1943 Dansey appointed Cohen to take responsibility for the MI6 element of Operation *Sussex* (Gilbert Renault was the BCRA lead and Colonel Francis Pickens Miller represented the OSS). This was a plan to parachute sixty-two-man intelligence teams immediately behind the enemy lines facing an Allied invasion, designed to disrupt enemy communications networks immediately after D-day, working to link up local *réseaux* with the advancing Allied forces and to make the most of this coordination in terms of German discomfiture. Indeed, the first *Sussex* drops were made on 8 February 1944, ten days before the raid on Amiens Prison. There was much at stake, therefore, in ensuring that the MI6 and BCRA *réseaux* across northern France were as little affected by enemy interdiction as possible, particularly following the devastation caused by German counter-espionage operations during 1943 (see chapter 6). MI6's intelligence *réseaux* were critical to Allied plans to counter German opposition to Operation *Overlord*, and it follows that in Dansey's mind, when it came to considering whether or not to support Ponchardier's request for action to be taken against Amiens Prison, everything that could be done to assist *réseaux* in the north to play their part in the forthcoming battle for the liberation of France was considered.

* See Chapter Five.

FOUR

MI9 and the *réseaux d'évasion*

An important additional aspect of MI6's work in France during the war and of the Amiens jigsaw puzzle was that of helping escaping or evading Allied servicemen to avoid the clutches of their pursuers. There were, at any one time, hundreds of these men wandering across both occupied France and the *Zone Libre*. They included soldiers escaping from capture by the Germans following the fall of France in 1940; those in the years that followed who found themselves left on French soil after commando raids; airmen evading capture after bailing out of their burning aircraft; and escapers making their way to Switzerland or Spain after breaking out of their prison camps in Germany or in Vichy France. Helping them became an honourable means of individual rebellion among that relatively small section of the French populace who were intent on doing something practical to fight back against occupation, but who did not find their way into the ranks of the saboteurs or spies.

One of those helped in this way in 1940 was the man who was to plan the raid on Amiens, Air Vice Marshal Basil Embry. After being shot down on 27 May 1940 over Saint-Omer, he was quickly captured by the advancing German army. A few days later, part of a column of prisoners marching to the rear, he spotted a chance to slip away unseen, thus beginning a two-month journey through a France in the throes of collapse. Escape was hard, however. He rapidly ran out of reserves of food, as well as physical and moral energy. Outside the village of Hesdin, he made a decision:

I was rapidly reaching a stage of exhaustion, for I had been without food or drink for over forty-eight hours, this being my third night without proper sleep, and the wound in my leg, although not serious, had not been attended to and was beginning to be troublesome. They say vitality is at its lowest at this hour of the morning. Mine was certainly low at that moment, and deep despondency came over me. I sat down and rested a few minutes, trying to think out a plan. It had just occurred to me that shortly it would be getting light and I ought to be finding a suitable place to hide-up for the day when suddenly I heard a dog barking not far off, and as I walked on it barked again. Realising I must have some food and drink, clean myself up and rest, or I would never reach the Somme, I decided to take a big risk. I would find the house where the dog lived, and if it were small and isolated I would boldly knock up the owner and ask his help. As I saw the outline of some small buildings and walked towards them, the dog barked furiously.

I tapped lightly on the door, and a man opened an upstairs window and asked who I was and what I wanted. I explained that I was a British aviator escaping from the Germans, and in a moment the door opened and I was pulled inside. Paul Beugnet and his wife welcomed me with open arms. They could not have shown greater kindness and care to their own son returning from the war. They took away my sodden clothes, which when returned were clean and dry; I was given hot water to wash in, and food to eat. After cleaning my wounded leg they bound it up and put me to bed, Paul promising to watch for any approaching German.

For several days Paul Beugnet, a veteran of the Great War, and his wife looked after Embry, washing the wound in his leg, feeding and sheltering him. Most important, they gave him back his hope: it ended up sustaining him throughout two further months of dangerous adventure on his journey across France, to Spain and thence back to Britain. He made the first RAF 'home run' of the

Second World War. Now, in 1944, he was being given a chance to repay some of that kindness. The memory of the risks taken by French civilians with everything to lose remained with him, and the impulse to help those who had once helped him was considerable.

Helping escapers and evaders became the business of the escape lines (*réseaux d'évasion*), initially an ad hoc and unorganised activity, but which in time developed their own structures, organisation, training and coordination. Escape lines often emerged in unplanned and spontaneous ways as French civilians came forward to provide succour to men – like Basil Embry – attempting to stay out of German captivity and, if they could, find their way back to Britain. In time whole 'lines' of civilian helpers – *passeurs* – were established in many different *réseaux* to coordinate the escape of these men. Men, women and children became involved in various ways: in hiding evaders, arranging identity documents and work and travel permits, accompanying them on public transport, acting as lookouts for German patrols, securing food, clothing and shoes and providing medical care for the wounded. Couriers would collect escapers and evaders from outlying areas, and then accompany them by road or train through enemy-patrolled territory to hubs or collection points (one of which was Amiens), where they could be prepared in groups for the final assault on the Pyrenees. It was an exceptionally dangerous undertaking for the French *passeurs* who engaged in this activity.

The most obvious and therefore most popular escape route was through neutral Spain, which entailed travelling long distances across France. Until November 1942 the Germans were content to occupy only part of France – the part that was most significant to them in strategic terms, namely the entire Atlantic coastline, and the north, the *Zone Occupée* – while their puppets in Vichy were allowed to administer the remainder, the *Zone Libre*. Captain Airey Neave escaped from Colditz Castle on 5 January 1942 and made his way by train and foot to Switzerland four days later. He was then spirited out of France via an escape route headed by the Belgian military doctor Albert-Marie Guérisse (who operated under the pseudonym of 'Pat Albert O'Leary'), who ran the Pat O'Leary line (often abbreviated to 'Pat line' or 'PAO'). It was the first properly organised escape line in France, managing to carry over six hundred escapers and evaders to safety before Guérisse was betrayed and arrested on 2 March 1943. Foot and Langley's account of MI9 suggest that over 5,000 Allied servicemen were repatriated to Britain as a result of the work of escape lines during the war. By the time of the Normandy landings in June 1944, some 1,500 Allied servicemen had crossed the Pyrenees to Spain.

In Britain the organisation established by MI6 to assist in the evacuation of Allied personnel from the continent was MI9. Headed by Major (later Brigadier) Norman Crockatt, in time it ran a secret army of *passeurs* across a wide range of *réseaux* behind enemy lines. Where they could, MI9 attempted to support, train and sustain these networks, which often operated like birds in winter, with few resources and very little money, eking out a precarious existence amid the frozen wastes of Nazi occupation. London helped to provide cash, radio operators, agents and training, as well as leadership to give often isolated *passeurs* a firm sense of direction and a feeling that the risks they took were contributing to an eventual Allied victory. Nightly BBC radio programmes were used to send messages to agents in the field. MI9 routinely used SOE's F Section's training school at Beaulieu in the New Forest, and its parachute and survival training schools, to prepare servicemen for the rigours of evasion. It also collaborated effectively with SOE in the design and development of all sorts of useful material: silk maps, a range of tiny compasses, language cards, explosive devices and escape kits, which contained emergency rations, local currency and survival aids.*

---

* Crockatt's post-war estimate of total British Commonwealth escapers from all thea-tres was '21,533, and of British Commonwealth evaders was 4,657 making a grand

In 1942 MI9 was staffed by two successful escapers. One was Captain James ('Jimmy') Langley of the Coldstream Guards, who had lost an arm at Dunkirk and found his way to Marseille, where he met many of the early escape-line organisers before being repatriated to England. He was joined the following year by the Colditz escaper (and Pat line 'parcel') Captain Airey Neave. Neave's codename became *Saturday*, hence the title for his best-selling account of this work, *Saturday at MI9*. Within MI6 Langley was known as 'P15' and, in Madrid, Michael Creswell was *Monday*. Donald Darling, MI6's man first in Lisbon and then in Gibraltar, and MI9's local escape coordinator (codenamed *Sunday*), esti-mated that at any one time during the war at least 500 escapers and evaders were at large across Europe, all making their way individually or with help towards the Pyrenees or, in 1944, toward evacuation by MGB off Brittany. Many *réseaux d'évasion* were coordinated by agents appointed and sustained by MI9 in London and supported by the apparatus of both MI6 and SOE. They became quite elaborate affairs. Airey Neave estimated that 12,000 people across occupied Europe supported the escape lines. For those escapers and evaders captured or recaptured by the Vichy police or the Germans, a short stay in prison would, on the whole, be their lot until transported to a POW camp in Germany or further east. For a *résistant*, however, the penalty was death, preceded, if one was unlucky, by imprisonment and torture. For their family members, it often meant arrest as well, and deporta-tion to a death camp in the east.

Few *réseaux*, however, survived intact for long, as the multifari-ous intelligence agencies of the Reich – the Geheime Staatspolizei (Gestapo), the Sicherheitsdienst (Himmler's Security Service, the SD), the Abwehr, the Secret Field Police and even the Luftwaffe

---

total of 26,190. Of these 4,916 were interned in Switzerland, but the rest were available for further service. It can be fairly claimed that of these 90% of evaders and 33% of escapers were brought out as a result of M.I.9 organisation and activities.'

security organisation – sought to eradicate this evidence of rebellion and destroy those involved.* General Otto von Stülpnagel, the military governor of France, produced thousands of posters to be pasted across the *Zone Occupée* setting out the penalties for supporting escapers, and the financial benefits of collaboration:

> All men who aid directly or indirectly the crews of enemy aircraft shot down by parachute or having made a forced landing will be shot in the field. Women who render the same type of aid will be sent to concentration camps in Germany. People who capture crews . . . or who contribute, by their actions, to their capture will receive up to 10,000 francs. In certain cases this compensation will be increased.

The Germans proved remarkably successful in their efforts to capture or kill *passeurs*. James Langley estimated that three died for every escaper who successfully reached safety.

It seems fair to assume that one of the several reasons why the RAF were willing to assent to the request to attack Amiens Prison was because of the work of local MI9 *réseaux* in rescuing and repatriating downed aircrew. The selfless contribution of volunteer *passeurs* in France rescuing these men from the prospect of German captivity, and sending them home to continue the war against the Axis Powers, created a sense of obligation on the RAF to support their French allies. Amiens was an important centre in the work of these networks, which had proliferated by early 1944: a collecting location, because of its good railway links to Paris, for a wide swathe of north-eastern France.

The story of one escape line, created close to Amiens by an

---

* The SD was the intelligence service of the SS and the Nazi Party. The Gestapo (the *Geheime Staatspolizei* (Secret State Police)) was the official secret police of Nazi Germany and the SD's sister organisation. Totalitarianism grows such organisations like viruses. All operated across France.

extraordinary family of Anglo-French *résistants* operating from the Hôtel de France in the village of Hornoy-le-Bourg, 22 miles due east of Amiens, is typical of many. Joseph (Joe) Balfe had served in the Irish Guards during the war (winning the Military Medal) and had stayed in France after marrying a local girl, Madeleine Gaudière. Now a naturalised French citizen, he managed his mother-in-law's twelve-bedroom hotel, many of whose rooms were taken by members of the occupation forces, unaware that the hotel had a double purpose.

Aged forty-six in 1943, it appears that Joseph began to look after escapers by accident, after being asked to help an RAF Spitfire pilot, Flying Officer Tom Slack, who had been shot down near Le Quesne on 18 July 1943. Slack stayed in Hornoy for a week, after which Joseph took him by train to stay with René and Odette Lemattre in Amiens, who hid him in the attic of their house behind their small hairdressing saloon located close to the station. Tom Slack described René as 'an ardent De Gaullist, Saboteur and Franc Tireur'. One of Lemattre's friends, he recalled, 'was a French pilot from the First World War who owned a garage and work-shop nearby. He ran a clandestine printing press and supplied me with the most beautifully forged papers and documents to see me safely through France.' The garage owner was Benjamin Lefebvre.

On 5 August, an unnamed woman travelled to Amiens from Paris to meet Tom and to escort him back to Paris, where he was passed on to the remarkable Belgian *réseau Comète*. He was success-fully taken across the Pyrenees to Spain on the night of 10 August 1943. The Comet line was run by a young Belgian woman, Andrée de Jongh (known as *Dédée*), who after accompanying three evaders to Spain in 1941 thereafter worked with MI9 to bring some 800 servicemen to Britain via Spain and Gibraltar, or by sea from Brittany. Airey Neave, who wrote her biography, described her as 'one of our greatest agents'. At the Hôtel de France on rue de Molliens, Joseph Balfe was helped by his two sons, Joe and John (who was married), and two daughters, Madeleine (who was fourteen at the time) and Marie-Thérèse. Both sons, after July 1943, lived a completely clandestine life to avoid being taken to Germany as part of Laval's STO, but in time Joe travelled as a 'parcel' along his own line to reach Britain, where he joined Airey Neave and James Langley in MI9. And when parts of the *Comète* line collapsed in 1943, Joe Balfe continued his work, linking his work and contacts to another escape line, the *réseau Bourgogne*, organised by Georges Broussine. Joe Balfe junior returned to France via *Comète* and John (Jack) Balfe with *Bourgogne* in November 1943.

Over time Joseph Balfe built up a strong group of supporters in the Amiens area, recruiting René and Odette Lemattre, Benjamin Lefebvre, Michel Dubois, Georges Tourdes, Morand Waquez, Jean Fourrage and his parents Marie-Antoinette and Sigismonde, and Madame Jeanne Vignon Tellier, among others. An Englishman resident in the city, Frederick Moore, who lived in rue Boucher de Perthes and who had two sons both serving with the British forces, one in the RAF and another in the Royal Navy, also supported Balfe by looking after evaders in his home. At the time of the Amiens raid, Balfe and his group were hiding nine US airmen on behalf of the US equivalent of MI9, MIS-X. All safely reached Spain after crossing the Pyrenees in two trips in April and May 1944.

Madame Vignon lived at 137 rue Vulfran-Warmé in Amiens. She sometimes had as many as twelve evaders living with her, some for many months at a time. She was 'petite, plump and grandmotherly', records the late Jack Fishman*. At least four US aircrew were with Madame Vignon at the time of the raid. Michel Dubois, who lived at 45 rue Delpech, was a 48-year-old former French army NCO, slightly bald and with a small moustache. He is described by Jack Fishman as a building contractor, although in other places as concierge of a Catholic school for young children. Georges Tourdes was an ex-officer in the French army who had escaped from a

---

* Author of *And the Walls Came Tumbling Down*, an account of the raid which draws extensively on extraordinarily detailed interviews with surviving participants.

prison camp and lived in Amiens. The 24-year-old Jean Fourrage, a member of the *réseau Bourgogne*, acted as a courier for Joseph Balfe, taking evaders between Hornoy and Amiens. Morand Waquez was a policeman in Hornoy-le-Bourg.

The stories of many of the evaders who were passed through Hornoy, revealed in their MI9 and MISX reports, provide testament to the extent of the aid provided by ordinary working-class French families struggling to get by in the midst of a brutal occupation. Any form of rebellion was extremely dangerous. Six weeks after the attack on Amiens Prison, Gestapo raids on 2 April 1944 resulted in the arrest of Jean Fourrage and his parents Marie-Antoinette and Sigismonde (all arrested in Hornoy), the Hornoy gendarme Morand Waquez and his nineteen-year-old son Raymond, together with Max Darras (aged seventeen). Jean Fourrage, Morand and Raymond Waquez were first incarcerated in Amiens Citadel (where they shared the same cell), before being tortured and shot in a forest at Gentelles, eight miles south of Amiens, on the night of 8 May 1944 with five other captured *résistants*. A further eighteen *résistants* were taken from Amiens on 28 May, tortured and executed, and their bodies thrown into an old First World War trench in the Bois de Gentelles. When their remains were uncovered following the liberation in September 1944, it was discovered that their faces had been pulverised by rifle butts in a last act of barbarity by their German killers. The young Max Darras and Jean Fourrage's parents, Marie-Antoinette and Sigismonde, were deported to Germany under the notorious *Nacht und Nebel* decree.*

An example of MI9's initiative in supporting escapers and evaders occurred in July 1943, when two agents – Dominique Potier

---

* Darras died at Bergen-Belsen, while the Fourrages both survived deportation, Marie-Antoinette to Ravensbrück. Fourrage is remembered at the memorial in Gentelles, which also records him as chief of the *réseau P3*, with the rank of second lieutenant in de Gaulle's FFI.

and his radio operator, Sergeant Conrad Lafleur – were instructed
to establish a *réseau* in north-eastern France – *Possum* – to organise the repatriation through occupied France to Spain (if evacuation by Lysander was not possible) of some of the large numbers of
Allied airmen who were being shot down en route to or returning
from their bombing targets over the Reich. Lafleur was in fact
already a successful escaper, and had volunteered to return to
France to help coordinate the activities of the men and women
who had enabled him to escape after the Dieppe raid in August
1942.*

The story of the *réseau Possum* demonstrates that supporting an
escape line was no sinecure. Three Lysander operations organised
by *Possum* were successful in September and November 1943,
returning eleven airmen to safety in Britain. The *Possum* network
very quickly grew to manage safe houses for evaders and escapers
and to coordinate their activities with other *réseaux* such as
Comète. It is estimated that perhaps seventy aircrew were passed
back to Britain through this line. The experience of Second
Lieutenant Alden Faudie USAAF, who was navigator on a B-17
shot down on 14 October 1943, is an example of what became
something of a common experience among aircrew finding themselves crashing in northern France. Faudie landed near Epernay,
south of Reims, where he was helped by members of *Possum*
(including Dr Robert Beaumont) for some months before being
brought to Amiens by Joseph Balfe on 11 February 1944 to be
hidden with Madame Vignon. He was with Madame Vignon

* One of those who helped Private Conrad Lafleur on 25 August 1942, dressing wounds he had sustained during the abortive assault on Dieppe on 19
August, was Dr Robert Beaumont. Lafleur was awarded a MM following his
first escape in 1942 (escaping through the 'Pat Line') and a DCM in 1944 for
his activities with *Possum*: see TNA WO 373/62/339 and WO 373/95/131.
His story is told by Lucien Dumas in *The Man Who Went Back* (London: Leo
Cooper, 1975).

during the RAF attack on Amiens Prison on 18 February.* He left Amiens on 18 March and was later picked up by a member of *Possum* at Chauny (halfway to Reims), who sheltered him until liberation on 31 August 1944.†

Another story among many is that of Flying Officer Raymond Sherk of the Royal Canadian Air Force, a Spitfire pilot from 401 Squadron RAF, who was shot down for a second time in his career (the first was in Libya in September 1942), this time during a Ramrod mission over northern France in March 1944. Sherk was found by Léopold and Renée Roussel, members of *Possum* who lived in the tiny village of Forceville on the Somme, 19 miles north-east of Amiens, where Léo was the village schoolmaster. Roussel forged Ray's identity papers and gave him the considerable sum of 3,000 francs (£10 at the time, about £310 today), before on 23 March his friend René Muchembled escorted Ray by bus and train to Bordeaux. Ray then crossed the Pyrenees into Spain by foot in April.

But the Gestapo were already on Roussel's trail. On 16 April he was arrested, incidentally the same day that René Muchembled was caught by the Germans and 'shot while resisting arrest', a euphemism for execution. Both men had come to the attention of the authorities in some way, perhaps through the work of an informer, or perhaps through information forced out of a *résistant* during torture. Torture was a desperate reality for captured *résistants*. When Raymond Bonpas found himself in Amiens Prison in January 1944, he was shocked to see the leader of his own *réseau*, arrested weeks earlier, in a terrible state, and without his fingernails. Likewise, André Pache, imprisoned at the same time, worried about how he and his comrades would react to torture. He

---

* At least four US airmen were hidden with Mme Vignon at the time of the raid: Second Lieutenant Ernest Lindell, Sergeant Gaetano A. Friuli, Second Lieutenant Faudie and Second Lieutenant John G. Harms.

† Chauny boasted a thriving *réseau d'évasion*, led by the one-legged Captain Etienne Dromas (*Le Noir*), who narrowly survived the war.

knew that some of his friends had already been arrested on the basis of information exacted from his Resistance chief, and feared that he would not be strong enough when his turn came: 'Perhaps under torture I would have denounced those who were working with me ... I don't know if I am strong enough to withstand torture.'

The Germans were skilled at infiltrating Resistance networks. Indeed, the capture of many *résistants* and the collapse of many *réseaux* was due to the work of traitors, as the *OCM* was to discover in north-eastern France with the turning of Roland Farjon. The eventual demise of the Pat Line was attributable to traitors, notably the French traitor and German infiltration agent Roger Leneveu. The entire Dutch section of the SOE in Holland was controlled by the Abwehr in June 1942 and remained in German control for eighteen disastrous months, at great loss of life. The Germans even infiltrated agents into the escape lines.

Léopold was taken to the Citadel in Amiens, where he was tortured. He was deported to Dachau on 2 July 1944. Of the 2,100 prisoners who were jammed into the cattle trucks without water for the journey of several days, only 1,630 survived. Léopold died of asphyxia within hours of the doors on his cattle truck being closed. In the Roussels' village, ten members of *Possum* were deported under the terms of *Nacht und Nebel*, seven never to return. But before he died, Léo and Renée had helped fifteen airmen to escape. The Gestapo managed to capture Major Dominique Potier, the head of *Possum*, in December 1943. Grievously tortured, he died on 11 January 1944 after throwing himself from a third-floor window of Reims Prison.

Dr Robert Beaumont (*Bistouri*) became an agent for *Possum* as the result of meeting and treating three wounded Canadian soldiers evading after the failed commando attack on Dieppe on 19 August 1942. He and his wife Liliane decided not merely to provide medical help to these men, but to provide identification documents, money and a contact in Paris. One of the men was Conrad Lafleur of the Mont-Royal Fusiliers, who came back in 1943 as part of MI9 to establish *Possum*, a key first recruit being Beaumont himself. The couple and their two children lived in Warloy-Baillon, 11 miles north-east of Amiens. At some time in the late summer of 1943, Robert and Liliane began organising a sheltering and evacuation centre for *Possum* around Amiens. As a doctor, he was able to secure precious fuel for his car, which enabled him to move evaders from one safe house to another between Reims and Amiens and the country in between. It is believed that he also established landing sites for Lysander and possibly Hudson operations. Through Lafleur, Beaumont had a direct radio link with London.

On the afternoon of 15 February 1944, Dr Robert Beaumont was arrested at his home in Hornoy and taken to Amiens Prison. No one knew why, although the suspicion was that he was denounced by someone who knew of his resistance activities, or who had been forced to reveal his name under torture. An American revolver was discovered in the house, which ordinarily would have condemned him to aggressive interrogation at the very least. He would be a prisoner for only three days before the Mosquitoes of 140 Wing arrived over the prison at noon on 18 February.

FIVE

Hitler's V-weapons

Agents reporting to MI6 in northern France began describing the emergence of strange new construction sites across the Pas-de-Calais and Cherbourg Peninsula in mid-1943. Nothing, however, linked this activity with the fragmentary but increasingly convincing evidence, which had begun to emerge six months before, about the development by the Germans of a secret weapon whispered to be able to wipe London from the map. The Nazi leadership was obsessed with the promise of technical innovations that they hoped would once and for all turn the tide of the war in their favour. Hitler for one never lost his faith in the prospect that wonder weapons – from new tanks to the jet engine, rockets and the products of nuclear fission – would provide a short cut to victory. His hope that these would soon translate into a tangible reality grew in direct proportion to the Wehrmacht's failure to achieve the increasingly absurd goals set it by the Führer.

Dr R. V. Jones, the Air Ministry's chief scientist since 1939 (the Assistant Director of Intelligence (Science), but to all intents and purposes MI6's chief scientist), had been convinced for some time that the claims made by the Nazi leadership about these weapons actually referred to stratospheric rockets, although the idea was derided by Lord Cherwell (F. D. Lindemann), the government's scientific adviser – rocket technology was unproven, the latter argued. While there was confusion and disagreement in Whitehall and Adastral House in Kingsway (the home of the Air Ministry) as to the chances of Germany successfully developing the technology that would drive a rocket all the way from continental Europe to the British mainland, carrying a sufficiently large payload to cause significant damage, there was no dispute that the enemy was up to something.

Fragments of intelligence about German ambitions began to cohere in August 1943 with the arrival of two reports from MI6 agents in France providing unparalleled detail about the German weapons programme based on Peenemünde, a test and experimental site on the Baltic coast. The second of these reports came from a remarkable female member of the *réseau Alliance*, Jeannie Rousseau (*Amniarix*), who confirmed that the Germans were developing two separate pilotless weapons: a flying bomb (later discovered to be the V1) and a rocket (the V2). She not only warned the Allies that these weapons were being manufactured, but linked them for the first time with the mysterious research facility at Peenemünde already identified as a site of unusual activity by intelligence reports going back to 1940, and confirmed by the Spitfires of the RAF's No. 1 Photographic Reconnaissance Unit (PRU) based at Heston aerodrome in West London. Peenemünde was attacked as a precautionary measure by a devastating raid on the night of 17/18 August 1943 by 596 aircraft of Bomber Command.

Rousseau, a gifted linguist, had become a member of Georges Lamarque's *réseau Druides*, part of *Alliance*, in 1942, but in fact by this time she was already an experienced spy. Evacuated with her family to Dinard in 1940, she had gained a job as interpreter in the headquarters of Walther von Reichenau's 6th Army, and had flooded London with information about early Wehrmacht plans for the defence of Normandy through a Resistance contact in St-Brieuc. Before the war she had attended the University of Paris, graduating in 1939, which was where she had first met Georges Lamarque (*Petrel*). She met him again by accident travelling by train from Paris to Vichy in 1942 when she was working as a translator with the French Chamber of Commerce, liaising daily with the occupation authorities in Paris. He told her of his resistance activities and invited her to join his cell within *Alliance*.* She agreed without hesitation. Her job brought her into contact with German officers who knew of the Peenemünde secret and, anxious to impress their pretty 23-year-old French interpreter, they bragged to her. On one occasion an officer showed her the security requirements for entry into the Peenemünde site. The information was immediately fed back, through Georges Lamarque's radio transmitter at 26 rue Fabert, to MI6. Rousseau's reports persuaded R. V. Jones that the Germans were in the process of manufacturing a stratospheric rocket, and that Peenemünde was its test and development site. What was not then known was how, and from where, the rockets would be launched against Britain.

This breakthrough was not long in coming. On 20 August, Rousseau was able to describe to MI6 in great detail the German plans for the deployment of the V1 pilotless missiles (FZG 76). Her extraordinary report, which demonstrated just how close she had got to her German sources, warned:

It appears that the final stage has been reached in developing a stratospheric bomb of an entirely new type. This bomb is reported to be 10 cubic metres in volume and filled with explosive. It would be launched almost vertically to reach the stratosphere as quickly as possible. The source speaks of 50 mph vertically, initial velocity being maintained by successive explosions. The bomb is provided with *Raketten* (vanes?) and guided to specific targets. The bomb is said to be fuelled with 800 litres of petrol ... The trials are understood to have given immediate excellent results as regards accuracy and it was to the success of these trials that Hitler was referring when he spoke of 'new weapons that will change the face of the war when the Germans use them . . .'

* Lamarque was caught by the Germans and shot on 8 September 1944.

Colonel Wachtel and the officers that he has collected are to form the cadres of an anti-aircraft regiment (16 batteries of 220 men), the 155 W, that is going to be stationed in France, at the end of October or beginning of November, with HQ near Amiens, and batteries between Amiens, Abbeville, Dunkirk.

The regiment will deploy 108 . . . catapults able to fire a bomb every twenty minutes. The army artillery will have more than 400 catapults sited from Brittany to Holland . . . Major Sommerfeld, Colonel Wachtel's technical adviser, estimates that 50–100 of these bombs would suffice to destroy London. The batteries will be so sited that they can methodically destroy most of Britain's large cities during the winter.

Reinforced concrete platforms are reported to be already under construction. They are expected to be fully operational in November.*

The extraordinary intelligence provided by Rousseau was supplemented on 28 October 1943 by a new source, routed this time through the MI6 station in Geneva run by Victor Farrell, warning that the Germans were building unexplained but nevertheless highly secret concrete emplacements in northern France, one at Yvrench, north-east of Abbeville and 30 miles from Amiens, each involving a ramp-like construction that was pointed in the direction of London. The information from an agent by the name of Michel Hollard neatly complemented that of Jeannie Rousseau, although there was no absolute proof at this stage, so far as a cautious London was concerned, that the two subjects were connected.

The story of the 45-year-old Michel Hollard clearly demonstrates the importance of MI6's espionage networks in northern

---

* Arrested in 1944 as she was attempting to travel by boat from the Breton coast to London, the Germans never knew whom they had captured. Rousseau narrowly avoided death in Ravensbrück and survived the war.

France to the discovery and ultimately the undermining of Germany's V-weapon programme. A soldier during the Great War (he had been decorated for bravery with the Croix de Guerre), to his great annoyance Hollard found himself rejected for military service in 1939 because of his age and found himself working in an armaments factory. When, after the armistice of June 1940, he discovered that the factory was making equipment for the Germans, he resigned and found work making vehicles that ran on wood gas, an increasingly important substitute for scarce petrol in occupied France. This job gave him permission to visit the charcoal-manufacturing areas of eastern France, and a cover to begin collecting information about the occupation forces. In 1941 he took a gamble and slipped into Switzerland, making his way to the British legation in Berne to offer his services as a spy. His biographer records how Colonel Cartwright, the British military attaché, showed him the door, concerned perhaps that he was a Nazi agent provocateur, a common problem for MI6 during the war. Who could be trusted when they arrived out of the blue on one's doorstep offering to provide information about the enemy? It was the perfect route into the heart of the enemy's intelligence system for a double-agent.

Fortunately for Britain, Hollard's credentials were quickly confirmed, and Victor Farrell took him under MI6's wing. It was the first of forty-eight separate journeys Hollard was to make across the border over the coming months, bringing extraordinary amounts of detailed intelligence about the Wehrmacht in France. The report about the strange site at Bois Carré, Yvrench, was his. In August 1943, hearing rumours about unusual building sites across the countryside, Hollard decided to take a look for himself. Through persistence and some trial and error he found one of the sites at Cormeilles-sur-Veau and just walked in, pretending to be a workman. He learned enough from the workers to raise his suspicions and so arrange for one of his friends, a draughtsman, to get a job there. This man was able in due course to copy all the construction drawings, which Hollard took to Switzerland. At the heart of each site was a strip of concrete pointing on the bearing of London.

Separately, MI6 had procured a detailed drawing of what the RAF reconnaissance pilots were calling 'ski sites'. The concrete strip was the foundation trackway for an angled metal ramp about 150 feet long, inclined at 15 degrees. Aerial photography demonstrated that in addition to the metal ramp each site had three long narrow buildings, each with a gently curving end rather like a ski lying on its side. Amazingly, Hollard discovered one of the V1 rockets in a railway siding between Dieppe and Beauvais. He promptly measured it and took the pile of diagrams and measurements personally to Victor Farrell in Berne.

Throughout most of November, however, considerable disagreement existed in London as to what these buildings were, and no lazy correlation was allowed between the rumour of a secret rocket weapon and the mysterious construction sites. It wasn't until the end of the month that the mounting evidence from the photographic experts at the Central Interpretation Unit (CIU) correlated photographs taken of ramps at Peenemünde with those found in northern France. This conclusion was accepted by the subcommittee of the Joint Intelligence Committee charged with investigating the reports of secret weapons, the Crossbow Committee.* It decided that the sites in France were designed to launch pilotless aircraft. The sites warned of by Jeannie Rousseau and observed, measured and photographed by Michel Hollard were the launch locations for the V1, of which Hitler originally planned that 5,000 would fall on London every twenty-four hours over a four-month period. This would mean building and launching a staggering 600,000 weapons.†

---

* Until mid-November it was known as the Bodyline Committee.
† In the event 5,430 were launched, causing 6,100 deaths and 17,300 injured, and destroying or damaging one million houses in Greater London.

The site became a target for the cameras of the PRU Spitfires, which first photographed the Yvrench site on 3 November, and gradually during the month the evidence that these sites were linked to the rocket weapons described by Jeannie Rousseau became overwhelming. Aerial reconnaissance had in fact been identifying these suspicious sites for some weeks. Hollard had reported six, but the numbers grew fast in November: 26 had been identified by 10 November, but by the end of the month MI6 reports listed 60, while the PRU had identified 38. All lay within 12 miles of the coast in a corridor that stretched for 200 miles along the length of the Seine-Inférieure and Pas-de-Calais *départements*, and as a group they were dispersed to mimic the southern coast of England. They were clearly launch sites for flying weapons that were timed onto their targets by volume of fuel, and pointed on their course by the direction set by the steel ramp.

The suspicious nature of these sites, long before any formal correlation was made between them and Hitler's rocket programme, warranted the attention of the Allied air forces. While attacks began on 5 November, the formal 'Noball' campaign against them began in early December 1943. Difficult to find because they were camouflaged by the woods in which they were hidden, they proved to be ideal targets for Embry's Mosquito squadrons. The combined squadrons of 140 Wing under the leadership of 'Pick' Pickard undertook their first mission against these targets, around Sainte Agathe-d'Aliermont, 17 miles south-east of Dieppe, three days before Christmas. The crews gathered at 8 a.m. that morning under conditions of great secrecy to be told the nature of their task. Forty aircraft, together with the single photographic Mosquito from the Film Production Unit, took part. Basil Embry also flew, in part to gain a solid understanding of the capabilities of his aircraft, their crews and the leadership of the Wing under Pickard. Although eight aircraft failed to find the target, over one hundred bombs were dropped, in what was considered to be a successful attack, with a follow-up strike made by a smaller number of aircraft later that same afternoon.

A window in the prevailing winter weather pattern allowed several more missions to be undertaken against similar targets in the days that followed. On 29 December a successful attack was undertaken by 29 Mosquitoes against sites at Pommerval, and the last operation of the year took place on 31 December against Le Plouy Ferme (19 miles north-west of Amiens), with 39 aircraft of 140 Wing. Squadron Leader Philippe Level flew his first Noball mission with No. 21 Squadron on 29 December. He has left a vivid account of the attack (written in 1946), starting with Embry's briefing at 8 a.m. that morning. Embry was dressed in his flying kit, the first evidence for Level that he was to fly with them:

We shall take off at about mid-day, as usual. The planes will be lined up to right and left of the take-off runway, and will move into take-off position in twos, some fifteen yards apart. When the first two planes are seventy-five yards away, the next pair will follow, so that our forty-eight planes will be airborne in the minimum time and heading for France in formations of six.

The sea is rough; we shall fly so low that the spray will cover our wind-screens. We shall have to watch out for seagulls, for we shall be flying at such a speed that any shock against our wings might crack the wing spar. We shall cross the coast over a lonely farm on the cliffs, about two miles west of Criel-sur-Mer, which will be easy to recognise as it is surrounded by a square shaped wood. We shall be flying over this farm many, many times in the next few months – but the Boches will never think of installing a few machine-guns along the cliffs.

We shall fly over the route from Dieppe to Tréport, and turn south. I shall lead the second section. The formation will be echeloned to starboard in close formation, only a few yards from each other. Our speed will be two hundred and seventy miles an hour. Coming down its valley, we shall be able to see Dieppe a few miles to our right. We shall cross the river and go up the valley, crossing swiftly over another smaller one. Along the higher ground to the south of this second valley we will see a road, and follow it for a few miles. The road winds through the peaceful orchards of Normandy. Then on the left-hand side of the road we will see the smoke from the bombs dropped by the first section. We will drop our bombs from thirty or forty feet, although the launching platform may already seem to be destroyed. In the light of the explosions, we shall see a group of typical Normandy houses very near the launching platform, with their half-timbering which is supposed to make their walls so solid. You will wonder how they will stand up to your bombardment. We shall swing left, flying over Londinières, ignoring the machine guns which will spit their fire angrily but without skill. We shall fly low, skimming the trees, crossing again the road to Dieppe, flying over our farm on the cliffs, skimming over the Channel, and so back to base, our mission completed. We shall have been over French soil for something like twelve minutes.

By January 1944 raids on Crossbow sites were commonplace across 140 Wing, with forty-one recorded. All the while Embry experimented with improving the tactics and techniques of his crews. In addition to the attendance on almost every mission of the FPU aircraft, he built models of the VI site targets so as to make the aircrew thoroughly conversant with what they were going after. The targets were tiny, comprising not much more than 500 yards square of buildings and ramps, all tucked away in orchards and small woods. The key targets were the ramp itself and the demagnetised building in which the V1 was fitted with its wings and had its compass fitted. Even a near-miss would litter the area with shrapnel that would make this preparatory process difficult, if not impossible, thereafter. The early missions were undertaken at medium altitude (1,500 feet and above), but every additional foot of height traded safety from flak for bombing accuracy. If attacks could take place at very low level – little above treetop height – accuracy could be dramatically enhanced and flak avoided, but flying so close to the ground required special skills from the pilots and navigators, especially as the targets were increasingly hard to find and were well defended.

It is clear today, therefore, in a way that had only gradually been dawning on policymakers in London since late 1943, that the Resistance could play and was playing an enormous and significant role in the effort in northern France to uncover and defeat the V1 (and later the V2) threat. Some information, of course, would continue to come through *Ultra*, and other material through the remarkable work of Photographic Reconnaissance, but an important source was the eyes on the ground provided by the intelligence-gathering networks of the Resistance, and the radio links between agents and the SIS signal-receiving station at Whaddon Hall.

Thanks to *Amniarix* it was known that the HQ of the Luftwaffe regiment responsible, 155 (W), was located in Amiens, and that the town was the centre of the V1 launch programme. It was the home of the Wehrmacht's 67 Corps (part of 15 Army), but from 8 January 1944 substantial reinforcements – an additional 45,000 troops – were transported to the region, bringing the total of fighting troops to over 75,000. The 2nd Panzer and 6th Airborne Infantry Divisions were based nearby in Abbeville, together with the 344th and 348th Divisions manning the Atlantic Wall respectively north and south of the mouth of the Somme. It was for this reason that Erwin Rommel visited Amiens on 17 February 1944 as part of his programme of visits designed to prepare the region for defence. His presence on this day, and the RAF attack the following day, were entirely coincidental.

It was in all likelihood this intelligence success by the French Resistance, among a number of other considerations, that helped persuade MI6, and the Air Ministry, to support the request for an attack on Amiens Prison. It would not have been difficult for them to appreciate the argument that released *résistants* could then provide a direct boost to intelligence efforts against the V-weapons in Picardy, especially since the German V1 programme was not yet under way, and much still had to be played for. In the months leading up to D-Day it was imperative that the volume and quality of intelligence along the length of the French coastline was maintained, and that every effort was made to ensure the health of local *réseaux* in these areas. Perhaps unwittingly, Hollard, known to history subsequently as 'the man who saved London', was also instrumental in a small way for the release of his compatriots from incarceration and eventual execution in Amiens Prison.

SIX

Disaster in France

For all their success, the SOE, BCRA and MI6 resistance networks in France remained vulnerable, and many suffered badly in 1943. The intensity and effectiveness of German counter-espionage operations dealt great harm to a large number of *réseaux* in mid- to late 1943, leading to considerable loss of life, the collapse of many networks and the arrest, incarceration, deportation and execution of many hundreds of committed *résistants*. The loss of so many mature networks and experienced agents across France threatened the critical flow of strategic intelligence to London – not just the secrets of the Atlantic Wall, but also critical information about V-weapon sites in Picardy and the Pas-de-Calais. These failures also threatened to lower the morale of those in occupied France who were daily placing their lives at risk to support the Allied cause. The negative impact on the morale of Allied aircrews posed by the rolling up of MI9 networks was a further consideration for London. Indeed, it is only possible to understand Operation *Jericho* in terms of the desperate struggle between the German occupiers and the various elements of *la résistance française* during the final six months of 1943 and the early weeks of 1944.

Underground activities always carry the risk of penetration by the enemy's counter-espionage services. The collapse of the *Interallié* organisation in November 1941, for instance, pointed uncomfortably to the damage that could be done when the enemy managed to turn key personnel at the heart of a network, especially if the network concerned did not operate a disciplined cell structure where groups in the same organisation operated entirely independently of each other. Likewise in 1942 the *réseau Gloria*, which provided intelligence for Dansey, was fatally damaged by enemy penetration orchestrated by Father Robert Alesch, a priest in the pay of the Abwehr. Run by Gabrielle Martinez-Picabia (*Gloria*) and Jacques Legrand, the network was decimated on 13 August 1942. More than eighty of its members were deported, most of them to die in horrifying conditions at Mauthausen or Buchenwald concentration camps.

Alesch, an extraordinarily manipulative individual, lived by day as a vocal *résistant* and devout Christian, but at night as a devourer of the souls he had persuaded to join the Resistance, who found themselves instead in a Gestapo torture chamber. He was paid a bounty for every person he handed over.* He had inveigled his way into the group, which included the playwright Samuel Beckett (who narrowly managed to escape arrest) and Germaine Tillion (who survived Ravensbrück), to such an extent that the entire edifice crumbled at the first push.

In 1943 German counter-espionage successes brought a series of disasters for the Allies. On 21 June 1943 the remarkable unifier of resistance politics in France, Jean Moulin, was arrested along with most of the senior members of the CNR in an Abwehr operation codenamed 'Grand Duke', led by SS-Obersturmführer Klaus Barbie in Lyon, in circumstances that remain disputed. General Charles Delestraint, arrested twelve days earlier, was deported under the terms of *Nacht und Nebel* to Germany, where he was executed in 1945 (at Dachau), while Moulin died following vicious torture at the hands of Barbie, revealing nothing to his persecutors. This was cold comfort to London, as Moulin's gallant death seemed to represent the beginning of the end of serious and united

---

* Alesch was executed by firing squad on 25 January 1949 at the Fort de Montrouge, Paris.

resistance in France. The man tasked with carrying on the work of Moulin, Captain Claude Bouchinet-Serreulles (*Sophie*), appears, by virtue of equal doses of inexperience and naivety, to have presided over further chaos and insecurity across many of the French networks in the ensuing months.

Likewise Maurice Buckmaster's F Section of SOE experienced the devastating collapse of Francis Suttill's *réseau Physician* (Suttill's codename was *Prosper*), which entailed mass arrests, partly as the result of the deliberate duplicity of one of its own senior agents, Henri Déricourt. In an act of treachery almost certainly driven by greed, Déricourt played both sides off against each other, growing rich in the process. A charming, urbane man, who made friends and won confidences easily, it seems clear that only one individual mattered in Déricourt's universe: Déricourt himself. Responsible for managing the in-country landing sites, he also handled the incoming and outgoing mail. This he passed to his Abwehr contacts for copying before resealing and forwarding to its destination. Through the capture of two of *Physician*'s agents the Germans managed to arrest Major Gilbert Norman (*Archambaud*) on 23 June 1943, Suttill's lieutenant and *pianiste*, and to roll up the remainder of the organisation, on the basis of information provided by Déricourt.* Noleen Baxter notes that with *Physician*'s collapse F Section's resistance in France threatened to come to an end:

> One thousand five hundred people were arrested, and hundreds of agents and locally recruited *résistants* belonging to the group were seized, tortured, deported to concentration camps and sent to their deaths. Among them was Prosper's organizer, Francis Suttill, who was brutally tortured before being sent to Sachsenhausen concentration camp and hanged. His courier, Andrée Borrel, was one of the four women F Section agents who

---

* Norman was executed at Mauthausen concentration camp, Austria, on 6 September 1944.

were burnt alive at Natzweiler. And the radio operator, Noor Inayat-Khan, having survived many months of solitary confinement in various prisons, terrible torture and, for the last four months of her life, being shackled wrists to ankles, was finally shot in the back of the head, too weak from starvation and torture to be able to crawl across the floor. It was said that when she died she no longer resembled a human being; she was just a mass of raw meat, the skin hanging off her back from her many beatings. But, like Suttill and Andree Borrel, she never once talked or gave the enemy any information.

Both the *OCM* and *CND* suffered grievously in late 1943. In the south the wife of the right-wing leader of the *OCM*, André Grandclément (*Bernard*), whose organisation was a significant partner of SOE's F Section, was arrested by the Gestapo in September. Fearful for her life, and persuaded by the Gestapo that the greater threat to the future of France was communism, he agreed to collaborate with the enemy. Within a matter of months his treachery had cost many lives and unravelled several local networks. In northern France the *OCM* (led by Colonel Alfred Touny [*Lacroix*]) also suffered severely from German penetration. One of its senior members, Roland Farjon, was arrested in October 1943. Like Grandclément he was swiftly turned, and began handing his erstwhile colleagues over to the Gestapo. The first to be arrested were Dr Antonin Mans and Captain André Tempez in Amiens. The danger to all connected *réseaux* was clear: Touny's *OCM* worked closely with Gilbert Renault's *CND*, utilising *Century* to coordinate intelligence collection from both networks.

But the *CND* was devastated in November 1943 by another hand, the Belgian traitor Georges-Henri Delfanne ('Christian Masuy'), who was working for the Abwehr.* In *Portrait of a Spy*

* Christian Masuy, the self-styled 'Chief of French Gestapo' (*Corps d'Autoprotection français*), was arrested and put on trial by a French court for

(1953) Gilbert Renault described how Delfanne destroyed the network that he had nurtured since 1940. It is estimated that by the hand of this man some 800 *résistants* were arrested. 'At the end of October 1943 the Abwehr arrested *Parsifal**, who was at the head of a network closely linked with my own which looked after the dispatch to London of its radio messages and correspondence,' recorded Gilbert. Abwehr interrogation of *Parsifal* (led by an agent called 'Gulliver') and their relentless accumulation of information about the *résistants* led to the unravelling of the entire *réseau*:

> In a few weeks Masuy managed the extraordinary feat of totally destroying a network in existence since 1940 which sent to London seventy lots of dispatches by air or sea and transmitted thousands of radio messages. Next Masuy undermined several other networks and would have wiped out the OCM had it not been for the heroism of our comrades. At this time I was in London, where I received and distributed the information arriving from networks operating in France and affiliated to the Free French forces. In November 1943 I observed a decline of almost 50 per cent in the amount of information sent to us. [During the period between 5 and 17 November 1943 Masuy's actions] all but wiped out a network which for three years past held its own with the entire German police.

By the time of its demise, the *réseau CND* was operating an ultra-short horizontal wave transmitter, codenamed *Ayesha*, which was virtually undetectable by conventional detection apparatus. This was hidden with a gendarme by the name of Picard, in Abbeville. Alas, it too was discovered and Picard arrested by Masuy

---

treason. He was convicted and sentenced to death on 18 November 1944 and executed by firing squad on 1 October 1947 at Fort de Montrouge, outside Paris.

* Robert Tainturier, who was arrested on 5 October 1943 and died at Dora Concentration Camp the following year.

on 9 November. The Germans expended considerable energy in tracking down the Resistance *pianistes*, for they knew well that an agent without means of communication to London was worthless, no matter how precious the material in his possession. Lieutenant Colonel Oscar Reile, head of Abwehr counter-espionage (Section IIIF) in Paris, considered that the devastation of British radio networks ranked among the greatest successes of his organisation. By the end of 1942 he had established a vast armada of radio detection vans which, with the assistance of Vichy, helped locate clandestine radio traffic to London. In 1943 alone 1,500 people were arrested and many small networks destroyed as a result of these successes. Hauptmann Dr Hubertus Freyer was the head of the specialist radio detection organisation of the Abwehr in France from the end of 1943, an organisation that hunted down *pianistes* with horrifying precision.

From the outset it was clear that Germany's counter-espionage services were engaged in a battle to the death against any flowerings of dissent or resistance, and the *CND*, along with all other *réseaux* in France, found itself battered and bloodied by this bitter form of warfare. *Alliance*'s Marie-Madeline Fourcade (*Hedgehog*) had been recalled to London by Dansey in July 1943. She could only watch helplessly as the Germans rounded up 150 of her best agents in the months that followed, including Raymond Bonpas, a veteran of the Great War who was incarcerated in Amiens Prison after having been arrested on 4 January 1944 for possession of false papers. Gabrielle and René Halbert, together with their ten-year-old daughter Renée, who lived in Amiens, were arrested by the Gestapo on 18 December 1943, accused of harbouring a radio operator for the *réseau* at their home in rue Claudius Sbocassaint. By the end of the year most of the *Alliance* groups in north-west France and the Rhône valley had ceased to exist.

The emotional response of this heroic woman to the destruction of her network dramatised for Dansey the scale of the enormous personal tragedy unfolding before him. She insisted on going back to rescue her *réseau*: he was determined to do anything possible to revive the flagging fortunes of the *résistants*, but this did not extend to allowing Fourcade to return to France, where he was convinced she would also lose her life. Meanwhile *Alliance* was taken apart by what they called the 'Gibbet', the combined efforts of the Abwehr and the Gestapo. By December 1943 Fourcade noted that:

> . . . the network was shrinking tragically. My only radio contacts were with *Swift*, *Petrel* (Georges Lamarque), *Opossum* (Henri Battu) in the north, and with *Grand Duke* and *Shad* (Jean-Claude Thorel) in the south . . . I began to wonder if British Intelligence perhaps considered us finished . . . I was constantly reviewing our miserable plight. In France there was the tragedy of the seriously damaged network, whose survivors were beginning to doubt whether they would ever be saved.

Dansey confided to Fourcade: 'The havoc caused by the Abwehr is terrifying. The emissaries that we send to France often find nobody at all.' Dansey eventually agreed to allow Fourcade to return to France, but his fears were borne out by subsequent events. Fourcade was arrested by the Gestapo, but by some miracle she escaped and narrowly survived the war.

Georges-Henri Delfanne was also responsible for the capture of another jewel in MI6's French crown, a man Masuy subsequently described as 'Commander Georges Bertrand', but who was in fact Major Gustave Bertrand, late of the cryptography department of the Deuxième Bureau, and a key player in France's pre-war intelligence war against Germany. The arrest was a major coup for the Abwehr, because Bertrand was the man through whose agency the Polish achievements in unravelling the Enigma mystery were first presented to the Allies in 1939, and the basis for Britain's celebrated *Ultra* operation, based at Bletchley Park. But Delfanne had no idea who he had caught, considering him useful only in so far as he could make contact with MI6, from which Delfanne hoped he might simultaneously secure the secrets of Operation *Overlord*. He also deluded himself that by establishing this contact he might be able to safeguard his own future after the war. If he could demonstrate some usefulness to the Allies they might then forgive him his working for the Nazis. Unbeknown to Masuy, Bertrand was in fact head of a covert intelligence network, run within the Vichy regime but working against the Germans and codenamed 'Kléber', led by Colonel Louis Rivet. Following Germany's invasion of Poland in September 1939, the then Major Bertrand continued the work of the pre-war Cipher Bureau, first outside Paris, then, after Germany's invasion of France (May–June 1940), at the secret cryptography centre based at Uzès, on the Mediterranean coast (codenamed *Cadix*) in the *Zone Libre*. In November 1942, following the German occupation of the *Zone Libre*, Bertrand fled to Algiers to join the Giraudist opposition to the German occupation.

Bertrand was arrested by Delfanne in Paris on 3 January 1944 during one of his many return visits to occupied France. Masuy claims that Bertrand and his wife Mary then managed to escape their confinement. The truth is more complex, outlined by Bertrand himself in his autobiography and by Paul Paillole, who as head of French Counter-Espionage was responsible for rooting out potential traitors. Bertrand had in fact pretended to collaborate with the Abwehr in return for his safety, terrified that torture would reveal the secrets of Enigma, the Allies' greatest and most closely guarded secret. Masuy was keen to get closer to MI6, and Bertrand told him that he could contact both Menzies and Dansey, which was true. It would have been a significant coup for Masuy to have managed to insert a double agent into the SIS, and thus learn the secrets of Operation *Overlord*, and much else. Given a limited degree of freedom in consequence, Bertrand seized the chance to escape, doing so on 11 January, although it wasn't until May that he and his wife were finally able to make their way to London in a Lysander that lifted them from a field in the Massif Central. Masuy grumbled that the last he heard of them was when his wife received a bunch of flowers from Mary Bertrand a few days after their disappearance. In Masuy's pre-execution testimony in 1947 he gave no hint of ever realising the size of the catch he had made, or the significance of his loss.

Bertrand's return to France had been designed to help prepare the various Resistance movements for the forthcoming invasion (although he had no personal knowledge of the details of Operation *Overlord*). The capture by Masuy of someone of Bertrand's significance was a shock to London (and Algiers), and demonstrated the argument of those in Dunderdale's organisation that he should not be allowed to return to France. It is clear that for all the period of his absence, hidden in occupied France, Menzies worried that Bertrand had been turned, and that the secret of Enigma was thereby at risk, and with it the entire structure of the *Fortitude* deception, intended to dupe the Germans into preparing for the now ineviatable Allied invasion to take place in the area of the Pas-de-Calais. Menzies reasoned that if Bertrand had been turned, the entirety of *Fortitude* might be being played back to the Allies, with the Germans pretending to accept the deception, whilst actively countering it by reinforcing other areas of the coastline vulnerable to invasion. In the event Menzies could do nothing about it, as the Bertrands were not spirited out of France until a few days before D-Day, but it undoubtedly played on his and Dansey's minds in the period leading up to their decision to refer the request to attack Amiens Prison to the Air Ministry for their military assessment of the possibilities of this sort of action.

Far from diminishing, state-sponsored violence against enemies of the German state increased dramatically as the war in Europe entered its final phase, beginning to take on some of the characteristics of German behaviour in the east. In Vichy Joseph Darnand, the head of the Milice, had entered the government in December 1943 and had taken responsibility for *le maintien de l'ordre*, allowing new depths of brutality to overtake the Vichy regime and its paramilitaries. On 20 January 1944 a law was enacted instituting military courts and effectively allowing summary executions, and the rate of transportations to the east of Jews and *résistants* was stepped up.

Between September 1943 and January 1944 some 9,500 were deported to Buchenwald, where many *résistants* became slave labourers at the notorious Dora Camp, which manufactured the V2 rocket. In a grim ironic twist, these *résistants*, many of whom had spied out the V-weapon launch sites in France, were now being forced to manufacture the weapons themselves. Over 380 *résistants* were condemned to death during the second half of 1943. On 3 September 1943 nearly 1,000 *résistants*, most of whom had been arrested as they were attempting to cross the Pyrenees into Spain, had set out for Buchenwald from Compiègne in cattle trucks. Another 1,000 began their terrible journey on 17 September, in trains also bound for Buchenwald and Dora, and on 28 October and 14 December 1944 more trains headed eastwards. Fewer than 10 per cent of their occupants would ever return. Between December 1943 and January 1944, 130 of these *résistants* were members of *Alliance*. Most were executed. Five more trains went east in January 1944, 5,500 men, women and children forced into cattle trucks on 17, 22, 27 and 31 January 1944 bound for both Buchenwald and Ravensbrück, the women's camp near Berlin.

The nineteen-year-old niece of General Charles de Gaulle, Geneviève, was taken from Fresnes Prison to Royallieu camp near Compiègne prior to transportation to Ravensbrück on 3 February 1944. Hundreds of other women from across France were squeezed into the transit camp:

I was amazed [Geneviève wrote] to discover the range and diver-
sity of my fellow prisoners: young and old, from very different
backgrounds and geographic locations. Virtually all of them had
been arrested for their involvement in the Resistance, but their
reasons for joining the Underground were many and varied: their
common bond was their unanimous refusal to accept the defeat

of their country at the hands of the Nazis. Some belonged to the intelligence units, others had housed and hidden Allied aviators who were shot down over France, still others had given refuge to those clandestinely sent by the Free French Forces from London into France to reconnoitre and report back.

The historian Gaël Eismann estimates that around 600 were sentenced to death between January and April 1944. On 21 May 1944 2,000 men were transported by train from Compiègne, the first large convoy of *résistants* to be sent to Neuengamme. It included many who had been rounded up after the Amiens raid. For the Germans the war against terrorism was now a priority, with the Milice directed to exterminate the Maquis. New horrors raged in the West – summary executions of *résistants*, deportations, the overruling of legal due process and mass killings of innocents – reaching a culmination of violence in the immediate aftermath of Operation *Overlord*. Indeed, German records counted 7,900 *francs-tireurs* killed in the month following D-Day. Most would have been innocent civilians caught up in the indiscriminate violence: typical behaviour by repressive regimes fast losing control over subject peoples. The mass murders in the Bois de Gentelles and Arras Citadel in May 1944 were evidence of what the Germans and Milice saw as an all-out war against those they considered gangsters and terrorists, and no holds were barred in their barbaric war.

The scale of the devastation wrought to Allied networks in France as a result of Abwehr and Gestapo action led to anxiety in Whitehall. Menzies took the opportunity to attempt to emasculate SOE entirely, arguing in a paper to the Joint Intelligence Committee on 1 August 1943 (subsequently known by its document reference – CX108) that SOE's 'resistance groups in France . . . [were] to a considerable extent compromised and that the enemy must be in possession of much detail regarding these resistance groups'. He was, of course, correct, but it is hard to avoid the conclusion that his purpose in writing was political. The subtext of his argument was that as SOE had clearly demonstrated its ineptitude on a grand scale, MI6 should be allowed to take responsibility for SOE, and that the operations of both organisations should focus on matters of intelligence (such as the effort to find the V1 rocket sites).

In the months that followed CX108 the true scale of the disasters that overwhelmed SOE operations in Holland became clear, reinforcing Menzies' argument. However, Lord Selborne, the minister for Economic Warfare and the man responsible for SOE, responded to these criticisms with a spirited defence of his organisation in two papers in which he emphasised the desperate venture on which his agents were embarked against the most vicious of enemies. Since its creation, he argued, SOE had undertaken over 3,100 operations and sent 1,467 agents into enemy-occupied countries, with remarkable success. This bitter squabble between the two organisations rumbled through until January 1944, but perversely shed much more light on the fate of the French Resistance than would have occurred without 'C's' initial, barbed proposal. Whatever the failures of the past, Churchill did not need to be persuaded of the importance of supporting indigenous resistance movements, not merely so as to damage the enemy's communications but to stimulate rebellion across Europe. Menzies' arguments, the Prime Minister considered, 'if anything convinced me of the wisdom of supporting the maquisards'. To General Hastings Ismay, Secretary of the Chiefs of Staff Committee, he remarked on 10 February 1944 that the 'warfare between SOE and SIS . . . is a lamentable, but perhaps inevitable, feature of our affairs'.

Although MI6 was quick to claim that many groups managed by SOE were most at risk from German counter-espionage activity, MI6 itself was not immune. Dansey's own organisation was badly damaged through the unravelling of many of its own *réseaux* in 1943, a subject that Menzies conveniently ignored in CX108. Three hit hard in particular, as has been seen, were *Alliance*, the *OCM* and Gilbert Renault's *CND*.

Watching the disintegration from afar of all that he had worked so tirelessly to create and build up, Dansey was devastated by these developments. It was Dansey who had secured the resources of the BCRA for MI6 in 1940, who established and managed some of the largest and most impressive *réseaux* in France (*CND*, *Alliance*, *Alibi*, *Jade-Amicol* amongst others), and who had come up with the ideas, in mid-1943, for what was to become Operation *Sussex*, the insertion of Jedburgh 'guerrillas' behind German lines in the run-up to D-Day in 1944. He was determined to do what he could to spare 'his' networks the depredations of the Nazis, and resurrect them where he could. His attitude to Marie Fourcade provides clear evidence of the true depths of his feelings, albeit well hidden beneath a stern and seemingly unforgiving exterior.

While the battle was raging within Whitehall between MI6 and SOE during the last quarter of 1943 and the start of 1944, the British government was under pressure to increase its support to the underground movements in France. For some months the newly combined French Committee of National Liberation in Algiers (CFLN: a collaboration between Gaullist and Giraudist parties, established in May 1943) had been pressing Britain and the United States for more wholehearted and substantial support to the underground movement in France, especially to the armed Maquis groups in southern France who were now actively engaged in open warfare with the Germans. But neither London nor Washington appeared to be moving at anything like the pace the Free French leadership in Algiers demanded, and the New Year of 1944 saw a dramatic growth in the pressure on both countries' leaders to act in support of the Resistance in France.

One of RF Section's most impressive agents, Wing Commander 'Tommy' Yeo-Thomas (*Shelley*), worked closely with the men and women of the BCRA, so his work was well known to MI6. In late 1943 the claws of the German state closed on many of his friends, including Pierre Brossolette. From bitter first-hand experience he feared that Britain was not doing enough to sustain the Free French agents in their hour of need, and in early 1944 he complained to a close friend, Major General Sir Ernest Swinton, about what he believed was the lack of serious support by Britain for the men and women struggling along alone in France. Swinton, a well-known military luminary in his day, had retired in 1919 but still retained the ear of the old friend who was now Prime Minister. He suggested that he meet Churchill to talk through his ideas. No. 10 Downing Street duly (but to Yeo-Thomas, surprisingly) responded, and at 3 p.m. on 1 February 1944 Yeo-Thomas found himself in front of the great man.

What Yeo-Thomas did not know was that his complaint had arrived on the Prime Minister's desk at precisely the time that Whitehall was embroiled in the dispute between MI6 and SOE about primacy in France, and when Churchill was being asked separately by de Gaulle and his recently appointed Minister of the Interior, General Emmanuel d'Astier de la Vigerie (who had previously headed the *réseau Libération-Sud*), to provide expanded support to the Resistance and to enable them to fight the occupiers now, as well as during the impending battle for France.

On 12 January 1944 Duff Cooper, the British Ambassador to the CFLN in Algiers, had sent an urgent telegram from North Africa to London summarising an official note handed to him by the political director of the CFLN's Commissariat for Foreign Affairs about the supply of arms to Resistance groups in France:

> After stating that sabotage in France is already causing the enemy serious inconvenience and quoting official Vichy report on acts of sabotage between 25th September and 25th October note states that when landings take place action of resistance groups will represent important support for the Allied forces.

Unfortunately the material available is small in proportion to number and quality of 'effectives' of resistance groups. While this is due partly to admitted technical difficulties the chief cause is insufficient means of transport for operations into France. Failure to arm and to use the forces prepared in accordance with the wishes of Allied propaganda to fight in the enemy's rear at the moment of landing would have grave military, political and psychological consequences.

The United States and United Kingdom Governments alone are in a position to furnish the necessary supplies for the battle behind the lines, preparation for which presupposes working out of precise plans as to the nature, quantity and use of material to be sent into France. This can only be done with the co-operation of qualified representatives of competent American, British and French services. To achieve this in the best conditions the Committee proposes that these representatives should meet in London as soon as possible.

Duff Cooper explained that the Allies' perceived failure to arm the resistance movements to the extent required was one of the 'hot topics' in Algiers, and one about which d'Astier often complained. The subject had been in contention between SOE and the Chiefs of Staff in London for at least six months, as SOE repeatedly demanded more aircraft from the RAF to be diverted to operations in support of the French Resistance than Bomber Command felt able, with all its other commitments, to support. Discussions took place during January, culminating in a special meeting of the Defence Committee on Thursday 27 January at Downing Street to discuss the issue of support to the Resistance, at which d'Astier de la Vigerie was present.

Although the Air Ministry was desperate to do nothing to detract from the bomber offensive against Germany, Churchill accepted that considerably more effort would be required from Britain and the Allies if the Resistance movement was to produce the results of which it was capable. For his part, d'Astier, while assuring the Prime Minister that the arming of underground forces in France would not result in the intensification of political rivalries among Frenchmen, warned that the fate of whole bands of Maquis was in Churchill's hands. If the Secret Army in France were not armed there was a very real risk of their disappearance. They were even now being intensively attacked, and the pressure was daily increasing. French guerrillas were killing two Germans to the loss of every one of their own number, but they could not go on much longer without help, opposed as they were not only by the German occupying forces but by those French elements who had been seduced by the Germans to do their handiwork.

The meeting reached a degree of unanimity. It agreed, subject to the needs of MI6, that the order of priority for aircraft after the air offensive against Germany should be the Resistance, other SOE operations, Crossbow (anti-V1 and V2) operations and sea-mining. By early 1944 few on the Allied side, despite perhaps some reluctance in United States political circles to see life through de Gaulle's lens, denied the pertinence of Anthony Eden's observation that: 'The resistance of the French people themselves, even more than the re-entry of French territories into the war, was vital for the future of France as well as important to our operations. It ought not to be weakened by us.'

This pressure is a vitally important context to the Amiens raid. The year 1944 saw the Allied High Command offer a new perspective on the utility of Resistance networks in support of the forthcoming invasion of Europe. The role that *résistants* were expected to play was clearly set out in instructions from Eisenhower's HQ, entitled somewhat long-windedly: 'Instructions Concerning The Employment Of The Resistance Movement Within The Framework Of The Military Plan Of Operations For Liberating Continental France'. It explained:

From the beginning to the end of the operations of liberation in Continental France, the northern area should be characterised more than any other by:

(a) the collection of information;

(b) activity against communications by a series of either local-ised or general reprisals, neutralisation activities (sabotage of rail-roads, various installations and material, seditious activities and finally stoppages of work), and by acts of destruction of a limited duration carried out by armed groups.

Only in the northern area would localised acts of armed aggres-sion against specific objectives take place throughout the entire duration of the operations.

Neutralisation of big-scale supply movements by temporarily knocking out all power cranes, railroad turntables, steam loco-motives, feeder lines of electromotive power at their source and in the distribution from power stations, transformer stations and sub-stations. Interruption of communication wires.

Although this still lay some months ahead, it is reasonable to assume therefore that MI6 gave the raid on Amiens Prison its sanction in part because of the political pressure to ensure that a Resistance 'force in being' existed in France at the time when it might support the Allied invasion. The purpose of the raid was genuinely altruistic – to release Ponchardier's friends – but at the same time it also sent messages to both the French, the French Resistance and to the Germans. The message to the former – in France and in the French National Council of Resistance in Algiers – was that they were being listened to by London and that their efforts were respected and valued. To the men and woman of the Resistance in France it was to boost morale at a time of otherwise unparalleled gloom: through such action *résistants* could escape, rebuild their networks and carry on the fight against the brutal tyranny which had oppressed them since 1940. To the Germans, the message was that 'something was up'. This was not true, of course, but it would keep them guessing, wondering at the secret that lay behind the raid, and would occupy considerable German energies at a time when they could least afford it.

SEVEN

The arrest of Dr Antonin Mans, 12 November 1943

André Dewavrin became intimately acquainted with the work of the various *réseaux* in and around Amiens when he visited the town in the spring of 1943. On 24 February 1943 two *CND* agents working to Gilbert Renault, Olivier Courtaud (*Jacot*) and Roger Hérissé (*Dutertre*), organised the arrival by parachute of 'Tommy' Yeo-Thomas and André Dewavrin at Bosquentin, 25 miles west of Rouen, on a landing site known as 'DZ Orange'. Dr Antonin Mans, the regional public health chief and head of the Civil Defence organisation in the Somme department, as well as being the secret head of the *OCM* in Amiens, subsequently described Dewavrin's visit to Gilbert Renault:

Passy came to visit us at Amiens so that he could verify for himself our network in the department, in particular the *Century* network which had recently been created to serve as a channel for the information picked up by the OCM. The Civil Defence was installed in the prefecture [building], one wing of which had been requisitioned by the Feldkommandantur. Passy took his place between Tempez and myself in the service car. It so happened that Herr Oberartz and several German officers came out of the door at that very moment. As usual, the Herr Oberartz gravely saluted us, having not the slightest idea that the fellow he saw sandwiched between his Public Health Officer and the chief of the Amiens

Passive Defence was none other than the chief of General de
Gaulle's secret services, whom we were taking for a little tour of
inspection round the Amiens countryside.

But the Germans were closing in. As he did every morning at seven
o'clock, on 12 November 1943 Doctor Antonin Mans was at home
at Cottenchy, eight miles south-east of Amiens, listening to the
BBC, when there was a ring on the doorbell. Knowing that listening to the BBC was sufficient reason to be thrown into a German
cell, he quickly switched the radio back to Radio Paris before
answering the door. It was, as he feared, the Gestapo. The serious-
ness of the situation was made apparent to him by the sight of
troops surrounding his house. Picking up his hat and coat, and
saying farewell to his wife and daughter, he accompanied the plain-
clothes agent and soldiers to the Citadel in Amiens. As the regional
head of the *OCM* he knew what lay behind the arrest – indeed the
knock on the door had been his daily expectation for many months
– but waited until he had heard the accusations: the enemy might
not know as much as they thought. As head of the Civil Defence
organisation in the Somme, Dr Mans was afforded the common
courtesies demanded by civilised behaviour, but he knew full well
that these would not last long once the Gestapo got to work.

As soon as the Germans left with her husband, the redoubtable
Mme Mans rang her husband's office, asking them to send a car for
her. When it arrived, driven by her husband's driver, M. Cavillon,
she hurried as fast as she could to her husband's office in an attempt
to get there before the Gestapo, and to destroy any incriminating
evidence she could find. She had only just reached the office when
François Vignolle, her husband's secretary, arrived. He was carrying a case full of documents destined for *Century* when he met her
in the typists' room. She had barely had time to say what had
happened when the Gestapo arrived. They went straight into the
doctor's private office and began to empty drawers and examine
medicine bottles, fortunately paying no attention to the large map

of the *département* that was fixed to the wall, on which was marked the disposition of the entire underground network of the Somme. With Gestapo officers hurrying about, Vignolle quietly instructed M. Cavillon to take the suitcase he had been carrying and to burn the contents. This he succeeded in doing.

At the same time Mme Mans managed to send a coded message to Émile Pelletier, so that he was able to escape arrest. She also sent messages to M. Jeanjean, of the *OCM*, and Raymond Vivant, putting them on their guard. But within twenty-four hours most of the members of the Amiens *OCM*, except the few who had been able to make good their escape, or had not been known personally to the man responsible for their demise, had been arrested. The net had been successfully cast thanks to the treachery of the one-time leader of the *OCM* in northern France, an industrialist by the name of Roland Farjon (*Dufor*), who had recently arrived in Amiens from Paris. Unaware that he had been turned by the enemy, who had persuaded him that the real enemy was not Germany but the communist chaos and blood-letting that would inevitably follow in France in the event of German defeat (a similar story had trapped André Grandclément), Antonin Mans and André Tempez allowed their trusted colleague access to their organisation. Farjon duly reported what he found to his new masters. Those who knew Farjon described him as naive rather than evil, but his actions nevertheless resulted in the destruction of the *OCM* in north-eastern France and the loss of hundreds of lives.

After his initial interview Antonin Mans was taken to Amiens Prison, where he was placed in a cell on the second floor and interrogated on the following day. Confronted by the wretched Farjon, Mans pretended to know nothing of the accusations against him, and denied even knowing his accuser. As the days went by Dr Mans was allowed visits by his secretary, François Vignolle, and it was through coded messages that members of the *OCM* who had met Farjon in the period before his betrayal had emerged were warned of the danger to them. By this means four of Dr Mans's principal *OCM* lieutenants – Captain Panier, in the village of Rue, on the northern mouth of the Somme estuary; Charley Vauquier, who had been wounded in the 1940 campaign and was now serving as butcher's boy in Saint-Valéry-sur-Somme; M. Chivot, factory manager in Friville-Escarbotin; and M. Hurdequin, deputy manager at a factory in Pont-Rémy – were all warned of their danger, and went into hiding. Over a week later the men were arrested, but they protested that it was their roles in the Civil Defence organisation that enabled them to be intimately acquainted with the work of Dr Mans, and the Germans released them.

Meanwhile, Antonin Mans had been moved into another cell on the ground floor – a change that was later to save his life. M. Gruel, 47-year-old chief of the bureau of the prefecture and another member of the group, was arrested at the same time (on 11 November 1943) and put in the cell on the second floor. Gruel was responsible for the Somme prefecture's identity department, and had been badly beaten by the Germans, who were determined to clamp down on the trade in false papers. There, with the other prisoners, he languished throughout the bitter winter months, awaiting his fate.

EIGHT

Dominique Ponchardier's proposition

When Colonel Georges-André Groussard of the reconstituted Deuxième Bureau first offered his services to the Free French in 1940 he was snubbed by de Gaulle because of his connection with the despised Vichy regime, which had already denounced the self-proclaimed leader of 'Free France' as a traitor. He was nevertheless given a ready welcome by MI6. Together with his colleague Captain Paul Paillole, he agreed to spy for Britain (reporting to Biffy Dunderdale), and managed the *réseau Gilbert* from Geneva. Ponchardier joined this *réseau* in early 1943, feeding intelligence, including material about the V1 programme, to London. He often crossed into Switzerland via a boarding school at Ville-la-Grand, which straddled the French/Swiss border next to the town of Annemasse.

In late November 1943 Ponchardier brought with him a dossier prepared by a police officer in Amiens, Lieutenant Marceau Laverdure, containing the names of *résistants* incarcerated in Amiens Prison, including those caught up in the recent sweeps against the FTPF, the *OCM* and *Alliance*. It was estimated that upwards of 200 *résistants* were held in the prison at the time, at least twelve of whom were due to be executed in weeks. None had any realistic prospect of surviving their incarceration at the hand of the Gestapo, an organisation not known for its lenience.

Laverdure was a member of the *réseau Zéro*, a network originating in Roubaix, north-east of Lille. It had begun in 1940 by helping

British soldiers to escape south to Marseille and then progressed to working with the underground Belgian secret service, providing intelligence that was ultimately to find its way to MI6. In May 1942 the Belgian army officer Captain Gérard Kaisan (*Alex*) was parachuted into north-east France to set up the spy network. *Zéro* was centred on the SNCF rail networks, with railway workers passing information along the lines for collection and dispatch to London. Active through to late 1943, and led by Joseph Paul Dubar, it provided intelligence for instance that led to the bombing by the Allies of the German V2 launch site in the forest of Éperlecques in the Pas-de-Calais on 27 August 1943. Lieutenant Marceau Laverdure could see the damage that was being done to the various Allied intelligence networks in the Somme region, especially that inflicted by the notorious collaborator Lucien Pieri, responsible for a swathe of arrests.

With Laverdure's dossier, Ponchardier argued strongly to Groussard that something needed to be done to revive the various *réseaux* battered by the Gestapo, as he feared that many of those arrested, all senior members of various networks in the region, were almost certainly destined for the firing squad and that the work of *Gilbert* was imperilled as a result. The Allies would lose their eyes on the ground in northern France if the situation were allowed to continue. He told Groussard that most of the *OCM* team in Amiens, including Dr Antonin Mans and André Tempez, had been arrested on 12 November 1943. Three weeks before (on 23 October 1943), Roland Farjon of the *OCM* had been arrested and taken to Gestapo HQ in the avenue Foch in Paris, although Ponchardier was not to know that it was Farjon who had effectively brought down the rest of the *réseau*. Nor did Ponchardier realise that *Alliance* too had been hit hard, with the Halberts arrested on 18 November. From the outset he entertained thoughts of a jailbreak, but wondered how it could be achieved. His *réseau* was being asked for more and more by MI6, but with such savage attacks on the secret intelligence organisations in France he wondered how they could play any role in supporting the long-promised liberation when it came.*

The names on Laverdure's list were Ponchardier's friends and comrades in the bitter struggle against the occupying German state, and most held important roles in local branches of the Resistance. The fate of all French men and women imprisoned by the Gestapo and its many companion organisations was a bleak one, and Ponchardier knew that execution or deportation to the east was all that could be expected for those unfortunate enough to have fallen into German hands. Life within the Third Reich's prison system was bleak and brutal, and often short. Amiens was no different from hundreds of similar desperate places dotted across the length and breadth of occupied Europe. 'From time to time an arrested man would be put to death,' recorded Gilbert Renault, of Amiens. 'German troops would march into the yard and halt there, while brief orders would be snapped out. Then there would be comings and goings in the corridors, the sound of keys in a cell door, and the groaning of the door as it swung open. A short scuffle, some hurried steps, more harsh shouting ... and another Frenchman would be shot.'

In his 1954 account Renault suggested that Ponchardier was motivated by a desire to save the two imprisoned members of René

---

* Jack Fishman argues on the basis of interviews he undertook with retired OSS officers in London (Colonel David Bruce, OSS Head of Station, and Major Justin O'Brien) that Ponchardier's request for action was transmitted to London simultaneously through OSS channels, as Colonel Georges-André Groussard briefed the OSS chief in Berne, Allen Dulles, separately from MI6. Although no separate documentary evidence appears to exist to confirm this argument in the now-released OSS files or the Dulles papers at Princeton University, there seems little reason to doubt that Fishman was right. Ponchardier's claim to be the author of the request that went to London was subsequently corroborated by Groussard in his memoirs. For their part the OSS were certainly concerned about the success of the forthcoming Jedburgh operation (Operation *Sussex*), and believed that the release of *résistants* from Amiens would assist. They also had a close relationship with Groussard, and it would have made sense for Groussard to use both routes – OSS and MI6 – to ensure that intelligence reached London.

Chapelle's local branch of the communist FTPF, a group of fire-
brands who were involved in anti-German sabotage primarily
against the railways, an especial target of the communist group as
they attempted, with some success, to attack German troop trains
heading to the east. Indeed Ponchardier, when assessing later the
merits of the raid, recorded that one of its benefits was that he 'got
two of his men back'. One of these men was a young *résistant*
named Jean Beaurin, Chapelle's right-hand man in the FTPF, who
had been told that he would be executed on or about 20 February.
He was imprisoned with his half-brother, Roger.

   It was certainly true that both Ponchardier and René Chapelle
were determined to do what they could to save Beaurin, a young
résistant who had already participated in at least two (and possibly as many as five) successful derailings of German troop trains
earlier in the year, one at Miraumont on the Paris–Lille line west
of Bapaume on 28 August 1943 and the other at the hamlet of
Frireulles (part of the commune of Acheux-en-Vimeu), on the Le
Tréport–Abbeville line as the railway crosses the Route Nationale
D925, in which the enemy had suffered grievous casualties (see
Appendix 4). But he was far from being the only person of interest in the prison: as has been seen several well-known and important members of a variety of *réseaux* were incarcerated there at
the time, among as many as 200 *résistants* in enemy hands.
Ponchardier acknowledged that the arrest of Vivant and Dr
Robert Beaumont on 12 February and 15 February respectively, a
few days before the raid – two men with close links with MI6 and
MI9 – helped his case with London by reinforcing the arguments
he had first begun to make in November 1943 about the grievous
impact the Gestapo and Abwehr operations were having on
réseaux across the north-east of France. Intriguingly, Gilbert
Renault recorded that he discovered after the war that it was
Vivant who had reluctantly 'authorised' Ponchardier's original
request to London:

It was some time later that one of my colleagues, then regional chief of the OCM, told me that the raid on Amiens prison had been at the request of several of the Resistance leaders in the region. He told me that it was he himself, although he had not been in agreement with it, who had sent the message to London.

The arrest of Vivant on 12 February, and London's hearing of it on 15 February, undoubtedly substantiated Ponchardier's warnings about Gestapo success in rolling up *réseaux* in a key zone, and increased the pressure on the Air Ministry to act. It did not, of course, initiate the call to attack the prison, which had come a few months before. Vivant then found himself in the ironic position of being arrested and imprisoned in the very place that only weeks before he had asked the RAF to attack. It is hard not to be convinced that Vivant's support for the pleas from Dominique Ponchardier and René Chapelle were the deciding argument for London in favour of an assault: this was a mission that the entire Resistance hierarchy in the region (what was left of it) were prepared to support.

But why was Vivant reluctant at first to support Ponchardier? The prospect of potential casualties is one possibility; reprisals against the innocent French population another. The argument that secured Vivant's consent was Ponchardier's insistence that in addition to freeing valuable Resistance leaders an attack would be a massive morale boost for the beleaguered underground whose key workers and leaders were languishing in Nazi captivity. Most of the *résistants* held captive by the Gestapo were the rank and file of the Resistance, those whose dogged, day-by-day bravery defined the nature of their heroism – men and women like the nine members of an eleven-person *réseau d'action* led by Pierre Bracquart, a telephone engineer, who worked within the orbit of the American OSS, reporting to Allen Dulles in Berne. They had been caught in a sweep by French police and now found themselves in Amiens Prison, among them Bracquart's fiancée, Elaine

Guillemont. On 8 February 1944 Bracquart was told that he would be shot on 16 February. That day came and went, however, without him being taken out. The father of one of the members of this group, Andrew Priestly, was English, a soldier who had settled in the area after the last war.

The arrests across the various *réseaux* that had so alarmed the leaders of the Resistance in late 1943 were compounded in early January by a raft of arrests of men close to Ponchardier. One of his men was the 29-year-old Maurice Holville – nicknamed 'the vicar of Montparnasse' by his colleagues in the Resistance on account of his peculiar, priest-like gait – who disguised himself as a uniformed member of the SNCF. In early January René Chapelle and Holville had set off to meet the 21-year-old Roger Collerais (*Serge*), in the Beaulot café, just behind Amiens station, to discuss initial plans for an attack on the prison. They had secured an ancient architectural diagram of the site from the Amiens Public Library: Roger Collerais kept one half and René Chapelle the other. Inside the prison Maurice Genest (*Henri*) had been dreaming up schemes for an attack on the prison for several months, and had fed information about the layout and daily routines to Chapelle. Three minutes before Chapelle arrived at the café Collerais was arrested, and Holville only just managed to save himself and Chapelle from the same fate. Holville wasn't free for long, however. He was caught trying to secure extra ration cards, a perennial risk for those living underground who were forced to rely on their wits to survive. Although not a 'political' prisoner in the sense that he had not been arrested for 'terrorist' crimes and his Resistance role was as yet unknown to his captors, he still found himself an unwelcome guest of the Germans in Amiens Prison.

The loss of both Collerais and Holville was a disaster for Ponchardier, and he reluctantly agreed with Chapelle to bury the idea of an attack for the time being. The Germans would now have Collerais's half of the map, and they would be on high alert. In January 1944 the local leader of the FTPF, '*Eugène*', launched an operation against the prison at Rouen, but it proved to be a complete fiasco. As a result, the Germans increased their prison security everywhere, including at Amiens. But it did not take long for them both to change their minds. With the heat on, Chapelle lowered his profile in the region, going into hiding at the house of a friend in his home town of Ponts-et-Marais in Seine-Inférieure. Here he was visited by both Jean Beaurin's mother and Maurice Holville's father, who both urged him to do something to save their children from certain destruction at the hands of the Gestapo. Chapelle could not bear to refuse them, so he promised to discuss the subject with Ponchardier. Ponchardier in turn agreed to talk the issue through with Edouard Rivière, and the three of them met again to consider the options they had for an attack. They quickly concluded that an assault from the ground would be foolhardy, given that the Germans would have been alerted after Collerais's arrest. Fishman suggests that Madame Beaurin attended this meeting, at the Chapelle home in Ponts-et-Marais, and that it was she who suggested a Resistance attack on the prison using a decoy raid by the RAF on the nearby Amiens railway station, a frequent target of Allied bombers, as cover.

After some time, the meeting fell silent as they pondered on difficult choices. Ponchardier then broke the silence by saying quietly: 'We should ask the RAF to break down the prison walls.' The others looked at him in astonishment – no one had dreamed of such a tactic – but once the incredulity had subsided, they started to weigh up the chances. A man of action, René Chapelle was thrilled at the prospect, and immediately proposed to do something similar at Saint-Quentin Prison, where a number of his men were also incarcerated. His *réseau* unusually boasted two German deserters (possibly coerced Poles or Ukrainians), who had come over to the Resistance with their weapons and uniforms, and Chapelle's plan was to gain entrance to the prison by using these men as a type of Trojan horse. The three men considered how best to get aircraft to drop their bombs on the external walls of the prison without causing too many casualties, but with the intention of releasing as many of the 'politicals' as was possible, and at a time of day when the Germans would be at their most vulnerable.

Not at all certain that his handler in London – a man he knew only as 'Captain Thomas' (almost certainly the *nom de guerre* of Lieutenant Neil Whitelaw, who reported to the principal organiser of MI6 operations in France, Lieutenant Commander Kenneth Cohen) – would even countenance such an idea, Ponchardier decided to break it slowly to the decision-makers in MI6 and the Air Ministry. Accordingly he proceeded to dispatch to 'Captain Thomas' a series of detailed descriptions of the prison and its environs, describing Amiens's anti-aircraft defences, together with a raft of intelligence intended to prove how much his men now knew about the habits of the occupying forces across the town. In a deposition he prepared on 25 October 1946 he recalled:

> At the end of the December 1943, two men from [René] Chapelle's group were arrested. In mid-January 1944, I decided to ask for the support of the British. Admiral [Edouard] Rivière; my second in command, along with Chapelle and myself, started to create a plan for the operation and without explaining [the reason to] London, I sent off the detailed plans of the prison and its surrounding areas. In particular I described the state of Amiens's anti-air defences. This included very precise details, to the extent of even disclosing the names of the men, their habits, the relaxation/ loosening of discipline and their procedures for changing the guard . . . Towards the beginning of February, I began to interest 'Captain Thomas' (my London [MI6] liaison officer) in the possibilities of an attack on this prison.

At least some of this information came from the hand of Maurice Genest, inside the prison. Gilbert Renault suggested that once Ponchardier was sure of this material's safe delivery to London, he followed it up with a series of radio messages to keep his bulletins up to date, while at no time specifically asking that the prison be targeted. These messages continued to be sent via an *Alibi pianiste* reporting to his friend Georges Charraudeau, who he knew was also in touch with 'Captain Thomas' and who had promised to give Ponchardier his support. While Ponchardier records that these messages were sent in January 1944, an otherwise incomplete study of the raid by the Air Ministry historian in 1957 revealed that 'the proposal was initiated in a WT [wireless transmission] message from Paris on November 25 or 26 1943, using the "*Alibi*" liaison network and Admiral Rivière's radio link in Paris'.

While this cannot be independently verified, Jean-Robert Fecan has told the author that one of the *Alibi pianistes*, a French-speaking Englishwoman known to him when a four-year-old child as 'Aunt Elizabeth', lived in the garret of his bachelor uncles' home, Robert and André Fecan, in the St-Pierre area of Amiens. Both men were doctors. The home was a hotbed of resistance activity, members of the family working for the *réseau Zéro* and close to both Georges Charraudeau and Dominique Ponchardier. Fecan says that Dominique Ponchardier brought a miniature radio with him to the Fecans' house on 3 January 1944, for Elizabeth to use, and that she started sending messages to London on 4 January 1944. This would tally with Ponchardier's own testimony as to the date on which he began sending messages to London about the prison.

At some time in early February 1944 Ponchardier sent a further message to London, addressed to an unidentified contact – presumably in MI6 – whom he recorded as 'Commodore Gentry', using Georges Charraudeau's radio transmitter and *pianiste* located in the town. He admitted to turning the screw somewhat, explaining in a detailed telegram that the morale of his men was low, that they were tired, and that it was time to carry out a spectacular attack. Referring to Charraudeau he wrote in 1950:

The head of the *réseau Alibi* (which helped us with radio trans-missions at the time) gave me a keen helping hand because he

knew personally the leaders of [MI6] who were responsible for
this sector . . .

In retrospect there seems little doubt that Ponchardier exaggerated
his case to London, almost certainly so as to gain their agreement
to his plans, and most notably in suggesting that there were at least
two, possibly more, 'British' secret agents held in the prison at the
time, awaiting certain execution. Gilbert Renault's account of the
raid in 1955 makes it clear that Ponchardier believed that these
two MI6 agents had been imprisoned in Amiens on 12 February
1944, although this may be a confusion with dates, and may in fact
refer to the arrests of Dr Robert Beaumont (12 February) and
Raymond Vivant (15 February). At this point in history, and with
no remaining MI6 records, the details of any such prisoners must
remain speculation, although it was the conviction of Jack Fishman,
who undertook extensive interview-based research into the story,
that at least five such agents were incarcerated there at the time of
the raid. When Airey Neave wrote to Jack Fishman in 1976 he also
observed: 'I think there were agents of MI6 and SOE in Amiens
prison, and that they must have been responsible for Group
Captain Pickard's operation . . .'

Fishman, who had been a wartime journalist, believed that there
was at least one British SIS agent in the prison (and four from other
organisations), but could not establish who was running him. If
this person was indeed a member of a secret service, we remain
none the wiser as to whether he reported to MI6, SOE or MI9, or
indeed to one of the many other organisations then active in France
– American (OSS), Free French (BCRA), Vichy (Deuxième
Bureau), Belgian or Polish. It is perfectly possible of course that
one or more of F or RF Section's agents, or of MI6's, was imprisoned in Amiens Prison at the time. We know that there were
several French operatives of networks working for MI9, a part of
MI6, in Amiens, among them Dr Robert Beaumont. At this
remove, and with so few files available, it is impossible to tell.

Fishman was supported by a number of Resistance witnesses, such as Maurice Genest, for instance, who all insisted that a British agent was incarcerated in the prison at the time. Jean-Claude Beloeil, a native of Amiens, insisted that he met this man in Famagusta in 1956, and Fishman retold Beloeil's story in his book.

There is no independent corroboration for Beloeil's assertion, but the argument that it *must* have required the presence of a British agent with top-secret information about D-Day, or some other aspect of the Allied war effort, to justify launching a raid does not withstand scrutiny. It was accepted by all who worked in the field across occupied Europe in a secret capacity that they existed outside the terms of the Geneva Convention and were not protected by international law if they were caught. London could not help them if they found themselves in enemy hands. Many were captured, and suffered appallingly as a result; large numbers lost their lives in brutal circumstances. For this reason agents were issued a potassium cyanide tablet with which to take their lives if captured. It seems inconceivable that MI6 would have deliberately secured support for and undertaken such a difficult and dangerous raid merely for the sake of one or two agents, no matter how important. Most prisoners of the Nazis were left to their fate: there was little else that could be done for them.

Likewise there can be no truth in the idea that one or more of the *résistants* (especially those linked directly to MI6) in the prison were party to D-Day secrets and had to be silenced (either by being enabled to escape, or deliberately killed in the attack). The secrets relating to *Overlord* were the most closely guarded of the war, kept to a tiny group of people on the Allied side (which did not even extend to General de Gaulle, for instance). Indeed, the only Free French officer privy to D-Day secrets prior to 6 June was Captain Paul Paillole, then the head of the Free French counter-espionage organisation.

Irrespective of the truth about the presence or absence of British agents, it would have been strange had Ponchardier not overstated his case, desperate as he was to assist his comrades. The request to bomb the prison was outrageous; he could hardly expect it to succeed. What other chance did a relatively minor Resistance leader have, hidden and at bay within his country, of influencing targeting policy inside the corridors of power in London? At the same time it is also possible that MI6 deliberately exaggerated the scale of the opportunity to the Air Ministry in order to get them to act, which could be part of the reason why the HQ AEAF orders mentioned 120 *résistants* expecting imminent execution. Ponchardier never claimed that the Germans were to execute any more than 12 *résistants* on or about 19 February: the number of 120 seems to have originated somewhere in London.

When the request from Dominique Ponchardier first reached Dansey, therefore, it was not as if it had come out of the blue, or from a stranger. On the contrary, Ponchardier was part of the extended MI6 family, and a friend, and considered as such by Dansey and those who worked for him. The concept of an air attack on a German-run prison was not out of character for Dansey. It would not be the first time that he had authorised a 'spectacular', a raid or attack designed as much for its psychological as its physical impact. It was Dansey, something of a romantic at heart behind his stern exterior, who came up with the idea of an attack by the RAF on the daily German marching band on the Champs-Élysées on 12 June 1942. In the end it didn't work, as a change of timetable meant that the band didn't appear when a lone Beaufighter flew the length of the Champs-Élysées ready to open fire with its machine guns. Dansey conceived of this as a morale booster for the French: a similar impulse may well have led him to support Ponchardier's request for a high-profile attack on Amiens Prison; it would have appealed to his sense of the dramatic. It would also perplex the enemy. What was it about Amiens, in addition to the simple fact of the freeing of *terroristes*, the Germans would be forced to ask themselves, that interested the British so much? Could there be someone or something of import in the prison whom or which they had missed? It's easy to imagine Dansey feeling a palpable sense of pleasure at the prospect of sowing concern amongst his foes. Ponchardier's request, though unusual, was treated in this context, and although Airey Neave recalled that it occasioned much debate within MI6's Broadway HQ at the time, the conversation nevertheless focused on the wider context of the war in France, the role the French Resistance was playing in Allied operations at the time, and their key place in the plans for 1944.

There were four primary components of this context, the first three closely related. As we have seen, the mauling most *réseaux* had suffered at the hands of German counter-espionage during the last six months of 1943 directly challenged MI6's ability to undertake what were increasingly important – even strategic – intelligence activities in France. Of note at the time was the fate of de Gaulle's new political emissary to the diverse Resistance movement, Pierre Brossolette. At that very moment he, the biggest catch for the Gestapo since the capture and death of Jean Moulin, the architect of unity amongst the Resistance, was cooped up in Rennes Prison following a failed attempt by MI6 to return him to Britain by sea from Brittany. The Germans took some time to work out his real identity following his arrest, but it is inconceivable that the possibility of springing *résistants* from German prisons, in Rennes as well as Amiens, would not have been discussed by the BCRA and MI6 as a result.

This was not the only time when consideration was given by the BCRA – and possibly also MI6 – to the notion of breaking *résistants* out of jail. Gilbert Renault acknowledged considering something similar against the large and notorious Fresnes Prison, south of Paris, and the Resistance – especially the communist FTPF – planned several, attempting at least one, against Rouen, but in the event an outside-in attack (as opposed to a breakout) was only successfully achieved at Amiens. SOE had certainly considered jail breaks from time to time. The pre-war playboy René Dumont-Guillemet was dropped blind by SOE near Tours in late 1943. One of his tasks was to organise a mass escape from Fresnes. M. R. D. Foot observed drily that what he described as this 'freak mission' was so perilous that Dumont-Guillemet had the good sense to abandon it.

The increasingly important intelligence activities described above include, second, the discovery of sites being built by the Germans as launch platforms for Hitler's new much-vaunted 'V' or 'Revenge' weapons (*Vergeltungswaffen*). As has been seen, the Allies found that there was a perfect storm centred on northern France at precisely the time that the request for the raid on Amiens Prison was received. French *résistants* working (albeit many of them unknowingly) for MI6 had uncovered vast secrets about what was now acknowledged to be the imminent and potentially disastrous V1 threat against London and other southern English cities (Portsmouth, Southampton and Bristol, for instance), and their role in providing continuing intelligence about enemy activity in northern France remained vital. The prospect of 300 or more tons of high explosive falling on London every day was a grievous threat, and meant that the role and usefulness of indigenous *résistants* was critical to the security of the United Kingdom. Ordinarily the request from one of its own networks to attack the prison at Amiens would not have received any more than a sympathetic nod in Broadway; now, with Amiens the acknowledged base of Luftwaffe Regiment 155 (W), the geographical centre of the forthcoming offensive on London, and the epicentre of one of the most spectacular SIS intelligence coups of the war, after some internal debate MI6 agreed to pass on the request to the Air Ministry.

Third, as has been outlined, Anglo-American-French plans (through Operation *Sussex*) included strengthening the support provided by the Resistance to operations undertaken behind enemy lines in support of the forthcoming invasion of France – Operation *Overlord*. With the rapidly developing plans for *Overlord* the usefulness of the existing *réseaux* both for intelligence (MI6) and for sabotage (BCRA and SOE) had become more prominent than hitherto, the arguments for their armed involvement in the forthcoming invasion receiving especial emphasis by the War Cabinet, and the Prime Minister, in early 1944. An attack on Amiens Prison to free imprisoned *résistants* would be seen as practical support. It is true that the pre-eminent concern of the Free French at the time lay in arming the Maquis in central and southern France – Free France in London and Algiers aimed to create a viable army in France to take the war to the occupiers in support of an Allied invasion. MI6 and the OSS, however, had their eyes firmly on the role the Resistance could play in providing intelligence to the Allied armies in advance of the invasion, and in its immediate aftermath. Although an attack on Rennes Prison to free Pierre Brossolette was not on the cards, an attack on Amiens would perhaps be a substitute.

A fourth and not insignificant element in MI6's deliberations was the role played by the Resistance through MI6's sister organisation, MI9, to rescue escaping and evading Allied servicemen from the clutches of the enemy, and bring them back to Britain, either on foot across the Pyrenees or by boat from the rugged and often treacherous Breton coastline. At least one MI9 agent, Dr Robert Beaumont, was imprisoned in Amiens Prison at the time of the raid. There were almost certainly several more, men and women who had been arrested for their roles in the work of *réseaux d'évasion* across north-eastern France whose names have since been lost to history.*

---

* Intriguingly, Jack Fishman's research revealed that Ponchardier was not the only one in Amiens spiriting information to London. His papers reveal an entirely separate document sent to London through the auspices of the *OCM* by one of their imprisoned *résistants*, Robert Bibaut. Drawn in pencil and passed by Bibaut to his sister, it was carried to London a short time before the bombing of the prison. Bibaut's colleague, Captain Etienne Dromas (*Le Noir*) of Chauny, a fellow *résistant* and member of the *OCM's réseau Samson* (led by Maurice Rolland), kept a hand-drawn copy. Bibaut and two *OCM* colleagues, Vandoyer and Coutte, were condemned to death by the Military Tribunal of Amiens for a sabotage attack they had launched on

A further intriguing series of relationships has emerged from the research accompanying this book. Group Captain 'Pick' Pickard, who led the raid, was friends with a number of individuals close to the heart of this story, members of both French and British secret services as well as senior leaders of the French Resistance. These coincidences are unusual. On reflection it is hard to see how these relationships could have failed to play a role in the process by which the raid moved from concept to reality in early 1944. In 1942 Pickard had led the airborne element of a successful MI6-initiated operation on the radar site at Bruneval, and for seven months in 1942 and 1943 he had commanded 161 (Special Duties) Squadron, which was responsible for flying MI6 and SOE agents in and out of France in tiny Lysanders and, later, fat-bellied twin-engine Hudsons. During this time he met Gilbert Renault through a mutual friend, and in wartime London moved comfortably in BCRA and MI6/9 circles socially as well as professionally. The mutual friend was Captain Philippe Level (*nom de guerre* 'Philippe Livry'), a wealthy Frenchman who had escaped to Britain after the fall of France and, despite his advancing years (he was forty-four in 1942), had been commissioned into the RAF as a navigator. Level was not only a great pre-war friend of Renault, but had also flown many missions as a navigator with Pickard, first in 161 Squadron and thence in 140 Wing, which Pickard commanded from August 1943 and which was to mount the raid on the prison on 18 February 1944. Indeed, Philippe Level was to fly as a navigator in one of the 21 Squadron Mosquitoes on the raid.

The close friendship between Level and Renault, and between both these men and Pickard, would have made it easy for the

a factory at Ham (36 miles east of Amiens) in December 1943. All three men were killed during the bombing of the prison. It appears therefore that information about the prison and its *résistant* inmates found its way to London from at least two different sources, and possibly more. Gilbert Renault mused that London must have been completely baffled by the raft of messages that were now arriving from Amiens from a number of different sources.

latter to become persuaded of the need to support his friends in the Resistance when told about Ponchardier's concerns in Amiens, and thus to encourage Embry to accede to the Air Ministry's request. Dominique Ponchardier claims to have met Pickard during a visit to London in late 1943, and suggests in his archival memoirs that he discussed the fate of *résistants* in Amiens Prison with him then. According to Jack Fishman, both André Manuel and François Thierry Mieg (the BCRA's counter-espionage chief) asserted that the entire BCRA team knew Ponchardier, and that he had been flown to London for forty-eight hours and met them both, introduced by Kenneth Cohen. Fishman describes how Cohen rang André Manuel at the 10 Duke Street offices of the BCRA and arranged for him to meet Ponchardier, and to look at the list of prisoners held in Amiens. Certainly, Level acknowledges that he spoke to Pickard about Amiens before the raid. In his memoirs he writes that Pickard told him of his concerns. 'I'm worried,' said Pickard. '. . . we have friends in the prison at Amiens, and somehow they must be freed. Shall we do something about it?' There is no obvious reason why Level would have made this up. The claim that Pickard had met Ponchardier, and that he had been briefed on the French Resistance leader's plans, is now impossible to verify. What is not in doubt is that if Pickard had been privy to Ponchardier's plans, as the latter claimed, and as Gilbert Renault believed, he would clearly have supported them.

It seems that Ponchardier had several strings to his bow: he fed material to ex-Vichy officers in Geneva (through the *réseau Gilbert*) as well as contacting friends in the Free French Secret Service in London, and in the RAF, to press the case for an attack. His persistence paid off. As Ponchardier had hoped, and after considerable debate, MI6 put the matter officially to Air Commodore G. W. P. (Tubby) Grant at the Air Ministry's Directorate of Intelligence.

Gilbert Renault recognised that, in the early weeks and months of

1944, the attitude of the Allies to the French Resistance had never been more positive. He eloquently observed the attitude in London among those acutely conscious of the agonies being experienced by France at the time:

There were many of us in England at that time who thought of France, and of the sufferings of those we loved. A few days previously the BBC had broadcast a speech which I had meant to be a Christmas greeting to them – not thinking that my words were to be so prophetic, at least for the men and women in Amiens prison: 'My dear friends, friends I know and do not know, it is one of your own people who is speaking to you. The walls of your prisons are not so high nor so thick that they can prevent you from hearing me.'

My speech had been recorded, so I was able to listen to the broadcast along with some of my comrades who had just arrived from France. One of them, Maurice Rossi, got slowly to his feet and a sob escaped his lips. He had been several months without any news of his wife and child.

The Liberation seemed to us then a thing of infinite promise. We had been struggling for it for four years. On the night of Pickard's famous party [New Year's Eve, 1943] – which for him was to be the last – we were all gathered together in the great ballroom of the Waldorf Hotel. The orchestra was playing slow waltzes and livelier tunes, but we had no desire to join the couples on the dance floor. Our table was strangely silent in the midst of so much gaiety, and people were beginning to notice us.

On the first stroke of midnight everything fell silent. The orchestra stood up, the dancers stood still. I was expecting the sudden burst of enthusiastic shouting which is usual with Americans and British on such an occasion, when I caught my breath with emotion. These men and women, who had recognised that we were French, slowly and almost religiously began to sing the Marseillaise, softly accompanied by the orchestra. We rose to our feet, so overwhelmed at their gesture that we could not sing a word. This was the first minute of the New Year, and our Allies had given to our country the first salute.

NINE

Planning begins

On Friday 11 February 1944 Brigadier General A. C. Strickland, US Army, the Deputy Senior Air Staff Officer (D/SASO) in the headquarters, Allied Expeditionary Air Force (commanded by Air Marshal Sir Trafford Leigh-Mallory), drafted a letter to its subordinate command, the Second Tactical Air Force – 2nd TAF – commanded by the New Zealander Air Marshal Sir Arthur 'Mary' Coningham. He attached a letter, dated the previous day, from the Directorate of Intelligence (Research) (DI(R)) at the Air Ministry*. DI(R) was the cover name for the department in the Air Ministry responsible for supporting 'special' operations undertaken on behalf of the Secret Intelligence Service (MI6) and SOE. DI(R)'s letter directed the Allied Expeditionary Air Force to undertake a mission against 'a certain important target in France'. The letter contained no further details of the target, presumably because all the details were attached in the accompanying letter. Strickland told Coningham's HQ that Leigh-Mallory had accepted the

---

* This letter is now lost. In April 1982 the BBC's *Panorama* programme accused the British authorities of deliberately 'weeding' files to remove or destroy evidence that they did not wish to get into the public domain. Henry Probert, late archivist of the MOD's Air Historical Branch and eminent historian, looked through the files carefully and concluded that they had not been deliberately weeded. I agree. There was no Civil Service archival strategy in place during the war – that was the last thing on people's minds at the time – and once it was over countless files were disposed of for no other reason than that the paperwork was now superfluous.

commission from the Air Ministry, and that a team from DI(R) would visit HQ 2nd TAF at Uxbridge at 11 a.m. the following morning to discuss the operation in more detail.

The letter to HQ AEAF from the DI(R) was written by Air Commodore James Easton, although it is clear from the correspondence carried on in October 1944 regarding publicity about the raid that the man in the Air Ministry who knew more than anyone else about the request from France was Tubby Grant. In fact, Strickland's letter merely confirmed what 2nd TAF had known for at least a week, and possibly longer. Easton had already explained the nature of the mission to Basil Embry (the Air Officer Commanding No. 2 Group, part of 2nd TAF). Embry had met with Group Captain Pickard, commander of the three Mosquito squadrons that comprised 140 Wing, as early as 8 February to discuss the feasibility of DI(R)'s request, and had gone as far as allocating the crews who would fly the mission. In his memoirs Sir Basil Embry recalled:

> Early in February 1944, I was asked by Coningham, the Commander-in-Chief of 2nd T.A.F., if I thought our Mosquitoes were capable of carrying out an operation to release about seven hundred French Resistance Movement patriots awaiting trial and death in Amiens prison. I said I thought it would be possible but I would want to examine the full implications of such an operation before giving a definite answer. Later I told him I thought it could be successful but that it would be with the loss of some of the prisoners' lives . . .

Coningham wanted to understand whether an operation could be undertaken by Embry's crews, one with considerable consequences for human life if it were to go wrong. There was no doubt that the Mosquitoes could strike the prison with the sort of precision that they had recently been achieving against VI sites. The question was whether they could do so without harming the inmates crammed into such a confined space while at the same time killing as many of the guards as possible, and enabling as many of the 700 or so inmates as feasible to go free.

After discussing the request in as much detail as was available to him with the members of his headquarters, including Squadron Leader Ted Sismore, Embry concluded that if planned well and executed faultlessly, the raid had a reasonable chance of success, although the threat of what today would be described as collateral damage inside the prison remained high. Little time remained to carry out the planning necessary to ensure a minimum of inmate deaths and casualties, but Sismore got straight to work, building detailed plans and pulling information together from a range of sources. These included aerial photographs from the PRU, as well as the material sent from Amiens by Dominique Ponchardier (and others), provided by MI6.

There has been a suggestion that none of the material Ponchardier said that he had sent to MI6 ever reached London, because Sismore appears to have laid great stress on determining the height and width of the prison walls by means of photographic interpretation. However, Gilbert Renault argues that the only information Embry's HQ lacked was the width and construction of the walls, information essential for determining the amount of explosives needed to create a breach. The details (guard rosters and timings and so forth) that had been sent through to London in the previous months appear to have been utilised effectively in the planning for the attack, as evidenced by the fact that London knew the exact times when the guards would be at lunch (12 noon) and the exact location of the German quarters, as well as knowing that many prisoners would be out of their cells undertaking duties associated with the midday feeding of prisoners – information that could only have come from intelligence sourced on the ground.

After undertaking this initial assessment, Embry spoke to Easton in the Air Ministry confirming his view that the operation was viable. This in turn prompted the Air Ministry to begin the process that led to the formal request, by letter to the HQ AEAF, on 10 February. Strickland then wrote to Coningham's HQ (of which Embry was a part) on 11 February, enclosing a copy of Easton's top-secret letter.* The exact wording of the request from the DI(R) can be seen from the information contained in the subsequent orders from 2nd TAF to its subordinate organisation, 140 Wing, which was to carry out the operation, dated 18 February 1944:

Mosquitoes of 140 Airfield [i.e. 140 Wing] are to attack the prison at Amiens in an attempt to assist 120 prisoners to escape. These prisoners are French patriots condemned to death for assisting the Allies. This air attack is only part of the plan as other assistance will be at hand at the time.

On 12 February representatives of 2nd TAF and No. 2 Group met those of the Air Ministry's Directorate of Intelligence at HQ 2nd TAF. The minutes of this meeting confirm that the reason that No. 2 Group was told not to launch the raid before 16 February was to give time to get a message to Amiens, and thus warn the *résistants* inside and outside the prison of the impending attack. This differed from the Air Ministry instruction of 11 February in which instructions had been given to attack the prison 'before the 16th February'. The disparity is almost certainly a typographical one, which the meeting on 12 February corrected.

Two days later an interpretation report was provided by the Air Ministry on the aerial reconnaissance photographs of the prison taken as early as 20 December 1943 by Spitfires searching for new V1 sites across the Pas-de-Calais. But the files reveal other photographs specifically of Amiens, capturing the town, with its Citadel

* The letter's reference was 55/44/DI(R) dated 10 February 1944. The relevant files (but not, of course, the original letter) are Air 37/806 and Air 37/15.

and the *Maison d'Arrêt* on the north side of the road that led east to the small town of Albert, with remarkable clarity. These were taken by Flying Officer Kenwright of No. 542 Squadron on 1 December 1943. An intriguing though unproven possibility exists that these photographs were requested to provide aerial interpretation of the prison following information that began to arrive in London the previous week. Kenwright's logbook does not suggest that he had specific orders to photograph the prison, but the results were nevertheless spectacular.

Building A, a cross-shaped building, was the prison. The height of the surrounding wall was judged to be 22 feet [it was in fact 20 feet], but 'it is difficult to make any accurate measurement of the thickness of this wall . . . [but it did] not exceed 4 feet in thickness and is probably considerably less than this.' [It was, as suspected, only 3 feet wide.]

The height of the main building was 49 feet to the eaves and 62 feet to the ridge. No machine gun nests were identifiable.

Buildings B appeared to be a small housing estate consisting of a number of semi-detached two story dwellings with gabled roofs.

Buildings C were marked on the town plan as 'Hospice St Victor' and their layout and design would correspond to that of an institute for the poor and aged. The grounds are surrounded by an 11 ft. wall but there is no photographic evidence of military occupation. Outside the grounds about 80 yards to the north there is a trench near the road junction.

Within days a plan had been formulated and a scale model of the prison constructed to allow the aircrew to plan the final details of the attack. Embry's conclusion was that semi-armour-piercing bombs should be used to break open the outer walls of the prison, with high-explosive bombs used to generate a concussive effect in the prison that would enable cells doors to be forced from their frames, so as to release the prisoners without necessarily destroying the cells. From the outset it was clear that the greatest danger posed by the attack was that of killing the very people the raid was designed to save. It was a terrible dilemma that was never fully resolved.

A claim made occasionally is that when asked about the dangers of collateral damage the message that came back from France was that the prisoners would 'prefer to die by British bombs rather than German bullets'. It is certainly conceivable that Gilbert Renault or any one of his colleagues in the BCRA, or indeed any Free Frenchman in London at the time, would have replied with this matter-of-fact observation. Even if it was a piece of hyperbole, or even fiction, dreamed up perhaps by the Air Ministry to counter worries about possible casualties on the ground, or by someone at No. 2 Group or the BCRA (or perhaps even Pickard himself), for the same reason, it eloquently captured the mood in France among the underground at the time. They had nothing to lose by such a raid, except lives that were already condemned, and everything to lose by inaction.

The size and depth of the prison walls, together with the construction of the internal buildings, was of vital importance to Sismore's team, because it provided the information necessary to make precise calculations about the optimal number and explosive payload of the bombs to be used. Too few would fail to breach the walls and to burst the locks on the cells. Too many would kill and maim inside the prison, instead of allowing people to escape. 'The difficulty was to achieve this kind of success without killing a lot of people,' Sismore wrote afterwards. 'It was a very difficult decision of what to drop and how much to drop.' Great efforts were made to gain precise calculations about the size and width of the walls from the evidence presented by shadows in aerial photographs. It is clear that the planners in the UK expected the fabric of the prison to be much harder to penetrate than it turned out. In fact, the construction of the walls was relatively weak (not of solid rock as expected) and those bombs that did not bounce off the frozen earth sliced through the weak walls like butter. The large number of 500-pound bombs (48) that were planned to be dropped on the prison during the raid were the product of a calculation that allowed for the number expected to miss the target altogether (as well as any aircraft unable to reach the target in the first place), the number that would fail to detonate, and the total considered necessary to do what Sismore planned.

His aim was to cut two holes in the outer wall on both the eastern and the northern sides of the site, to allow prisoners the physical means to escape, while at the same time killing as many guards as possible with attacks on their quarters. The decision to attack at precisely 12 noon was made on the basis of intelligence – received, as he described, from Ponchardier – that this was the usual time for the guards' communal lunch and the time when many prisoners would also be out of their cells on lunch duties. A well-aimed bomb would hopefully remove a large number of enemy at a stroke, and give the prisoners the greatest chance of escape.

Embry's discussions with Sismore had made it clear that the mission would need to be led by a commander experienced in low-level precision attacks. Pickard, for all his flying experience, did not have vast amounts of this specific expertise, with a mere six anti-V1 site attacks under his belt, none of which had entailed countering a simultaneous threat from the Luftwaffe. For this reason Embry considered that it would be risky to place him in charge. Embry determined from the outset that he would himself lead the raid, and Pickard would be his deputy. He agreed this with Pickard when they talked the operation through on 8 February.

On 9 February, however, a day after briefing Pickard and agreeing the outline of a plan, Embry managed to brief Sir Trafford Leigh-Mallory, Commander-in-Chief of the Allied Expeditionary Air Force. In response to the question: 'Who is leading the raid?' Embry responded: 'I am, sir.' Leigh-Mallory said nothing at the time, but he clearly reflected on the potential loss to the AEAF if

Embry were to be lost on the raid. Later that night Embry received a telegram making Leigh-Mallory's wishes plain:

> ON NO ACCOUNT, repeat NO ACCOUNT, are you to fly on operation discussed this afternoon. Acknowledge.

This decision is not surprising. A three-squadron raid required no more than the Wing leader – a group captain – to command the mission, not an air vice marshal. Embry was well aware of this, but he had always led from the front, and wanted to do so this time. He was also concerned that Pickard lacked the requisite experience. With something of a heavy heart, and after first conferring with 'Mary' Coningham, his immediate superior, he did as he was told, and informed Pickard that he would instead be in command. Embry was certain that Pickard would do an excellent job within the extent of his abilities, but he wasn't his first choice to lead the raid. Nor could he, without undermining Pickard's position as Commanding Officer of 140 Wing, offer the job to any of Pickard's more experienced but subordinate commanders. Some have suggested that Embry was refused permission to fly because he knew of the *Ultra* secret, but this is fanciful. The network of people who knew anything about the work of Enigma and its various permutations was tiny, and was one of the closest-guarded secrets of all time. The reason was simply his importance to preparing his group for the impending demands of *Overlord*, now only months away. It would have been foolish to risk his life in operations over occupied Europe when there were others just as capable on call.

Sismore's plan was that the first wave of six aircraft would strike at 12 noon exactly, the targets being the 20-foot-high eastern wall, the northern wall and the guards' quarters inside the prison. The eastern wall was the first that would face the aircraft as they approached from the direction of Albert, east-north-east of Amiens, a line of attack designed to mislead German air defence observers (and radar) as to the location of the intruder's ultimate

target. Three minutes later the second squadron of six Mosquitoes
would place its bombs against the western and south-eastern walls
of the prison. It was hoped the bombs of the second wave could
create sufficient blast to knock open the doors to the cells and free
the prisoners. Pickard would fly at the rear of this wave, and determine whether he needed to call up the third wave – standing back
some ten minutes behind – in the event that the first twelve aircraft
were unsuccessful.

TEN

The Wooden Wonder

The aircraft that 140 Wing would be flying on 18 February 1944 was the de Havilland Mosquito Mark VI FB (fighter-bomber), a variant of one the war's most extraordinary and successful aircraft. The Wing had been progressively equipped with this unusual aircraft from August 1943, although earlier variants had first come into operational service as early as September 1941 and the RAF had received the first of its Type IV B (Bomber) version in mid-1942. What set this aircraft apart from all others in the combat service of the air forces of all belligerents at the time was that it was wooden, which to the uninitiated seemed a throwback to the stringbags of the first era of propeller aviation. Its plywood construction for the fuselage (birch and balsa laminate) and main structural members (such as wing spars) of spruce and birch ply, however, was the aircraft's secret weapon. Wood made it incredibly light and also remarkably sturdy and resilient to flak, which tended to punch holes in the airframe without creating secondary stresses, which was a problem in all-metal aircraft.

Until the advent of the first operational jet fighter (the German Me 262) in April 1944, the Mosquito was one of the fastest and most versatile aircraft in the air, the brainchild in 1938 of Geoffrey de Havilland, who envisaged a lightweight, long-range, unarmed bomber able to fly to Berlin and back. De Havilland's idea was to build a streamlined twin-engine, two-seater bomber out of laminated wood that would be too fast to be caught by conventional metal-framed fighters, and thus require no defensive armament. His design team at Salisbury Hall, near the de Havilland headquarters at Hatfield, Hertfordshire, suggested that the overall weight of an aircraft made from laminated wood and stuck together with glue and brass screws, equipped with two powerful engines, would deliver speeds at heights of 15,000 feet and above (and therefore above the range of anti-aircraft fire – flak) in excess of 400 miles an hour, and carry some 4,000 pounds of bombs. This far exceeded the speed of the single-engine fighters of the day, even that of the remarkable Supermarine Spitfire, which had recently entered RAF service, and would be able to outstrip them all for range. A thousand of these aircraft, de Havilland suggested, would serve to act as a deterrent to any ambitions Hitler might have to act aggressively against the Western Powers.

Ridiculed by conventional wisdom, which insisted that the future of air warfare was via armoured aircraft, and that wooden aircraft belonged to the past, not the future, the proposal was rejected by the Air Ministry. Convinced of the soundness of his idea, the decision failed to deflect de Havilland from his vision and he decided to fund a prototype himself, taking comfort in the knowledge that recently successful aircraft procurements, such as the Spitfire and the Vickers Wellington, had triumphed as private ventures in the face of early and official opposition. He knew that there was merit in the idea: the sleek wooden twin-engine de Havilland Comet had been designed to compete in the England–Australia race in 1934. It had won, in the staggering time of 71 hours (steamships took four weeks), and yet utilised relatively old engine technology. It was made with a conventional wooden airframe clad with plywood, with a final fabric covering on the wings. A fully laminated airframe, aerodynamic cleanness and a high power-to-weight ratio through the use of two modern Rolls-Royce Merlin engines – the same that powered the Spitfire – would, the de Havilland team contended, make their aircraft unbeatable. The aircraft would also be cheap to build, with construction of its wooden parts easily replicable in hundreds of separate facilities in every corner of the country, exploiting the vast pools of skilled labour in Britain expert at working in wood.

The build concept was also unique, and enabled replication in carpenters' yards up and down the country. Built like an Airfix model, with the two halves of the fuselage manufactured separately and then bonded together, six tons of wood and nearly 50,000 brass screws were used in each aircraft, an assembly undertaken in 400 different sites across the country, with components brought to the factory at Hatfield for final assembly. The two Merlin 25 engines provided extraordinary power, each engine delivering 1,635 horse power, so that the Mosquito could climb at an unprecedented 2,500 feet a minute, a rate not matched until the arrival of the jet engine. The process from concept to design led the de Havilland team through 1939 and into 1940, as the nations of Europe fell one by one, like dominos, to the German aggressor.

An order for fifty aircraft from the Air Ministry off the drawing board gave de Havilland some breathing space, but repeated design interference came with this new contract. Then, for a period in mid-1940, he was ordered to stop work altogether, as precious resources were concentrated on building Spitfires and Hurricanes. When it was accepted that the Mosquito would make negligible demands on the metal required for the other programmes, he was allowed to continue. The prototype aircraft flew at Hatfield on 25 November 1940, and was an immediate sensation. This stream-lined wooden bomber was 20 miles per hour faster than the single-engine Spitfire fighter. It was a revelation and delivered everything that de Havilland had promised. The Air Ministry, suddenly won over to what had been known as 'Freeman's Folly' after the only member of the Air Ministry who had supported de Havilland's vision from the beginning, ordered 150 immediately.

Ten months later, on 17 September 1941, the first operational sortie of a Mossie, as it was now being affectionately called, took place: a photo reconnaissance flight over occupied France. The first delivery of aircraft prepared for these duties was made in July 1941, only twenty-two months after the first design concept had been sketched out. By mid-1942 the Mossie had become an integral part of the RAF in the various roles of bomber, night fighter and intruder. It had by then come to the attention of a man who was to play a significant role in the Amiens story. The then Group Captain Basil Embry, station commander at RAF Wittering, where 151 Squadron – a night-fighter squadron newly equipped with Mosquitoes – was based, lauded the aircraft as 'the finest aeroplane, without exception, that has ever been built in this country'.

Sergeant Mike Carreck recalled the moment in late 1942 when some of the assembled aircrew of No. 2 Group saw their new Mark IV aircraft for the first time. Piloted by Geoffrey de Havilland, Mosquito W4064 landed at their base at Swanton Morley near Norwich, but not before doing an impromptu aerial display:

> On 15 November it came suddenly out of nowhere, inches above the hangars with a cracking thunderclap of twin Merlins. As we watched, bewitched, it was flung about the sky in a beyond belief display for a bomber that could outperform any fighter. [It was an] impossible dream of an aircraft. No other word for it, it was beautiful. An arrogant beauty with a 'job-to-do, get out of my way', slim, sleek fuselage high cocked 'to-hell-with-you' tail. It had awesome power on the leash in those huge engines and was eager on its undercarriage like a sprinter on the starting blocks who couldn't wait to leap up and away.

But it was only when deployed from mid-1942 onwards as a light bomber that its extraordinary potential as a hedge-hopping precision attack aircraft became apparent to the pilots who flew it. They found that their wonderfully stable aerial platform could fly at little more than rooftop height and, at 400 miles per hour, be gone before anyone on the ground was aware that the aircraft was even coming.

What began to impress itself upon the RAF was the particular usefulness of low-flying precision attacks where, with good planning, the enemy's defensive flak screen could be mapped and avoided. The ability to strike hard and fast, and without warning, was to become one of the Mossie's distinctive hallmarks. But much needed to be learned about the best way to operate these unarmed aircraft in the hostile environment of occupied Europe. A number of aircraft were lost through inexperience, or even extreme low flying. On a raid against U-boat slipways at Flensburg in July 1942, Sergeant Peter Rowland felt his aircraft shudder alarmingly, and his port engine begin to vibrate. Glancing sideways to his navigator, he saw, sitting in Sergeant Mike Carreck's lap, a piece of chimney pot. The same German chimney had taken a large chunk out of the fuselage, and Rowland was forced to abort the mission and return home.

This was not the first or last time that aircraft returned home wrapped in wire or foliage they had encountered on their journey over enemy territory. Pilot Officer Max Sparks of the Royal New Zealand Air Force, who was to fly on the Amiens raid, recalled that: 'Many a Mossie pilot would come back from a mission with telephone wire draped around his tail wheel ... [On more than one occasion] I came back with branches of trees that weren't planted in England.'

The perils of Mossie low flying are borne out by tales recorded by the New Zealand official historian, H. L. Thompson:

During one March raid Squadron Leader Kain swerved to avoid another Mosquito and hit the top of a tree. A second pilot flew into some telegraph wires, setting an engine on fire, but he was able to make a safe crash-landing on return. Warrant Officer Ward was flying over the [V1] site at Hambures [22 miles southeast of Dieppe] when his machine was damaged by blast from exploding bombs and he just managed to get back to an airfield in Kent. Flying Officer Greenaway was involved in a remarkable episode early in January. He was navigating a Mosquito of No. 21 Squadron which set off from Hunsdon to bomb a site near Abbeville. As the formation crossed the French coast Greenaway's pilot saw a flock of birds ahead, and in going a few feet lower to avoid them one propeller hit a sand bank in the middle of the Somme estuary. The machine shuddered violently but remained airborne, so the bomb load was jettisoned and the pilot turned for home.

This proved only the start of an extraordinary sequence of events for Greenaway. Right after he turned for home, both engines seized up and the Mosquito crash-landed on a beach. Made captive, Greenway was being taken by truck from the civil prison at Beauvais (33 miles south of Amiens) to the Gare de l'Est in Paris, en route for a POW camp, when he made good his escape. He and three other RAF prisoners were being guarded by four Germans who were distracted by a task they had been given. Making use of a moment when his guards' backs were turned, he simply ran out of the station into the darkness. 'He turned up a side alley, saw a light in a building and "taking a chance", as he put it, knocked at the door.' Amazingly he had arrived on the doorstep of a fully fledged member of a *réseau d'évasion*. He was given a complete civilian suit and some money, allowed to shave off his moustache and the beard he had grown since capture, and then guided to the Gare du Nord. By midnight, he was well clear of Paris. He continued his journey across country during the next few days, receiving help from time to time from French people. He arrived in England early in April.

The threat of being pounced on by waiting fighters diving from a great height, and thus able to accumulate high attack speeds, proved to be a constant hazard to these low-flying daylight sorties, although statistics were to prove in due course that the greatest threat to low-flying Mosquitoes was ground-based anti-aircraft fire. The aircraft's considerable speed gave it the advantage of surprise, but that advantage was modified by the fact that being much closer to the ground it presented a larger, though more fleeting, target than at higher altitudes. Of the other threats they faced, the chief worry to pilots was bird strike. On the Eindhoven raid (see below) on 6 December 1942, twenty-three aircraft were damaged by birds, several after encountering a flock of ducks en route to the target. On 3 October 1943, on 140 Wing's first operation equipped with Mosquitoes, the aircraft flown by Air Vice Marshal Basil Embry, leading the attack, was struck and badly damaged by a duck.

The ability of Mosquitoes to fly at such low altitudes enabled them to make very accurate attacks on pinpoint targets, something that could not be achieved by bombers flying at the high altitudes (15,000 feet and above) necessary to avoid flak. And the aircraft's advantage in surprise was enhanced by its wooden construction, which tended to minimise its radar signature. Targets especially vulnerable to the type of accuracy delivered by low-flying Mosquito attack included buildings of special note, such as those of the enemy's secret police. The first such attack was delivered by four Mosquito IVs of No. 105 Squadron RAF against the Victoria Terrasse building, the headquarters in Oslo of both the Sicherheitspolizei (SiPo) and the Sicherheitsdienst (SD), on 25 September 1942. This famous and distinctive building dominated the Oslo skyline, and since the invasion it had boasted a swastika flag that flew provocatively over the subjugated Norwegian capital. Information had been received in London that Vidkun Quisling, the Norwegian collaborationist leader, was attending a rally in the city. With luck both the Gestapo and their local supporters would be hurt by a surprise attack, and the morale of the loyal population given a boost.

In the event three aircraft managed to deposit their bombs directly into their target, while a fourth fell victim to a diving Focke-Wulf FW190 fighter before the target was reached. The desired effect of the Oslo raid – to demonstrate that the RAF could find, and strike with deadly precision, a pinpoint target anywhere in the heart of enemy occupied Europe – was achieved, although the aim of killing Quisling was not. He had managed to find his way to the basement before the bombs struck home. The bombs were not fused instantaneously, but were instead on eleven-second delays, enabling the bomb to stop before exploding, rather than detonate on impact. Of the four 500-pound bombs that struck the target, one failed to explode and the remaining three unexpectedly went straight through the building, exploding on the other side. Eighty civilians were killed or injured in the resulting blasts. Yet the raid was a harbinger of things to come. Four Mosquitoes had successfully flown a distance of 1,100 miles from Leuchars in northern Scotland to Oslo, crossing the cold grey surface of the North Sea at heights less than 100 feet, to strike a high-value enemy target precisely where it had been intended, in broad daylight. It was also the first time that the British public were made aware of the new weapon in their nation's inventory: the BBC carried an account of the raid on its radio programmes the following day. The Mosquito began to be known as 'the Wonder Weapon', and shortly thereafter as 'the Wooden Wonder'.

Two months later, on Sunday 6 December 1942, the low-level precision capabilities of the aircraft were decisively demonstrated by a daylight attack on two Philips radio factories at Eindhoven in Holland, an operation undertaken on a weekend to avoid casualties among the Dutch factory workers. Operation *Oyster* involved ninety-three light bombers of No. 2 Group flying an assortment of Mosquitoes, Douglas Bostons and Lockheed Venturas. The two targets were the Philips radio factory and the smaller Emmasingel valve and lamp factory, three-quarters of a mile to the south-east, these sites producing over one-third of all of Germany's radio valve requirements at the time. Aircraft casualties were high: nine Venturas, four Bostons and a Mosquito were lost, and three more aircraft crashed on return to England, a rate of loss of 18 per cent. The Ventura, slow and cumbersome, was unsuited to low-level raids: it was not nicknamed 'The Pig' for its looks alone. The raid was led by a legendary Mosquito pilot, Wing Commander Hughie Edwards, VC. Squadron Leader Charles Patterson flew a Mosquito in the second flight that day with an RAF cameraman on board taking film footage of the raid, a practice that had begun so as to provide direct evidence of the effects of an attack, and to assist planning and training for subsequent operations:

Ahead of me I saw the front formation of Mosquitoes in the distance already climbing up to 1,500 feet so I immediately took my formation up as fast as I could to 1,500 feet to catch Edwards' formation. We caught up about two-three miles south of Eindhoven.

We banked over to port and started to dive down on the Philips works in the centre of the town. The moment I turned to port I could see this factory standing out unmistakably, very prominently, right in the centre of Eindhoven.

We all went down in this shallow dive, full throttle, and at the appropriate moment, dropped the bombs. As I went across the Philips works the whole factory seemed to erupt in a cloud of smoke and flashes. It looked as though the whole thing was completely eliminated. In the distance I could see masses of Bostons whizzing about across the trees at low level to port. I came straight down to ground level. Now the Mosquitoes all split up and we all had to come home separately.

The West Australian on 8 December 1942 printed a report of the raid from an unnamed RAF wing commander who took part:

As we came in over the mainland all the Dutch people came out to have a look. They were standing in their backyards waving handkerchiefs and even flags. Soon we saw two big columns of smoke coming up from the target. The Philips factory is a huge place built in 2 separate parts. We took it in sections and attacked each of them in waves. It was a very methodical business and we went in as low as possible. We did this to make sure of hitting each target properly and to avoid hitting any Dutch people by accident. We came in at right angles to the factory. The bombers were very close together and so there was a lot of slipstream and those in the rear had a very rough time keeping their aircraft under control. We had both incendiaries and high explosives with delay action fuses. We made for the north-west part of the factory. I pulled back the control column and pressed the bomb release and scraped over the tops of high buildings. Germans were firing at us, both from the base and the roofs of the buildings. I could see some firing from the roofs of buildings while the buildings were blazing underneath them. My rear-gunner saw our bombs enter the building we had aimed at and as we came down towards the ground again he told us it was on fire. We kept straight ahead so that our automatic cameras would do their stuff. We were still very low. We had to lift over electric cables and twice we brushed the tops of poplar trees and when we got back many of us had souvenirs of the low flight, some twigs and pieces of shrapnel, lots of birds and one aircraft even brought back a duck.

It is fair to say that the crews of these remarkable aircraft fell in love with them, a fondness that has lasted long since the demise of the aircraft itself. It was 'the ultimate aircraft' recalled Pilot Officer Arthur Dunlop of No. 487 Squadron RNZAF. The historian Edward Bishop noted:

it was scarcely surprising that the Mosquito was accumulating experiences from which was to flower a mystique such as existed around no other military aircraft of the Second World War. A sentimental relationship developed between crews and their beloved Mossies and the regard of the airmen for their planes amounted to something very much more than admiration for the machine's clean cut appearance, smooth handling and mechanical efficiency. Their attachment for their aircraft was such that an entire squadron of pilots and navigators would solemnly take their drinks out to a Mosquito with an outstanding operational record and drink a toast to the plane . . .

The film composer John de Lacy Wooldridge, a wing commander in No. 105 Squadron RAF who experienced the Mosquito on both low-level daylight and high-level night-time sorties across the length and breadth of Europe, wrote in 1944 of his experiences:

The Mosquito bomber is in every way an outstanding aeroplane – easy to fly, highly manoeuvrable, fast and completely free from vices of any sort. From our point of view it has a further quality, a highly important one in wartime – and that is an extraordinary capacity for taking a knocking about. Owing to the high speed and rooftop height at which defended areas are crossed, the Mosquito very often tends to be immune from flak, but there are, of course, occasions when someone 'cops a packet'.

I myself had an experience of this kind a short time ago. While approaching a target at approximately 100 feet above the ground, with the bomb doors open, my aircraft was hit by three Bofors shells. Apart from the distinct thud as the shells exploded and a rather unpleasant smell of petrol, the behaviour of the aircraft after impact appeared to be normal and the bombs were dropped successfully. Actual damage was as follows: the first shell entered the lower surface of the port mainplane, approximately four feet from the wing tip, and burst inside, removing three square feet of the upper wing surface. The aileron was fortunately undamaged. The second shell hit the port engine nacelle fairly far back, wrecking the undercarriage retraction gear, severing the main oil pipe line, damaging the airscrew pitch control and putting the instrument on the blind flying panel out of action. The third shell entered the fuselage just in front of the tail plane and severed the tail wheel hydraulic line, rendering the air speed indicator useless.

After a while, on the way home, the port engine began to give trouble and eventually it failed.

Although the airscrew could not be feathered, a ground speed of almost 200mph was maintained on the return journey and the aircraft was landed in pitch darkness on its belly without the assistance of flaps.

John Terraine concluded that 'this astonishing machine, with its ceiling of 36,000 feet, its range of 350 miles, its cruising speed of 315 mph at 30,000 feet and maximum speed of 425 mph at 30,500' was a 'priceless gift' to the Allies, and that with the Lancaster and the Spitfire it was one of the three 'outstanding British aircraft of the Second World War'. All those who flew the Wooden Wonder certainly agreed. So too did the Germans. The man tasked with the fighter defence of the Reich, Adolf Galland, described the Mosquito as 'a plague to our Command and the population'. Its 'activities over Germany caused a lot of trouble':

In daytime they flew without loss and went wherever their mission took them; at night they chased the population out of their beds. The latter, who were justifiably annoyed at this, started to grumble: 'Fatty [Göring] can't even cope with a few silly Mosquitoes.'

Andre Dewavrin, head of the Free French BCRA and General De Gaulle's secret service chief. *Renault Papers*

Claude Dansey, Assistant Chief of MI6, responsible for forming and maintaining close links throughout the war with Dewavrin's BCRA.

Dominic Ponchardier, the author of the request, through his MI6 handler in London, to ask the Air Ministry and RAF to sanction a raid to relieve pressure on the hard-pressed *résistants* in north-eastern France. *Renault Papers*

Gilbert Renault (Colonel Rémy), the BCRA's star spy in 1940–43. *Roger Viollet/Getty Images*

Dr Antonin Mans, head of the Somme region's OCM *réseau*, who survived the raid and subsequent incarceration in Germany. *Renault Papers*

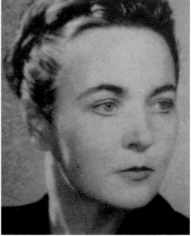

Dr Odile Regnault, Dr Antonin Mans' deputy and a secret member of the OCM *réseau*, who carefully recorded events in the immediate aftermath of the prison bombing. *Renault Papers*

Michel Hollard, the 'Man who saved London'; by reporting on V1 operations in northern France to MI6 through Colonel Groussard's Gilbert *réseau* in Geneva.

Raymond Vivant, the *sous-préfet* of Abbeville, who escaped from the prison after the attack and survived in Paris through to the Liberation. *Renault Papers*

LEFT: René and Maria Chapelle, members both of the FTPF and the Sosies *réseaux*. *Renault Papers*

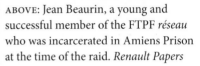

ABOVE: Jean Beaurin, a young and successful member of the FTPF *réseau* who was incarcerated in Amiens Prison at the time of the raid. *Renault Papers*

LEFT: Dr Robert and Liliane Beaumont. He was the MI9 agent who died in the raid. *Paul Fishman*

A photograph taken by a German member of a firing party at the execution of a *résistant*, Amiens, 1941. *Yad Vashem*

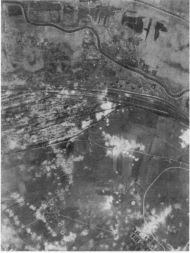

A V1 launch site ramp in northern France, bent out of shape following an RAF strike. © *Imperial War Museum*

Problems of accuracy. A USAAF attack on Amiens Railway, 6 September 1943.

The prison model constructed for the briefing of pilots on the morning of 18 February 1944. *Australian War Memorial*

RIGHT: The officers of HQ No 2 Group who planned the raid: David Atcherley, Wyckeham-Barnes, Shallard and Basil Embry. © *Imperial War Museum*

LEFT: Pickard (centre, with his Old English sheepdog Ming), when he was Officer Commanding 161 Special Duties Squadron, RAF Tangmere. © *Imperial War Museum*

RIGHT: Officers of No 487 Squadron RNZAF, the men who laid the first ten bombs on the prison. Sitting by the stove with hands folded is Merv Darrall. Warrant Officer Frank Wilkins (Bob Fowler's Navigator) sits next to him. Above Frank is Max Sparks. Fred ('Steve') Stevenson is at the top of the picture. *Kim Stevenson*

Wing Commander Irving ('Black') Smith, RNZAF. © *Imperial War Museum*

Max Sparks and Alfred Dunlop, who flew the second Royal New Zealand Air Force Mosquito MKVI to drop its bombs on the prison. *Max Sparks*

Philippe Level, the French member of the RAF, who flew on the mission and was good friends with both Gilbert Renault and Pick Pickard. *Renault Papers*

Pickard and Broadley, pilot and navigator respectively of 'F' for Freddie, and commanders of the raid against Amiens Prison. © *Imperial War Museum*

ABOVE: The view during the attack from Mosquito MK IV 'O for Orange'. *Australian War Memorial*

The breach in the main wall, caused by bombs dropped by the very first RNZAF Mosquito to attack the prison, flown by Wing Commander Irving ('Black') Smith. © *Imperial War Museum*

The ruins of the prison a day after the raid, taken by a reconnaissance Spitfire. © *Imperial War Museum*

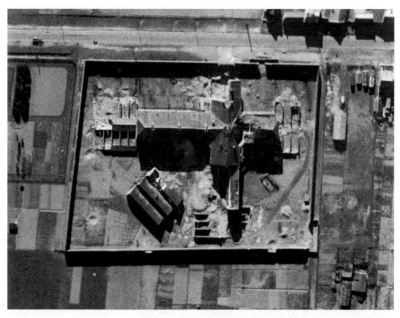

A bird's eye view of the prison after the raid, showing clearly the breaks in the walls caused by the bomb strikes. © *Imperial War Museum*

ELEVEN

No. 2 Group and 140 Wing

On 1 June 1943 Basil Embry's No. 2 Light Bomber Group had been transferred from Bomber Command to 2nd TAF in a reorganisation designed to prepare for the invasion of France. Part of Leigh-Mallory's Allied Expeditionary Air Force (AEAF), an amalgam of the US 9th Air Force and 2nd TAF, it was a grouping of several fighter and light bomber groups intended both to achieve air supremacy over the battlefield and to perform ground-attack missions. No. 2 Group, commanded by Air Vice Marshal Basil Embry, consisted of four Wings of Douglas Bostons, Mitchells and Mosquitoes. Its primary task was to provide tactical air support to ground forces, something that required low-level precision attacks on enemy targets, many of which were small and difficult to find and required specific tactics and expertise.

The experience required was hard to come by: a small number of high-profile attacks, although spectacular and well publicised, had been neither frequent nor well practised enough to count as an adequate basis for grasping the complexities of this type of air attack. Embry therefore set himself the task of learning every nuance of the role, as well as equipping his group with the most appropriate aircraft to play it. He intended to build up expertise on the basis of the learned experience of his crews, and to establish a training programme that would establish what worked best in terms both of low flying and of precision attacks on small targets. One of the first subjects he needed to master was that of the current imprecision in bombing accuracy. In *Mission Completed* Embry explained that he sought to improve the overall bombing error in No. 2 Group from 1,200 yards to 300 yards at medium altitude and to no error at all at low level, through a combination of training and repeated practice. He largely succeeded. In six months the visual bombing error had dwindled to 200 yards.

But there wasn't much shared understanding in the Allied air forces at the time of the best way to mount low-level precision attacks. Prior to the formation of 2nd TAF the four outstanding low-level operations of the war had been the daylight attack on Cologne by 55 Blenheims in August 1941; the destruction of the Gestapo headquarters at Oslo by Mosquitoes in September 1942; the successful low-level daylight attack by the mixed force of 94 Venturas, Bostons and Mosquitoes on the Philips works at Eindhoven in December 1942; and two audacious raids on Berlin by Mosquitoes on 31 January 1943.

The latter were carefully timed to disrupt important Nazi Party speeches being delivered by Hermann Göring and Joseph Goebbels at the Grossdeutscher Rundfunk, the state radio station, in Berlin's Wilhelmstrasse to mark the tenth anniversary of the Nazi Party's ascension to power. The sound of twelve exploding 500-pound bombs from three Mosquitoes led by Squadron Leader Reggie Reynolds and navigated by Ted Sismore were heard across the airwaves and caused rejoicing in London. The raid showed not just that small targets could be struck by high-quality crews flying long distances at low level, but also that small precise attacks could have a profound psychological value that far outweighed their physical impact. It also became famous for rousing Göring's notorious ire. In early 1943 he is recorded to have 'harangued aircraft manufacturers that he could "go berserk" when faced with the Mosquito, which made him "green and yellow" with envy'.

This and previous raids displayed the efficacy of low-level precision bombing as a counterpoint to the generally high-level (and high-volume), though less precise, attacks carried out by Bomber

Command. Embry's careful observation and subsequent training of his crews developed an effective modus operandi for his group. Daylight raids enabled the pilots to identify their targets exactly. Flying fast and low, formations of Mosquitoes would cross the Channel or North Sea at heights scarcely above the wavetops, rising to hurdle the cliffs of occupied France or skim over the coastal villages of Holland, manoeuvring at high speed between village steeples and clumps of trees across enemy-held territory, and often bringing back evidence of just how low they had flown. The first wave would cross their targets – a building, ammunition yard, train, factory or U-boat pen – at the same height before releasing their eleven-second-delay high-explosive or semi-armour-piercing bombs. The second wave would rise before their arrival on target to observe the strikes of the first wave, before diving from 1,500 feet to deliver their instantaneously fused 250- and 500-pound bombs on the smoke and debris caused by the first wave.

The first wave of a low-level attack could only be mounted with bombs fitted with delayed fuses, otherwise instantaneous bombs would destroy the carrying aircraft – a fate that caught a number of aircraft in the early days of operations. First-class navigational skills, high-quality flying, careful timing and teamwork and plenty of training in bomb aiming and delivery were the essential components of a successful mission. The New Zealander Merv Darrall considered that: 'Daylight operations required much concentration on the part of the pilot and navigator. The navigator became very expert in map reading – one quarter of an inch to a mile maps at tree-top level. It has been likened to rally-car driving.' Teamwork, which in many cases resulted in lifelong friendship, as in the case of Darrall and his navigator Fred 'Steve' Stevenson, was an essential ingredient in the success of these operations. So good did they become, as Darrall jested, that they could 'take out any phone booth on any given street corner of any European city'.

The right aircraft was also essential for success, and there was no doubt in Embry's mind that the outstanding aircraft in his group for its low-level tasks was the Mosquito. At the outset, however, he had four types in his inventory: in addition to small numbers of Mosquitoes he had Bostons, Mitchells and Lockheed Venturas, and No. 2 Group had initially been allocated the American Vultee Vengeance dive-bomber as its new low-level attack aircraft. Embry refused point-blank, campaigning hard for his strike forces to be issued with the far more flexible Mosquito Mk VI. By a blend of persuasion and good fortune he won the argument, and was able to reduce his aircraft types to two, deploying in the autumn of 1943 two Wings of three Mosquito squadrons each, with a third Wing comprising two squadrons of Douglas Bostons.

By the end of August 1943 No. 464 Squadron RAAF moved within Norfolk to RAF Sculthorpe from its previous base in Feltwell in order to join its sister squadrons in the group, as all three began to receive their first Mosquitoes. The powerful Mk VI was not to be trifled with: the barrels of four 20mm cannon together with four 0.303-inch machine guns poked menacingly out of the nose, while two 500-pound bombs would normally fit into the bomb bay in the belly of the aircraft, with one each attached to the wings. They trickled through in the following months to No. 21 Squadron RAF and to the New Zealanders of No. 487 Squadron RNZAF. The excitement of receiving the new aircraft even found its way into the New Zealand squadron's operations log: 'Two Mosquitos should have arrived today. Perhaps tomorrow.' Disappointingly they did not arrive that day, but the excited crews did not have long to wait. The record for the following day is as follows, scribbled across the page like an insert in the diary of an excited child:

> Here they come! Just two today; bags of excitement ... The Mossies that arrived last night have been exercised fairly hard all day in glorious weather. It is a pretty aircraft. The squadron is generally as pleased as a child with a new toy ... All anybody talks about here is Mosquitos.

ROBERT LYMAN   153

Security was stepped up. Not only was this a new aircraft, but it presaged a new series of targets, many of which would emerge from secret sources in enemy-occupied territory. It soon became common for operational briefings to be accompanied by the full panoply of secrecy: RAF policemen on the door checking passes, the 'Need to Know' principle strictly enforced. It was without much sense of loss that the last Venturas were flown away in late September, and ceremonies to say farewell to 'The Pig' were carried out with the enthusiasm of men who knew that their new aircraft was a different proposition altogether.

Pickard's 140 Wing was ready for operations with its newly issued Mosquitoes on 2 October 1943. The early operations were designed by Embry to be 'fly and learn' missions, in which future approaches and tactics were developed from experience gained of actual attacks, an approach that complemented the exercises that otherwise filled the group's training programme, and built upon the experience of low-flying attack missions in the past. The first operation by 140 Wing was an attack by twenty-four Mosquitoes on 3 October against the power station at Mur-de-Bretagne, which supplied electricity to the Atlantic coast region between Saint-Nazaire in the south and Brest in the north. Six aircraft approached at low level and dropped their eleven-second-delay bombs; the second group of six followed some minutes later, approaching the target in a shallow dive from 2,000 feet, before dropping their instantaneous detonation bombs from 300 feet. All aircraft returned safely, although one suffered a duck strike and four others, including 'Pick' Pickard's (who led No. 487 Squadron RNZAF for the mission), were hit by anti-aircraft fire. Pickard was forced to fly on one engine direct to RAF Predannack on the Lizard Peninsula in Cornwall.

Embry flew on the raid, partnering Wing Commander David Atcherley, No. 2 Group's Senior Air Staff Officer (SASO), who acted as navigator. It was their aircraft that suffered the duck strike. Embry was to fly nineteen operations during this time in command of No. 2 Group, not through any misplaced yearning for glory, but because he had resolved to learn how best to deploy his squadrons in battle, and sought every opportunity to experience operations for himself before he decided the tactics for the missions he would subsequently authorise. He was liked by his men. Arthur Dunlop described him candidly as 'an extremely impressive person and a very pleasant person to talk to . . . He was a very sort of understanding person . . . he listened to me . . . his feet were very firmly planted on the ground. He was a very likeable chap. If he said that we were to do an operation, we would do it without any second thoughts.'

Embry enthusiastically adopted the earlier innovation of including in each raid a Mosquito aircraft dedicated to filming the entire operation. For him this aircraft had a number of purposes, especially as the science of low-level precision attacks was still in its infancy and required testing and evaluation. These included the need to provide accurate damage assessment, as well as feedback for the crews on their performance, as part of raising the level of the group. The Amiens raid was no different: the aircraft – 'O' for Orange – was allocated to the raid not by the Air Ministry or HQ AEAF, but by Embry. On the 3 October mission against Mur-de-Bretagne this aircraft was flown by Flight Lieutenant Charles Patterson, DSO, DFC, and navigated by Pilot Officer Lee Howard; the latter would do likewise for the Amiens raid.

Major Hereward de Havilland, Geoffrey's brother, who spent the war years flying around the country in his personal De Havilland Leopard Moth reporting on the RAF's use of his company's aircraft, visited Sculthorpe after this attack, noting some of the lessons of the attack on the power stations:

The first wave bombed from treetop height and the remainder from 800 feet. Both targets were well covered with direct hits, but several of the delayed action bombs bounced 400 yards. No fighters were seen but there was considerable flak over the targets.

According to the historians Mark Lax and Leon Kane-Maguire, in line with his desire to learn as much as possible about the best way to execute future attacks, Embry had taken extensive notes on the trip:

> He could see the outcome of the planning and the effectiveness of both the tactics and the bombing accuracy. He noted that check points, route navigation and run-in speeds and altitudes needed more work and that bomb fusing had to be set to allow aircraft a safe escape from the ensuing blast. Embry re-wrote the operations manual to ensure targets were hit. Formation station keeping was also to be revised, as bomb fuse timing would play a big part in aircraft safety.

But while the Mur-de-Bretagne raid could be judged a success, the next, six days later by the Australian and New Zealand squadrons against an aircraft factory at Metz, was a disaster. Hereward de Havilland was at Sculthorpe with Pickard when the surviving aircraft returned, and captured the detail in a letter to his brother:

> Twenty-four aircraft of 464 and 487 Squadrons took off from Sculthorpe at 11.15 am . . . After crossing the English coast they ran into thick weather and about eight miles out had to go off course to miss a very large British convoy flying balloons, of which they had had no warning. Visibility decreased to 400 yards and the formations lost touch before reaching the French coast, where Squadron Leader Davey saw a flak battery winding their guns round like mad to bring them to bear, as they had luckily been pointing in the wrong direction.
>
> In France the clouds were right down to the hills and no aircraft reached the target. Unknown to me, or I think anyone else outside Sculthorpe, the intercom switches of these aircraft had been altered to press-buttons on the control column, close to the

bomb-release switch, and it is probable that this accounts for two of the four aircraft that were lost. All were flying at near sea-level, and one was seen to disintegrate with a colossal explosion just before, and another sometime after, crossing the French coast. The explosions were consistent with the bursting of bombs with instantaneous fuses, released at this sort of height. The second wave of aircraft carried instantaneous fuse bombs only, and for this reason were unable to attack any targets they happened to see owing to the low level at which the weather forced them to fly. Some pilots carrying eleven-second delay bombs did have a go at factory buildings and canal barges.

I drove round with Pickard to each aircraft as they came in to Sculthorpe. Most crews had little idea where they had been to and all were roundly cursing the weather, the convoy, and instantaneous bombs. All windscreens were plastered thick with flies which didn't improve some of the landings. Four leading edges and two main spars were damaged by birds.

In the words of the official New Zealand historian, the failure of most aircraft even to find the target 'may be partly attributed to the weather, which led to a succession of errors in navigation, but it would also seem that the mission was rather too ambitious for crews relatively inexperienced in low-level attack and flying a new type of aircraft.'

One of the less well-known issues facing Embry at the time was a general paucity of targets for his crews. He had struggled for months to find enough precision targets to keep his aircraft flying and his aircrew trained and motivated. At the point at which he had been approached to consider an attack on Amiens Prison in the early days of February 1944, 140 Wing had only just begun a sequence of Noball attacks – operations against V1 sites in northern France. On 18 October 1943 Embry had written to HQ 2nd TAF complaining that the target directive recently published by the Air Ministry was overwhelmingly weighted towards heavy bomber operations, a fact that denied his No. 2 Group the opportunity to fly missions against targets appropriate to its own type of aircraft. He noted that of the list produced, 'only ten are suitable for our aircraft'. One of the suggestions he made was to undertake more operations in support of the Ministry of Economic Warfare (MEW). He was referring here to Special Operations generally; SOE was part of the MEW.

It is notable that Embry did not mention the Foreign Office (and by inference, support to MI6 operations) in his letter, presumably because he assumed that his reference to the MEW would capture this point, or because he was unaware of the operational differences between the two organisations. The latter is possible given the traditionally intense secrecy surrounding the work of MI6. Even those involved closely with the work of Special Operations (for example, through the work of 161 Squadron RAF) would rarely have understood who their masters were; for some operations it was SOE, for others MI6. It was even more confusing for those in the French Resistance. Most of its leaders who had reason to do so merely referred to the 'Intelligence Services', and on at least one occasion Gilbert Renault, who as has been seen was on intimate terms with MI6, demonstrated profound confusion between the two organisations.

With the bomber offensive in full swing, and in particular at the time, the Battle of Berlin, light bomber operations were not high on the Air Ministry's list of priorities, so rather than argue with the policy Embry stressed the operational issues involved in finding suitable targets for the eight initial Mosquito squadrons in his No. 2 Group. The nuances of Mosquito operations were not well understood in Kingsway House. In particular, to be effective Mosquitoes needed to enter enemy territory at low level, but the enemy had deployed light flak to close off most entry points. Because the range of a Mosquito was 350 miles this meant that, keeping ten per cent in reserve for emergencies, the distance flown to a target needed to be no more than about 157 miles. A diversion to ensure a secure low-level entrance into France or Holland added an average of twenty-five miles to each journey.

A month passed, and Embry had still had no response to his letter, so on 26 November he pressed his case again with HQ 2nd TAF, enclosing an evaluation of the targets listed under the current directive, detailed enough to demonstrate how many were entirely unsuited to operations by Mosquitoes. Embry wanted to deploy his raw crews against lightly defended targets with reasonably easy approaches to build up their confidence before committing them to major operations. 'To my way of thinking, this should form the main diet of their training, in the immediate future,' he argued. To achieve this, many more suitable targets were required:

> In our present elementary stage of operational training, attacks are carried out by aircraft in pairs, so as to give experience to the optimum number of Pilots and Navigators in a given time. I intend in the next stage to increase this number up to fours and sixes, and thereafter to the culminating stage where Squadrons will be put on to vital and, maybe, difficult targets . . .
>
> You will appreciate that only three of our five Mosquito Squadrons have so far had operational experience, 613 still in process of conversion and 305 just beginning to equip. Judging by present form I am hoping that 487 and 21 Squadrons will be fit to undertake difficult operations within the next three weeks and 464 . . . similarly a fortnight later. It may be February before both the other Squadrons have reached this stage and you will see therefore that I shall require plenty of [appropriate] targets to maintain the necessary operational training momentum.

HQ 2nd TAF agreed, but were unable to help, noting in response only that 'the number of learner targets at present available for 2 Group is, to all intents and purposes, negligible . . .' Of the seventeen targets listed in the Directive all but four were judged to be 'Poor', 'Very Poor' or 'No' target material. The dearth of adequate

targets was granted to be a significant hindrance to plans to ensure that all No. 2 Group crews were 'sufficiently trained in time for the operations next year'.

The emergence of the V1 threat in November and December 1943 ironically proved a godsend for Embry, as it solved this problem, as well as helping in the systematic destruction of the static V1 sites in northern France. As has been seen, the Germans were known to have approximately 140 sites in various stages of construction, and of these 103 were destroyed in due course by the Allied air forces, many of them by virtue of intelligence provided on the ground by men such as Michel Hollard, Dominique Ponchardier and others.* Embry observed in 1945 that 'history may decide that this battle was nearly as important as the Battle of Britain'.

No. 2 Group was responsible for approximately one-third of the destruction of these V1 sites. Between December 1943 and May 1944 it carried out a total of 4,710 sorties against them, at a cost of 41 aircraft and 120 lives. In addition, 419 aircraft were damaged as a result of enemy action, chiefly anti-aircraft fire – an overall casualty rate (aircraft lost and damaged), relative to sorties flown, of nearly ten per cent. Right from the start, flak proved the biggest challenge. 'This has varied from being very troublesome at times to a free run,' Embry recorded.

Over the last twelve months, we have averaged by day 8% damage from flak. On certain occasions, particularly recently, against bridge targets as much as 90% of the attacking force has received damage. However, our comparatively small loss from flak has been achieved by careful routing to and from the targets. We pay

* In his 1945 deposition Ponchardier asserted that his work, with Groussard's *réseau Gilbert*, in identifying and defeating the V1 threat was of far greater import than the Amiens raid, but that the latter received much more publicity. He never could understand why.

special attention to the best lines of approach and getaway, rather than by extensive evasive tactics . . . For low level daylight attacks, exact pin-pointing of all heavy and light gun positions en route and in the target area is of vital importance.

Early in 1945 Basil Embry found himself talking to students at the RAF Staff College at Bracknell about the work of his group. It was an important lecture, revealing much about the way in which missions such as that against Amiens Prison were selected and organised. Pinpoint targets required specific tactics, he explained, and 'an exceptionally high degree of skill and efficiency on the part of aircrews'. It was important to train Mosquito aircrew, and send them on operations, as a team, rather than as two separate individuals brought together for each raid. Trust between pilot and navigator needed to be absolute. For this reason crews stayed together, only being split by reasons of death or injury, or incompatibility. Many crews spent their entire operational careers together, forming extremely close relationships that, for those who survived, lasted for the rest of their lives. Merv Darrall and 'Steve' Stevenson are examples of such a friendship, as are Pickard and Broadley.

In his lecture Embry described a number of special targets that required accurate bombing, including 'launching sites for V1 and V2 weapons, Gestapo headquarters, SS barracks and other special targets in support of the French Forces of the Interior [i.e. the French Resistance]'. He explained that targets offered by the Resistance in France found their way to 2nd TAF via the Air Ministry, and described the process of planning that followed:

The planning of operations is done at [No. 2] Group level, the amount of detail depending on whether the target is a customary or an unusual one. In Group, we usually specify the armament, including bomb load and fusing, the number of aircraft to take part, the times of attack and heights and for day operations, the routes to be followed and the fighter rendezvous. Group are responsible for arranging fighter cover . . .

If the target is an unusual one, presenting new problems, it is the usual practice for us to make a relief model of it, and we use this model for the planning and subsequent briefing. We have found that the models have been of tremendous value for our low attack targets, particularly in planning the lead-in to the target and the routing around flak positions.

The tactics used by the Mosquitoes evolved over time and through experience:

We have found that the box of six aircraft as the basic unit is the best and these are built up into one or more waves of three or more boxes. The leading crews are picked not only for their ability to lead their box in plain flying, but also for their proved bombing accuracy and navigational skill. Normally, each box bombs on its box leader . . .

But the arrival of perfect targets, in the form of the V1 sites identified by the French Resistance and the PRU and scattered across farms and woods in northern France, was accompanied by additional problems, which made the progress of No. 2 Group frustratingly slow. When the harsh winter weather allowed, operations were undertaken every day, but these rarely meant deploying more than half of the 36 Mosquitoes available in each Wing, given the limitations of individual training, aircraft maintenance and the availability of full crews for each sortie (a significant problem for the RAF at this stage of the war). Indeed, the norm was for many fewer even than half of the available aircraft to make it into the sky for a mission, and then it was rare for all aircraft to find, let alone hit, the target.

The statistics for the first two weeks of February 1944 are instructive – the first period of sustained operations against the V1 sites by the crews of 140 Wing. The Wing's Operations Record Book reveals that in the fourteen days before the attack on Amiens, that is between 3 and 17 February, a total of 128 sorties were undertaken, representing a utilisation rate of the aircraft available of a quarter. However, because of poor weather only ten of the fourteen days were flyable. Of the total of 128 sorties undertaken during this period 113 were flown against V1 ('Noball') sites in northern France, but during these missions only 80 aircraft successfully located their targets and dropped 80 tons of bombs. This meant that 30 per cent of all aircraft leaving the airfield at the start of the mission failed to drop any bombs on the target, whether because they got lost en route, or suffered some kind of malfunction or incident (such as a bird strike) that forced them to return to base, or failed to locate their targets. During these 128 sorties two aircraft were lost.

The pattern therefore was that a portion of the aircraft available in 140 Wing would attack allocated targets every two days, with longer delays between missions if – as was the case in February 1944 – the weather closed in to produce difficult flying conditions. It also meant that few crews actually became immersed in the rigours of low-level precision flying and bombing. It is instructive that the logbook of Group Captain 'Pick' Pickard revealed only six such missions before the Amiens raid.

TWELVE

Charles Pickard

The man who was tasked with commanding the raid, and who died leading it, Group Captain Percy Charles ('Pick') Pickard, was one of those larger-than-life characters who expend their all in the service of their country, and whose legend, strong in life, continues equally strongly into death. Twenty-eight at the time of his death, he had flashed briefly into prominence when in July 1941 he was seen by millions across the free world in the drama documentary *Target for Tonight*. This was a propaganda film designed to raise the morale of war-weary Britons, and to encourage Britain's friends around the globe to believe that it was striking back successfully against the aggressor, and would continue to do so with every fibre of its being. The film, produced by Harry Watt, was a triumph. Pickard played Squadron Leader Dixon, the pilot of Wellington bomber 'F for Freddie': all other roles likewise were played by serving personnel. Few of these amateur actors survived the war. Every aircraft Pickard subsequently flew was designated 'F for Freddie'.

Known across the RAF as 'Pick' (but to his family as 'Boy'), Pickard had already had a long war by the time he was promoted to Group Captain and appointed to the command of 140 Wing in October 1943. He had joined the RAF on a Short Service Commission in 1937, in common with many young men at the time concerned that Hitler's aggressive rhetoric and menacing behaviour would soon lead to another European war. A life of practical adventure in the colonies – initially in Kenya – followed a school career at Framlingham undistinguished by academic achievement, but one in which his huge appetites for field sports, horses, dogs and shooting had flourished. His life as a pilot began and ended with bombers: first the slow and ungainly Handley Page Harrow, followed by the Hampden, and then, when war started, the Wellington.

It was on his twenty-first mission, flying a bombing mission over the Ruhr on 19 June 1940, that Flight Lieutenant Pickard's aircraft was fatally damaged. He attempted to coax the stricken bomber home, but before they could reach the British coast he was forced to ditch in the hostile waters of the North Sea. He succeeded, however, in saving the lives of his crew, a feat for which he was awarded the Distinguished Flying Cross. Bringing the Wellington low over the water, he managed to stall it just above the waves, to drop like a stone over the remaining few feet. They were able to stay afloat for the two minutes necessary for the entire crew to evacuate into the inflatable life raft. The impact of landing nevertheless was enough for Pickard to smash one of his wrists on the instrument panel. The crew were in their tiny dinghy for thirteen hours before being rescued by an inshore lifeboat.

In late 1940 Pickard was promoted to Squadron Leader, taking charge of the only Czech bomber squadron in the RAF, No. 311, during which time he was awarded his first Distinguished Service Order. His citation captures something of the dynamism of this natural leader:

Since joining No. 311 Czech Squadron in July 1940, this officer has invariably taken out new Czech crews on their initial operation, or first long distance mission. On such occasions, he has been the only British member amongst the crews who have been inspired by his splendid leadership and example. On one occasion it was undoubtedly due to his determined efforts that one Czech crew was rescued after being adrift in the North Sea for over 13 hours. On another occasion when a crew was forced down in the North Sea, his persistence, and good airmanship in failing light, and his sound use of recognition signals, enabled surface craft to effect a rescue. His complete disregard for danger was particularly shown on an occasion when a fully loaded bomber crashed and caught fire. He led a rescue party and personally extricated two members of the crew and succeeded in eventually conveying them to safety, although compelled to remain prone in the danger area during the explosion of some of the bombs. He has displayed coolness and courage of a high order and, by his magnificent work, contributed largely to the present efficiency of the Squadron.

Tall and physically imposing (Pickard was well over six feet), this blond Yorkshire-born giant was always to be found at the heart of the action, social or otherwise. A pipe seemed to be permanently jammed between his teeth and his Old English sheepdog, Ming, was as well known around the station as his master. He was liked and admired by all who came into contact with him. 'Bunty' Anderson, a pretty young YMCA worker at RAF Hunsdon (since the end of 1943 Hunsdon had been the base of all three squadrons of 140 Wing that had previously been scattered across airfields in Norfolk) who provided hot tea and refreshments to aircrew return- ing from flights, was struck by his 'tremendous personality' and observed that 'everyone thought he was marvellous'. Lax and Kane- Maguire relate how Pilot Officer Bill Binnie recalled sharing the Officers' Mess at RAF Sculthorpe (a Nissen hut) with the larger- than-life OC:

There was little in the way of entertainment apart from a piano in the Mess. My navigator, Stan Adams was a very good pianist and Pickard used to have him play as often as he was willing. Pickard's favourite was 'Why they whisper green grass'. I remember him coming into the Mess late one night well-oiled and asking 'Where's Stan?' When informed he was in bed a mile away, Pick persuaded me to take his Humber Snipe and bring Stan back – he could be very persuasive. I was terrified I would prang his precious Snipe – however, I got to our digs and dragged poor old Stan back. I don't think he was too impressed.

But Pickard was not self-important. Once, during the period of introduction to the Mosquito, as crews familiarised themselves with the aircraft, he became annoyed with the number of minor accidents the Wing was suffering. He left a notice in the briefing room that read: 'The next clot to prang a Mosquito through finger trouble will be posted to the bloodiest job in the Air Force.' Sure enough, the next day a Mossie swung and snapped the tail wheel. Out stepped Pickard, his only comment being 'There's always bloody something!' In many ways he was a law to himself. Flight Lieutenant Charles Foster, DFC RAF recalled his first meeting with the Station Commander:

The CO at my Mosquito conversion course considered me too ancient (32 years) and suggested I join Transport Command. On Bob Iredale's advice I travelled to Sculthorpe to see Pickard, who I met at the bar of the Officers' mess. After hearing my story over a beer, he said 'That's OK, we've got grandfathers on this unit'. Just then a chap (Wing Commander Meakin) put his head around the corner – 'Jack', he said, 'I've got another crew for you'. Another chap then came in and said 'the crews are complaining about the food'. Pickard got angry and said to me, 'What really matters is that they've got the right aircraft – the Mosquito. You know, Foster, the Station CO should have the option of shooting one man per week – what do you think, Foster?!' Pickard was living in the wrong century. He should have been a buccaneer like Drake.

Pick's buccaneering spirit was designed for war. When he was a young pilot officer at No. 99 Squadron at Newmarket Heath at the start of the war, a member of the ground crew, Norman Didwell, had cause to observe and admire the characteristics of this young officer:

> He was the most decent and straightforward of men. Whilst he had made an early career in the RAF, Pick was far from being a Service zealot, shrugging off officialdom and avoiding paperwork whenever he could. At the same time he had an intense pride in what he was doing, and deep fulfilment in the mastery of flying with the perfection of touch that it demanded. Its close affinity to the skills demanded by horse riding had not evaded him. He was unimpressed by hierarchy's cold formality and pomp. He took a pride in being at one with his men, which was different from attempting to be one of them. He was brave and patriotic, he led by firm discipline and fine example to the extent that people felt secure in his command.

In May 1941 Pickard returned to Wellingtons, taking command of No. 9 Squadron RAF. It was here that he was joined again by a man who had experienced the ditching with him in the North Sea, Alan ('Bill') Broadley, and who was to fly with him, with few exceptions, to the end. The two became inseparable. By the end of August 1941 they had completed sixty-five missions, and were fast developing reputations as men with unwavering commitments to complete the tasks allocated to them, no matter how hazardous.

In November 1941, accompanied by promotion to Wing Commander, Pickard took command of No. 51 Squadron, flying Whitley bombers in support of HQ Combined Operations. It was during this posting that he planned and executed the RAF element of the second British parachute operation of the war, the successful raid on the German radar site at Bruneval on the night of 27 February 1942. It was this operation that introduced him for the first time, indirectly, to the work both of MI6 and of the French Resistance, a connection that would link both him and Broadley directly to the Amiens Prison raid two years later. Professor R. V.

Jones had asked Dansey to attack the site of the German Würzburg radar on the cliffs at Bruneval and bring back components of the equipment for examination in Britain. Men of Gilbert Renault's *réseau CND* conducted the close target reconnaissance and Dansey duly asked the RAF to help. Pickard's squadron was tasked with carrying the newly trained parachutists to their drop zone nearby.

The newspapers in Britain on Sunday 1 March 1942 were full of news of this small and daring venture, described by some excited editors somewhat prematurely as an 'invasion'. Photographs of the triumphant parachutists returning to Portsmouth next morning on board a motor launch show Pickard greeting them at the dockside. Something of Pickard's character can be seen in his description of the visit of the King and Queen a few days later to Dishforth to meet the men who had executed the raid. George VI asked him about a series of dirty marks covering the ceiling in the Officer's Mess anteroom. Pickard came clean:

> I am afraid it's the result of the Mess party to celebrate our return from Bruneval. At the height of the proceedings my shoes were removed, my feet blacked with boot polish, chairs stacked on each other, and I was perched at the top making footprints as you can see. I'm sorry, Sir.

When questioned by the King as to the 'large blobs at the centre of the ceiling', Pickard could only reply: 'I'm afraid to say, sir, those are the marks of my bottom.' Pickard received his second DSO for his role in this raid.

Both Pickard and Broadley now cemented their involvement with the work of both MI6 and SOE by taking up a posting for ten months in October 1942 with the famous 161 (Special Duties) Squadron, supporting the underground movements across Europe in their resistance to German occupation. Flying Hudsons and Lysanders from RAF Tempsford in Bedfordshire, both men became intimately bound up with the business of ferrying secret agents into France and collecting returnees, escapees and the documentary intelligence gathered by the various *réseaux* of the resistance movement. Pickard flew 100 operations between October 1942 and April 1943, at which point he, and Broadley who had completed 80, met Gilbert Renault and his friend Philippe Level. A number of sources, including Renault, suggest that he also met Dominique Ponchardier during this time. Hugh Verity, wartime pilot and author of *We Landed by Moonlight*, met Pickard at Tempsford, and while impressed with his qualities considered 'that he was driving himself hard and burning himself up'.

After the excitement of this job a long administrative posting should have beckoned, but after pressing his case with Embry, Pickard was brought back to operational flying in October 1943 with command of 140 Wing. This, however, left Embry in something of a quandary. Although Pickard was a vastly experienced operational flyer, he had absolutely no knowledge of low-level daylight flying. His experience had been in night-time operations in both bombers and Special Operations aircraft such as the Lysander, and evidence suggests that this magnificent character, as Verity suggested, was in fact exhausted, pushing himself beyond all reasonable limits. This was also the verdict of Flight Lieutenant Charles Patterson, who had been flying Mosquito DZ414 ('O' for Orange) – the FPU Mosquito that would accompany the 140 Wing raiders to Amiens – operationally since 6 December 1942. He regarded Pickard as a 'splendid character. But it was quite plain to me that he should never have been allowed to go on. He was a nervous wreck . . . he was obsessed with getting on operations . . . but his brain was really too tired to really sit down and tackle the detail . . . it was quite obvious that he should have been rested, no matter how much he wanted to go on . . . A man who'd made a staggeringly splendid contribution to the war was denied his future.'

Patterson blamed Embry for giving in to Pickard's persistent badgering to be allowed another operational posting. 'Embry ought to have recognised that after so many trips on light bombers there was no basis on which to start off a completely new career on low-level daylight bombing.' Adrian Orchard, one of Pickard's biographers, dismisses this accusation. His view is that:

Embry was acutely aware of the dangers to Pickard of this change in role, and planned a period of apprenticeship for him. This mainly entailed Pickard, now re-united with Broadley as co-pilot, flying in a subordinate role on missions to his squadron command-ers. His new Mosquito was of course marked F-Freddie, and he and Broadley were soon after launched into their first combat. Attacking the Pont Chateau power station at low-level, their star-board engine was damaged, but made it home. On their very next sortie attacking Cleve, F-Freddie was again damaged, but again made it back to base. By the end of January 1944, 140 Wing had been moved south to Hunsdon. Pickard and Broadley had racked up another four low level missions on Mosquitoes.

But after the war, Embry acknowledged his feelings of guilt in continuing to allow Pickard to lead the Ramrod raid on Amiens. Embry had felt that Pickard lacked experience in low-level opera-tions, but his hand was forced.

. . . I shall always regret that decision because, although he was an exceptionally experienced operational pilot at night, he had carried out only a few missions by day, and I believe this may well have been the reason he was shot down by enemy fighters . . .

It is probable that Embry knew of Pickard's close association with the men of the French Resistance through his work with both 51 Squadron (Gilbert Renault) and 161 Squadron (Philippe Level). He would have entirely understood Pickard's personal motivation to support a raid against Amiens. The months he had spent taking and recovering so many MI6 agents, *passeurs* and SOE operatives to and from the field of operations by Lysander and Hudson, illuminated only by moonlight, meant not only that Pickard knew several of the BCRA and MI6 agents involved in the Amiens affair personally, but that he recognised the extraordinary risks that these brave men and women were taking. There can be little doubt that Embry's experience of escape and evasion in 1940 and Pickard's familiarity with the work of the Resistance and personal knowledge of some of the men involved were to have a profound impact on their attitude to the request to support incarcerated *résistants* in February 1944. Now their chance had come.

THIRTEEN

RAF Hunsdon, 8 a.m.,
Friday 18 February 1944

There was a heavy greyness to the morning of Friday 18 February 1944, a typically miserable English winter's day. Well after dawn the sky was still dark, due partly to the intensity of the snow swirling thickly over the airfield, partly to the low cloud. Widespread snow over most of southern England that morning and for the past two days had limited all but the most essential flying, and the aerodrome was blanketed with snow. On the day before, the weather had ruled out an urgent operation planned for 140 Wing. Merv Darrall's logbook listed a total of two hours and nine minutes' flying time in the previous week, all Night Flight Training (NFT). This comprised twelve minutes on 11 February, twenty-seven minutes the following evening, an hour on 13 February and thirty minutes on 15 February. The logbook is blank on 14, 16 and 17 February, the weather just too bad to think of flying.

Bomber Command had not flown a mass raid for two days. On the night of 15 February a total 891 aircraft – heavy bombers such as the Lancaster and Halifax, which the German public fearfully called 'Four Motors' – had bombed Berlin, and on the following night 823 aircraft had attacked Leipzig. On this night also – 16 February – the records list 48 aircraft undertaking operations in support of the French Resistance. For all of 17 February, Bomber Command had sat idle, while freezing temperatures and swirling snow offered the beleaguered citizens of Nazi Germany a brief respite from the otherwise relentless terror from the skies. Likewise, for 2nd TAF, Fighter Command and Coastal Command, operations were severely curtailed, if not abandoned altogether. Indeed, the original plan had been to launch this raid the day before – Thursday 17 February – but the harshness of the weather forbade it, and a delay of twenty-four hours was imposed.

On waking to their customary cup of tepid tea from the messing assistant, the crews at RAF Hunsdon who had been chosen for the mission were told to prepare for a briefing at 8 a.m. Pilot Officer Arthur Dunlop, Max Sparks's navigator in No. 487 Squadron, remembered the morning well:

> I was awakened at 6 o'clock in the morning, and looked outside, where it was very dark and it was snowing and looking extremely unpleasant. I went over to the mess at Hunsdon and after breakfast went in the crew bus down to the aerodrome which was about a mile and a half away. We had to go there for a briefing at 8 o'clock in the morning and I went to get my flying gear and then went into the briefing room.

Armed RAF policemen stood at the door, admitting only those whose identity documents tallied with the list they consulted. Because the source of information about the target came from France through the auspices of MI6, the utmost secrecy surrounded the subject all the way to the point of embarkation by the Mosquito crews on the day of the attack. This was an increasingly common protection afforded to highly sensitive information when lives might be lost – those of *résistants*, for instance – if it were compromised. Indeed, for some months now the crews of 2nd TAF had been undertaking raids against V1 launch sites across northern France, about which new and strict secrecy procedures had been enforced. RAF policemen had begun to guard the briefing rooms at airfields as a means of impressing upon the crews the sensitivity of their targets, to ensure that they did not blab about them if captured.

The men filed in, one by one, and began filling up the seats from the front of the room. Already present were two officers from No. 2 Group, Squadron Leader Ted Sismore and Wing Commander Pat Shallard, the Group Intelligence Officer, together with 'Pick' Pickard and Basil Embry. A few select individuals had already been briefed on the target, including the commanding officers of the three squadrons (Wing Commanders Irving 'Black' Smith (No. 487 Squadron), Robert Wilson ('Bob') Iredale (No. 464 Squadron) and Ivor 'Daddy' Dale (No. 21 Squadron), together with Tony Wickham of the FPU. Bob Iredale later recalled:

> Curious faces looked towards me as I walked past the armed guards outside and into the briefing room. Tense, expectant faces. From me their eyes swung back towards the large box which stood on the Commanding Officer's table beneath the flight map affixed to the wall. It was several inches deep, that box, five feet square at the top. What was hidden beneath it?

Flying Officer Lee Howard was equally mesmerised by the big wooden box:

> It was about five feet square and six inches deep. Clearly a model of the target; it couldn't be anything else. I was particularly intrigued by the thing. Unlike most of those present I had been given preliminary details of the raid the evening before, because there are certain additional preparations the film cameraman has to make which take time. Most of the other members of air crew were quite used to my knowing what was happening long before they did, and several of them asked me what the raid was all about. Normally I could have answered their questions; but this time, when I had seen Group Captain Pickard the evening before, he had done nothing other than indicate the nature of the attack in the most general terms.

He had told me where it was; he had told me the route by which we were getting there; and he had told me I would like the raid. 'It's going to make a grand story for you', he said. 'You should get some damned good pictures; I think you'll find it's very photogenic'.

'A big factory of some kind?' I hazarded.

'Well – something like that, in general,' he replied. 'You'll understand the need for absolute secrecy when you hear all about it at the briefing,' and with that I had had to be content . . . I had already ready fitted my two fixed cine cameras into the Mosquito and had stowed away my two hand-held cameras in the nose, ready for use. My hands were numb with the cold, and I warmed them by the stove while we waited for the briefing to start.

The briefing was formal and careful. Pickard and Embry arrived and began by revealing the nature of the mission. Lee Howard recalled Pickard's words clearly:

Your target today is a very special one from every point of view. There has been no little debate as to whether this attack should be carried out, and your A.O.C. more or less had to ask for a vote of confidence in his men and his aircraft before we were given the chance of having a crack at it. It could only be successfully carried out by low-level Mosquitoes; and we've got to make a big success of it to justify his faith in us, and to prove further, if proof is necessary, just how accurately we can put our bombs down.

The story is this. In the prison at Amiens are one hundred and twenty French patriots who have been condemned to be shot by the Nazis for assisting the allies. Some have been condemned for assisting Allied airmen to escape after being brought down in France. Their end is a matter of a day or two. Only a successful operation by the RAF to break down their prison walls can save them, and we're going to have a crack at it today. We're going to bust that prison open. If we make a good job of it and give the lads inside a chance to get out, the French underground people will be standing by to take over from there. There are eighteen of you detailed for this trip. In addition, the Film Unit's special aircraft is coming along to see what sort of a job you make of it. The first six of you are going to breach the walls. Now, these walls have got to be broken down if the men inside are to get out successfully. This will mean some real low-level flying; you've got to be right down on the deck. The walls are only about twenty-five feet high, and if we're not damned careful our bombs are going to bounce right over them and land inside the prison and blow everybody to smithereens. We have told the men inside of this risk, through the underground movement, and they're fully aware of the possibility.

We've got to cut that risk down to the minimum. You've got to be below the height of the wall when you let them go; down to ten feet, if possible. There are no obstructions in the way on your run up, so you should be able to make it.

The listening crews were spellbound. After a pause and without any fanfare – but in complete silence – the lid was then removed from the box. Bob Iredale:

It was a plaster of paris model of the Amiens prison and environs, based on photographic reconnaissance photos and information supplied by the French. Clearly shown in three dimensions was the appearance of the jail and its proximity to houses on the western side.

Pickard then continued with the detail of the attack, recalled by Lee Howard:

We have here a model of the prison, which you are all going to study in detail shortly. You will notice that the prison itself is in the form of a cross, and that at its east and west ends are small triple buildings which, according to our information, are the quarters of the Nazi prison guards. The second six aircraft are going to prang those quarters. I don't suppose all the Nazis will be inside at once, but we're sure to get some of them and it'll all add to the general confusion and give the prisoners a better chance.

The crews were then briefed on the detail of the route and flying instructions. Ted Sismore followed with details of the attack, each crewman scribbling in his notebook. The attack was to take place at 12 noon that day. The outward leg would take the aircraft in six waves (two waves per squadron), each a few minutes apart, to Littlehampton, where they would rendezvous with their Typhoon fighter escort via a checkpoint above Henley-on-Thames. Other Typhoons would go directly to Amiens and meet them there, providing top cover during the raid against any Luftwaffe intruders. The first squadron would leave Hunsdon in pairs, followed two minutes later by the second squadron. The third squadron would leave exactly ten minutes later. Each squadron would then cross the Channel at wavetop height to Tocqueville; then to Senarpont; then to Bourdon; a point one mile south of Doullens; then to Bouzin, followed by Court, two miles west-south-west of Albert. At this point they would line up on the Route Nationale 29 and follow it due west until, on the right-hand side, just short of Amiens, they would see the large, dark mass of the prison.

Each aircraft was even then being bombed up with its load of four 500-pound bombs, all fused to explode 11 seconds after release. The attack would be undertaken at low level, which meant that the target had to be approached at little more than ground level – between 20 and 30 feet, where the greatest danger was trees and telephone cables – the aircraft rising above the target as they dropped their bombs in order to avoid hitting the target them-selves. Six aircraft would attempt to break the outer wall in at least two places. In the first attack the leading three aircraft would attack the eastern wall using the main road as lead-in, while the second three aircraft, when at ten miles from the target, would break to the right, rise high enough above ground level to allow them to watch the first attack, and then line up to release their bombs on the northern wall on a north–south run. Three minutes later, the leading three aircraft of the second wave would attack the south-eastern end of the main building, before another three aircraft attacked the north-western end. The third and final attack would take place by the reserve squadron thirteen minutes later, but only if Pickard believed that the first two attacks had failed.

Once the attack was over and each aircraft had made its single pass, they were all to hightail it for home. On the return journey aircraft were encouraged to fly together, rather than individually, for added safety. The route was to fly from the target to Saveur, then following the track to Senarpont, Tocqueville, Hastings and then home to Hunsdon. There was one final warning. Merv Darrall remembered Pickard giving strict instructions to the pilots to undertake just one run at the target before heading for home. If they loitered and became 'battlefield tourists' they would present wonderful targets for any lurking FW190s, which were known to fly high-level combat patrols in these skies in the hope of swooping on any unsuspecting, low-flying Mossies darting in and out of northern France.

The room was a cauldron of barely contained excitement following the briefing, even among the most experienced of the crews. At last, here was an operation that the men could relate directly to the desperate predicament of those whom they were attempting to save. But who, someone asked, would fly in each wave? Bob Iredale recalled that this question 'was solved by the flip of a coin'. Much to the chagrin of both the Australians and Britons, the New Zealanders of No. 487 Squadron (call sign 'Dypeg') won the first crack at the prison's defences. The Australian No. 464 Squadron ('Cannon') were to come in second, with the RAF's No. 21 Squadron ('Buckshot') in reserve, only to be deployed if their antipodean colleagues failed in the first two waves. Take-off order would be the same as the bombing order and the commanding officers were to lead their squadrons. Ian McRitchie takes up the story:

> At the end of the briefing Pickard asked Smith and Iredale who would comprise the last flight (to bomb the prison). Bob Iredale pointed to me as I was walking up to join them because I had been pondering a question which it would be wrong to have asked so that all could hear. The question was, had HQ considered that there had to be a speed limitation on putting bombs into a brick or bluestone wall? That is, faster than about 240 mph the bomb casing was likely to fracture and render the bomb useless. Pickard asked me a few questions and I gave him the answers. He then called all to silence and said pilots were to keep their bombing drop speed down to under 240 mph.

Wing Commander 'Daddy' Dale of No. 21 Squadron then asked how they would know whether or not the attack had been successful, and therefore whether or not No. 21 Squadron were to continue with their attack. Pickard's solution was simple:

> I shall be flying towards the end of the first twelve. When I've dropped my bombs I shall pull off to one side and circle, probably just to the north of the prison. I can watch the attack from there; and I'll tell you by radio. We'll use the signals 'red' and 'green', repeated three times; so that if you hear me say 'red, red, red' you'll know you're being warned off and will go home without bombing. If I say 'green, green, green' it's all clear for you to go in and bomb. As an additional precaution, the film aircraft will have just as good a view as myself of the whole show – perhaps even a little better – so it can act as cover. If you don't hear me give the signal and hear the answering acknowledgement, Tony, you can give the 'red' or 'green' yourself before the third six come in to bomb.

The briefing over, Pickard escorted Embry from the room and went to his office. A telephone call to HQ No. 2 Group gave him the latest meteorological report, which indicated that weather conditions were improving over the Channel. He determined that the mission would proceed: a delay or postponement because of difficult weather conditions over southern England did not outweigh the obligation he felt to assist his friends on the ground in Amiens in their hour of need. Some records suggest that at this stage a further message was received from France, pleading for an attack to take place, but there is no evidence for this, nor does Ponchardier mention it. It also ignores the reality that there was a significant time delay between sending radio messages from occupied France to Whaddon Hall and thence to Bletchley before dissemination to its intended recipient. As Ponchardier knew to his cost, this could take two days and more. The suggestion that there was a last-minute intervention from France, therefore, is likely to be fiction, although in sentiment it exactly captures the desperation that Ponchardier and his friends on the ground in Amiens would have felt at the time: if the RAF did not arrive, for whatever reason, men and women would die, and *la résistance française* – both in what it was able to do, and in what it stood for – would be much the poorer for the failure of the Allies to act when requested.

Returning to the briefing room an hour later, Pickard told the expectant crews that the mission was on. They were to disperse to their aircraft. Lee Howard recalled Pickard's final words:

It's still snowing, and the visibility is not so very good; but we can get off the deck all right. I've just had a final word with Group on the phone and they've given us the O.K. to go. This is one raid where a cancellation is unthinkable; if the slightest hint of what we are going to try to do were to leak out, every one of those men would be shot instantly. So, let's get going and make a good job of it.

Renault recorded that Pickard concluded by commenting: 'It's a job of death or glory, boys! You'll have to burst open the gates of this jail.' Pilot Officer Max Sparks recalled Pickard assuring the assembled crews: 'If it succeeds it will be one of the most worthwhile ops of the war. If you never do anything else you can still count this as the finest job you could ever have done.'

> The idea of going to their rescue was simple enough, and the very thought of it sent a thrill through all of us. But we could see that the exact task of breaking the prison open, and doing it in such a way that the prisoners would have a reasonable chance of getting away across the open ground, was not going to be so easy. It would call for the best we could give to it in the way of absolutely accurate timing and bombing.

Smith agreed. 'We heard the details of this mission with considerable emotion,' he recalled:

> After four years of war just doing everything possible to destroy life, here we were going to use our skill to save it. It was a grand feeling and every pilot left the briefing room prepared to fly into the walls rather than fail to breach them. There was nothing particularly unusual in it as an operational sortie but because of this life-saving aspect it was to be one of the great moments in our lives.

A recurring myth associated with the raid suggests that the French Resistance had asked the RAF that, if they were unable to destroy the walls to allow the prisoners to escape, they should nevertheless bomb the prison to smithereens and destroy all within, friend and foe alike. The rather fantastical argument has it that the Resistance thought it would be better for the *résistants* in the prison to die at the hands of their allies rather than their enemies. Ian McRitchie, for example, interviewed many decades after his release from POW

camp, suggested that Pickard made mention of destroying the
prison at the pre-operation briefing at Hunsdon on the morning of
the raid. McRitchie was mistaken. As dramatic as it might sound,
the claim is bizarre, and supported by no other testimony from
that morning.* The role of No. 21 Squadron, as Wing reserve, was
to attempt to open gaps in the prison walls if the efforts of the first
two squadrons had failed. It was not to destroy the prison and all
within it in an attempt to take the prisoners' lives before the
Germans could do so. Gilbert Renault clearly never heard this
claim, observing instead just how careful the pilots had to be to
place their bombs:

> However, in order to kill as few prisoners as possible, they would
> have to drop their bombs with the greatest precision, almost as if
> they were setting them down by hand. Not an easy job.

Later in his account Renault wrote that Embry told his aircrew
during the briefing (details of which he had received first-hand
from one of those present, Philippe Level):

> You must not only do your best to cause the least possible number
> of casualties among the French prisoners; you must also try to
> cause heavy losses in the German garrison, which is quartered
> within these same walls.

It seems clear that what Pickard meant was that if the first two
waves failed, he would order No. 21 Squadron to attack the walls as
well. It is inconceivable that he would have suggested the

---

* Martin Bowman records in his account of the attack in March 1945 on the Gestapo
  HQ in the Shellhaus in Copenhagen that the resistance leader advised that 'the
  Resistance members in the attic would prefer to die by RAF bombs than be shot by
  the Gestapo' (*The Men Who Flew the Mosquito*). It is possible that history has confused
  the two raids in terms of this comment, for nowhere can it be found in relation to
  Amiens, although it has become very much part of the accepted narrative of the raid.

wholesale obliteration of the prison, after spending considerable effort during the briefing explaining just how important it was to prevent collateral damage by the careful placing of their bombs. The No. 2 Group 'Digest' written after the raid observed matter-of-factly: 'The problem in this operation was to ensure that the right weight of attack "Opened up" the building sufficiently to enable those inside to make their get-away without killing them in the process.'

The men then spent the remaining time over sandwiches and hot tea examining the model, talking through their notes with their fellow crewmen and preparing to go out to their aircraft. Morale was high. Gilbert Renault quoted a New Zealand officer as saying: 'The feeling of the men was that this was a job where it did not matter if we were all killed. We set out on that raid more intent and more keen than we had ever been before or since.' An hour or so later Howard's cine camera captured some poignant moments, as Pickard and Broadley stood below the entrance to the Mosquito, checking each other's Mae Wests and sharing a smile as they prepared to enter their aircraft.

Out on the exposed Tarmac of Hunsdon airfield, 26 miles north-east of London, the snow was being driven in violent flurries by the spinning propellers of the 19 twin-engine Mosquitoes that were lined up in pairs on the taxiway running parallel to the airfield's long single runway. For the two-man crews perched in each cramped cockpit, visibility was a matter of yards, the aircraft ahead a blur only 75 yards away. For the ground crews huddled in the open, watching with jealous pride their carefully prepared charges waiting to take off, the roar of the deep-throated Rolls-Royce Merlin engines was even more deafening than usual, somehow redoubled by the closeness of the weather. Max Sparks later observed that the weather was so bad that when the order to 'to fly in this stuff' was given he thought it was 'either some form of practice or some form of practical joke':

So we went outside and looked at the weather again. It was terrible! Snow was still falling, sweeping in gusts that every now and
then hid the end of the runway from sight. If this had been an
ordinary operation we were doing it would pretty certainly have
been scrubbed – put off to another day. But this was not an ordinary job; every day, perhaps every hour, might be the last in the
lives of those Frenchmen. We got into our aircraft, warmed up the
engines, and sat there thinking it was no kind of weather to go
flying in, but somehow knowing that we must. And when we saw
the Group Captain drive up in his car, and get out of it and into
his own Mosquito, we knew for certain that the show was on.*

To avoid the chance of mid-air collision in conditions of near-
zero visibility, each pair of aircraft had been instructed to take off
at five-second intervals and to make their way independently
through the low cloud to rendezvous above Littlehampton, on
England's south coast between Bognor Regis and Worthing,
where it was known that visibility that morning was much
improved. From there they would cross the English Channel,
flying in formation and accompanied by their Typhoon fighter
escorts from Nos. 3, 174 and 198 Squadrons towards their target
in occupied France. The role of the escorts was to protect the
Mosquitoes when they were at their most vulnerable during the
raid, which meant being at their wing tips when crossing the
English Channel and sitting above them as they launched their
attack. The German fighters at the nearby airfield at Glisy were an
especial concern, but the Luftwaffe were also known to fly continuous combat air patrols across this area, not just to protect the VI
sites being constructed across the Pas-de-Calais but also to catch

* 'Black' Smith suggested in 1982 that a final delay on the runway at Hunsdon was
caused by Pickard having second thoughts, and that he returned to the office to ring
Uxbridge for a final weather check. Smith believes that a favourable weather report
over the Channel, together with Embry – who was still at Hunsdon – persuaded
Pickard to fly.

the lumbering bombers that almost nightly made their way to and from the Reich.

The second Mosquito squadron was to depart from Hunsdon three minutes after the first, and the third, No. 21 Squadron RAF, was to follow ten minutes later. Pilot Officer Lee Howard, navigator in the FPU 'O for Orange', recalled:

> I just had time to check over my cameras, and then were taxying for the take-off. A moment or two after the second six had gone we, too, belted down the runway in a shower of fine snow. Airborne, we climbed to 300 feet and set course. The aircraft ahead were invisible; the ground below us could be seen only vaguely through the swirling snow.

The first aircraft to leave Hunsdon and disappear into the murky sky was piloted by Wing Commander 'Black' Smith, the CO of No. 487 Squadron RNZAF. Max Sparks took off next. 'By the time I got to 100 feet I could not see a thing except that grey soupy mist and snow and rain beating against the Perspex window,' he recalled. 'There was no hope of either getting into formation or staying in it, and I headed straight for the Channel coast.' Pilot Officer Arthur Dunlop was Sparks's navigator:

> The Wing Commander and No. 2 went up the runway to take off. They got to 50 feet and disappeared into cloud. We then went up the runway and took off, and similarly went into very, very dark cloud. The snow was going horizontally past us and it was impossible to see anything in front: we were behind the Wing Commander, about half a minute behind, so we couldn't see any navigation lights. We had decided that we wouldn't turn immediately on our ETA [Estimated Time of Arrival] at Henley because of the risk of collision and we would overshoot Henley slightly. We did this, keeping a very close look out making sure that there was nothing in our path, and proceeded down towards

Littlehampton. The cloud was just as thick and the snow just as
heavy and we saw absolutely nothing: we were in a little world of
our own. I think it must have been somewhere south of Petworth
when the cloud became grey rather than black and lighter and
ultimately before we reached Littlehampton we came out into the
grey overcast but out of the snow, out of the clouds, which was
now above us, and the ground was visible. We looked ahead of us
but there wasn't a Mosquito in sight. Thinking we were way
behind schedule and we were going to miss our 12 o'clock target
time we increased our speed but after we had gone a comparatively short time I discovered that there was another Mosquito –
two in fact – flying on our port side, behind, and this turned out
to be Wing Commander Smith with No. 2. So we got back into
formation, got down towards the sea; we had to decrease our
height to go to Littlehampton. Now because we could see where
we were going, we went out over the coast right down on the sea
and out to pick up the Gee line the coordinates of which I had set
on the Gee set that would take us in to Tocqueville.* Visibility
now was improving and you could see 5–7 miles, possibly a little
bit more, and we came in towards Tocqueville right in on course.

Lee Howard was very pleased to meet the Typhoon escort at
Littlehampton. Because of the poor weather not all of the planned
escorts were available that day. The FPU Mosquito arrived off
Littlehampton about three minutes later than planned:

This was the first time I had experienced the joys of a fighter
escort; normally Mosquitoes operate alone, being well able to take
care of themselves, but this target was very near to an enemy-
occupied fighter airfield and the boys needed a free hand to ensure
their doing a good job of work, so the powers above had provided
us with two Typhoons each to chase away inquisitive Huns.

* 'Gee' was a radio navigational system designed to improve bombing accuracy.

In addition, we were to be given further fighter cover of two [sic] squadrons of Typhoons which would be around and about the target when we got there. Being a few minutes late at our rendezvous with the Tiffies I thought perhaps we might miss them. As we tore over the coast – we were going pretty fast, in an endeavour to catch up with the second six – both Tony and I saw aircraft ahead, and as we gained on them we were able to identify them as Mosquitoes and Typhoons, we were still belting along when, as if from nowhere – I made a mental note of it, to remind me how easy it is to be 'jumped' by fighters if one doesn't keep a good look out – a couple of the Typhoon boys were sitting, one on each of our wingtips . . . They stuck to us like glue; I'm sure if we'd gone down a railway tunnel they would have come right with us.

As we crossed the Channel the weather changed, and nearing the French coast it was quite sunny. We climbed to cross the coast, and as we went over France lay spread before us, carpeted in white. It altered the appearance of the ground quite a lot but this didn't seem to trouble the leading navigators, who found their way unerringly to turning point after turning point, finally bringing us right on to the main Albert–Amiens road, which led straight to the target and provided an unmistakable guide.

Squadron Leader W. R. C. 'Dick' Sugden later recorded that it was possibly the most atrocious weather he had ever encountered. It was very nearly his last flight. Coming out of the cloud over Littlehampton another Mosquito flashed across his path. Shocked, he shouted into his microphone: 'Get the hell out of it, you bastard!' As it turned in front of him he saw that the aircraft was Pickard's. He spent the rest of the flight worrying about the reprimand he would surely receive when he returned to Hunsdon, not just for abusing his commanding officer, but for breaking radio silence. New Zealand Pilot Officer Merv Darrall recalled that 'it was a stinking day, snow most of the way. You had to hang on by your

eyeballs to keep in touch with the joker in front of you.' Pilot Officer
Arthur Dunlop:

> Just before we reached Tocqueville Wing Commander Smith
> suddenly began climbing. Although this wasn't in the flight plan,
> and although No. 2 went up with him we didn't manage to do it
> and we were about 2,000 feet below him. He went up to about
> 4,000 feet because he suddenly had a thought that they might
> have moved their light ack-ack into Tocqueville because we had
> used this for a couple of months to go in to bomb the rocket
> launching sites. We crossed the coast right about 2,000 feet but we
> didn't experience any gunfire at all and we were supposed to go to
> Doullens ... but we short-cutted because the first two were
> coming down from a greater height at a faster speed so we
> reformed at Senarpont. We turned there south eastwards to
> Albert. The visibility at this point was very much improved. There
> was snow on the ground but it made things stand out very clearly.
> The air itself was very clear. It was at this point that a Typhoon
> shot straight through the formation. I initially thought it was a
> Focke-Wulf 190 but was relieved to find it wasn't when I could get
> a good view of it and we turned at Albert along the Albert–Amiens
> Road, which is about 7 miles long, and from the moment we
> turned I could see the prison building standing on the north side
> of the road. We throttled back to 220 miles an hour and got really
> down on the ground, because the aim was to be below the level of
> the 20 foot outer wall so that the bombs at the reduced speed and
> at the lower height would hit the wall and wouldn't go through it
> and would explode in the wall.

They flew low over France. At one point Merv Darrall noticed that
'Steve' Stevenson, sitting in the right-hand seat, had winced. He
pressed the intercom and asked his navigator what the matter was,
to be told that they were so low they had nearly hit a fence post.

Squadron Leader Philippe Level flew as the navigator in

Mosquito YH-D, one of the No. 21 British Squadron fighter bombers flying on the mission that day. He recalled sitting on the runway, another Mosquito a mere 15 yards away, waiting for the aircraft ahead to move off. As soon as they had rumbled a hundred yards two others moved off behind them, and then the third.

> Then it was our turn. It's impossible to describe the constant thrill of taking off: the fierce roaring of the engines, the machine moving forward, slowly and heavily at first, as if with difficulty, then the tail coming up, the wheels leaving the ground, faster and faster, until you're flying at two hundred and fifty miles an hour, and the plane has become light and responsive. Then we, too, set off towards the east. We crossed the Thames, and as we left the English coast behind I loaded our guns and machine-guns. We were flying low, our propellers only fifteen or eighteen feet above the water, and there were no waves. The crossing took a quarter of an hour. Then we were over our little farm on the cliffs, with its square wood. So far, so good. We cleared the trees with only a few yards to spare, and flew over the road from Dieppe to Tréport, indistinguishable now in the thick snow. With our Mustangs [*sic*] clinging close, we followed the valley down one side, and back up the other, crossing the Somme valley. Amiens lay to our right. To deceive the enemy we flew north again then, over the vast white plain with its single main road, swinging round in the direction of Albert. From there on we followed the road that led to Amiens and our objective.

'Along the Albert to Amiens road went four flights of Mosquitoes like a swarm of bees,' recalled Squadron Leader Ian McRitchie. 'Nearing the jail I turned to starboard and climbed up to watch.'

*

It is not entirely clear when Ponchardier received the radio message from London, through *Alibi*'s *pianiste* in Amiens, telling him that the RAF had accepted the mission and would undertake it at precisely 12 noon on any day from 16 February. It is not hard to imagine his response. Astonishment, perhaps, that his request was about to bear fruit. Terror even, in case he could not put the teams together in time to back the prisoners' escape when the walls came crashing down. Perhaps in his heart of hearts he didn't quite believe that he could pull it off. In any case Ponchardier now struggled to assemble the men needed to deliver an evacuation plan with the care he had wanted. 'I was a nervous wreck for days,' he admitted a few years later when he penned *Les Pavés de l'enfer*.

His first concern was that René Chapelle was not with him. *Pépé* had inconveniently chosen that moment to undertake a reconnaissance of the prison in Caen, where he was continuing to study the possibility of breaking in using his two German deserters as the vanguard for a rescue bid. In the event the attack never took place, and his absence from Amiens meant that Chapelle was unable to join Ponchardier when he was most needed with the 'additional twenty men and three trucks' that he had offered. In desperation Ponchardier asked the help of the local FTPF, whose leader *Eugène* promised him a hundred men and some trucks, 'on condition that he himself would swear on his life that the RAF would not fail their rendezvous'. Renault was later to observe that: 'Ponchardier was by then willing to swear on whatever they wanted.'

'Many of the prison neighbours were involved in the attack,' Ponchardier recalled in 1950. He managed to smuggle this information into the prison through his colleague 'Clément',* whose son-in-law was a prisoner (and according to Ponchardier awaiting execution on 25 February), so that selected prisoners at least might be forewarned of the possibility of escape. René Chapelle had long recruited sympathetic prison warders to smuggle material and

---

* This may have been a pseudonym for a *résistant*, perhaps a member of the *Sosies*; I have been unable to determine an exact identity. Dr Antonin Mans, however, mentions a Clément Leboeuf in the prison at the time of the attack. Gendarme Achille Langlet subsequently recorded that Leboeuf had survived.

messages into and out of the prison, among them Gaston Brasseur, who had been arrested on the morning of the raid. The message to prepare for an attack by the RAF was received by perhaps as many as a dozen people, including Maurice Genest, Antonin Mans, André Tempez, Maurice Holville and Jean Beaurin. Robert Glaudel, a member of Antonin Mans's Civil Defence organisation in Amiens, located in the town hall and a well-known home of resistance sentiment, recorded in 1980 that on the morning of 18 February he received a visit from a person he had never met before warning him that within an hour the prison would be bombed.

In Amiens 16 February passed quietly by, with not even the sound of an aircraft engine to break the stillness of the cold Somme air. The weather had been terrible, Ponchardier considered, with low cloud and snow. That might explain the silence in the sky. Nothing happened on 17 February either, which gave him some more precious time to prepare what he could. Ponchardier's not unnatural fear was that the RAF would not arrive at all. Late on the morning of 18 February he and six comrades made their way again through the snow towards the prison, making themselves as inconspicuous as possible as they attempted to blend in with the surroundings and to keep away from the attentions of any watching guards. It was now or never.

FOURTEEN

Maison d'Arrêt, Amiens,
12:03 p.m., 18 February 1944

Philippe Level describes how with a howl overhead of multiple Merlin engines Ponchardier and his six comrades saw three aircraft appear from the direction of Albert and hurtle just above the ground towards the prison. It was 12.03 p.m. In an instant they had passed, swooping in from the east and skimming the top of the prison before disappearing towards Amiens. 'For safety, we flew in somewhat loose formation until we came near to the run up,' recalled Wing Commander 'Black' Smith, piloting the first aircraft in this wave, for whom this was his first operational flight with his new squadron, 'and then everyone tightened up wing tip to wing tip'. 'The actual bombing was done by the leader of the section in each case,' Smith explained.

> The other members of the section bombed on his bombs, that is, the moment they saw the bomb released from the wing they then pressed their bomb release also. They couldn't possibly look at the target, they had to look at their leader. It all depended on the leader entirely for the accuracy of the bombing and secondly to pull up over the building. We bombed at very low speed but I assessed the speed as the minimum I needed to have sufficient speed to pull up over the wall of the building. It was impossible to see any results of our bombing as we had to clear the target area immediately as 464 Squadron was one minute behind us to bomb the ends of the building.

One of his fellow New Zealanders in that wave, Max Sparks, remarked afterwards: 'It's the lowest I've ever flown. I wouldn't want to fly any lower.' He recalled the final seconds of the approach:

We skimmed across the coast at deck level, swept round the north of Amiens and then split up for the attack. My own aircraft, with our Wing Commander's and one other, stayed together to make the first run-in; our job was to blast a hole in the eastern wall. We picked up the straight road that runs from Albert to Amiens, and that led us straight to the prison. I shall never forget that road – long and straight and covered with snow. It was lined with tall poplars and the three of us were flying so low that I had to keep my aircraft tilted at an angle to avoid hitting the tops of the trees with my wing. It was then, as I flew with one eye on those poplars and the other watching the road ahead, that I was reminded we had a fighter escort. A Typhoon came belting across right in front of us and I nearly jumped out of my seat. The poplars suddenly petered out and there, a mile ahead, was the prison. It looked just like the briefing model and we were almost on top of it within a few seconds. We hugged the ground as low as we could, and at the lowest possible speed; we pitched our bombs towards the base of the wall, fairly scraped over it – and our part of the job was over. There was not time to stay and watch the results. We had to get straight out and let the others come in; and when we turned away we could see the second New Zealand section make their attack and follow out behind us.

Seconds later, with the sound of the first RNZAF Mosquitoes ringing in their ears, from the north, skimming directly over the position on one of the side streets near the prison where Ponchardier was standing, two further aircraft thundered in at rooftop height and planted their bombs on the northern wall.

These belonged to Merv Darrall (navigated by 'Steve' Stevenson') and Bob Fowler (navigated by Warrant Officer Frank Wilkins). It was a stunning display of flying and bomb aiming by these young pilots. As he turned to line up against his target – the northern wall – Darrall was astonished to see the wake of snow thrown up by the aircraft's prop wash. They were little more than 10 feet off the ground.

The five aircraft that remained of Smith's New Zealanders had planted their bombs exactly where they had planned. (At 11:54 a.m. and ten miles out, Flight Lieutenant Brian 'Tich' Hanafin had to abandon his part in the raid when his port engine, which had been giving him trouble since the coast, caught fire a second time and he was forced to make for home.) These aircraft dropped ten 500-pound high-explosive and ten 500-pound semi-armour-piercing bombs, all on eleven-second fuses. Smith's bombs were seen by the second wave to hit the eastern wall, although it appears likely that they travelled through the wall without exploding. Darrall's and Fowler's bombs breached the north wall successfully, although one overshot, hitting a corner of the north wing where the Germans held their terrorist suspects. Philippe Level, who was flying in No. 21 Squadron ten minutes behind, interviewed 'Black' Smith after the raid:

We didn't have any trouble finding the prison. My section went right in for the corner of the east walls, while the others drew off a few miles and made their run in on the north wall. Navigation was perfect, and I've never done a better flight. It was like a Hendon demonstration. We flew as low and as slowly as possible, aiming to drop our bombs right at the foot of the wall. Even so, our bombs went across the first wall and across the courtyard, exploding on the wall at the other side. I dropped my own bombs from a height of ten feet, pulling hard on the stick. The air was thick with smoke, but of all the bombs dropped by both my section and the other, only one went astray.

Standing on the roadside on the south side of the prison and looking east, Ponchardier and his colleagues saw a flight of aircraft
head south, and assumed that they were off to bomb the railway
station at Amiens as a diversion. They weren't: this was Wing
Commander Bob Iredale's six aircraft of No. 464 Squadron RAAF
using up some time before their own attack, as they were too close
behind the New Zealanders and risked being caught up in the
explosions of the first delayed-action bombs. Squadron Leader
Dick Sugden was in this wave:

> As we commenced our run up to the gaol, down the road leading
> north to Albert, either the leading squadron was a few seconds
> late or ours a few seconds ahead of time, which would have meant
> probably being over the previous squadron's bomb bursts. So Bob
> Iredale very wisely took us left around a 360 degree turn, which
> also brought us over the airfield at Glisy, where we collected a fair
> amount of light flak, fortunately no casualties, and were able to do
> a good bombing run.

One of the pilots in No. 464 Squadron who completed the
360-degree circuit to create some distance from the first wave of
attack aircraft from Black's No. 487 Squadron saw the New
Zealander's bombs explode:

> There were two annexes to the prison, one of which was occu-
> pied by the German guards. We were trying not only to open the
> prison itself, but also to demolish the enemy quarters and kill a
> whole lot of Germans. And that's what we did. We flew so low in
> order to drop our delayed-action bombs that we fairly had to
> jump over the wall in order to drop a bomb on the annexe. And
> all the time we were having to fly through thick smoke from the
> New Zealander's bombs. All this time, Pickard's [sic] Mosquito
> was circling above the prison, slightly higher than the attacking
> planes, so that he could see exactly what was going on and

decide whether the third wave should be brought into action or not.*

The Australian attack was equally accurate, coming in at 12:06 p.m. Wing Commander Bob Iredale recalled:

> From about four miles away I saw the prison and the first three aircraft nipping over the top. I knew then it was OK for me to go in. My Squadron was to divide into two sections – one to open each end of the prison, and it was now that one half broke off and swept to attack the far end from the right [i.e. from the north]. The rest of us carried on in tight formation. Four hundred yards before we got there, delayed action bombs went off and I saw they'd breached the [eastern] wall. Clouds of smoke and dust came up, but over the top I could still see the triangular gable of the prison – my aiming-point for the end we were to open. I released my bombs from ten feet and pulled up slap through the smoke over the prison roof. I looked around to the right and felt mighty relieved to see the other boys still two hundred yards short of the target and coming in dead on line. They bombed and we all got away OK, reformed as a section, and made straight for base.

Elsewhere Iredale recorded:

> I pinpointed the guards' quarters, let go my bombs so that they would skid right into the annexe, then pulled up into a steep climb. It was all over as quickly as that, with the sloping roof of the prison inches from the belly of my plane as I climbed over it. Back behind me my bombs exploded. The building housing the German guards seemed to shudder and disintegrate.

---

* In fact, this pilot confused 'O for Orange' with 'F for Freddie', as Pickard at this time was behind No. 464 Squadron, not above it observing the attack.

Ian McRitchie's flight followed Iredale's. The Australians dropped ten 500-pound high-explosive and ten 500-pound semi-armour -piercing bombs, also on eleven-second fuses, the first section against the eastern wall, the small building extension to the east of the main building, and the western extension.

All in all ten Mosquitoes from the New Zealand and Australian squadrons attacked the prison, and dropped a total of forty bombs on the target, twenty of which were high-explosive and twenty semi-armour-piercing, designed to penetrate walls that were thought to be built of solid rock. Of these, seven or eight bombs failed to explode and eighteen bounced outside the prison after striking the frozen earth, exploding well beyond their intended target. Nevertheless, enough bombs had struck precisely on target. The post-operation report summed up the damage:

> Numerous bombs only hit the prison building after having gone through the brick wall encircling it (about 33 to 40 centimetres thick). They made 80 cm to 1.20m holes in the wall; those which hit the wall half-way up or higher, continued their trajectory to the foot of the prison facade (about 12 to 15 metres away). Others hit the wall lower down (50 cm. above ground) and exploded within the perimeter wall, but without hitting the building. The shell-holes are 4 metres in diameter and 2 metres deep. The main part of the prison is destroyed. All the remaining walls are cracked and crumbling. Some of the bombs ricocheted or scored direct hits on houses 200–300 metres away. A pavilion of the Hospice St-Victor, 600 metres away was hit and damaged by a bomb.

From his vantage point in 'O for Orange' Flight Lieutenant Tony Wickham saw that the operation had been a complete success:

> Both ends of the prison had been completely demolished, and the surrounding wall broken down in many places. We could see a large number of prisoners escaping along the road. The cameras

fixed in the plane were steadily recording it all, and the photographer [Pilot Officer Lee Howard] was crouched in the nose taking picture after picture, as fast as he could. He was so enthusiastic that he got us to stay over the objective longer than I considered healthy. After each run I would suggest to him that we about-turned and made for England, and he would answer: 'Oh! No . . . do it again! Just once more!' But eventually he was satisfied, and we headed for home. The photographs turned out well – they showed clearly enough the ruined parts of the building, the walls crumbled and scattered over the snow-covered ground . . .

Lee Howard's recollection differed slightly from his pilot's:

As we charged down the road we saw the leading aircraft's bombs exploding, though we were too far off to make out much detail. Tony did a broad sweep to starboard to lose a little time and when we came up to the target we did a couple of fairly tight circuits to the north of it to allow the remainder of the bombs to explode. I went down into the nose to do the filming, and as I peered out of the side I saw the Group Captain's aircraft orbiting near us. I believe this is the last time he was positively seen by anyone on the trip; he did not return from the operation.

I had just time to note the Group Captain's aircraft, and to think I'd never seen so many Typhoons apparently playing at figure-skating over the target, when Tony's voice warned me 'Here we go'. I switched on the fixed cameras and started operating the one in my hand, too. The target was a remarkable sight. There was a strong east wind blowing and smoke was streaming in thick clouds across the western end of the prison; but the hole in the wall, a beautiful round hole – ideal for getting out of prison – stared us straight in the face. We could both see tiny figures running like mad in all directions; then we were over and racing round in a tight turn.

'Going round again,' said Tony, and round we went. Again I stared, more at the hole in the wall than anything; it fascinated me. We were so tightly banked in this turn that I could scarcely move; but it was obvious that things were happening very quickly down below, and that the band of patriots who had to escape were not standing upon the order of their going. 'Like another?' asked Tony, so we made our third and final run. It was as we did this that I realised how one could tell Nazis from prisoners; on our every run the Germans threw themselves flat on their faces, but the prisoners went on running like hell. They knew whose side we were on. As we flew away from the prison Tony switched on the radio and gave the 'red, red, red' signal that sent the last formation home with their bombs.

Inside the prison, the timing of the attack was impeccable. Most of the guards were at lunch in their quarters, and a particularly obstreperous NCO by the name of Rosel Otto, together with two young Belgian *résistant* prisoners, were carrying between them a large cauldron of what passed in the prison for soup: hot water impregnated indifferently with potatoes and other old vegetables left over from the autumn vegetable harvest. When they reached the second floor, on the right-hand side of the arm of the cross, the first wave of New Zealand Mosquitoes screamed overhead with only feet to spare. The deafening explosions followed quickly thereafter. In his first-floor cell Dr Antonin Mans rushed to the window to see one of the Mosquitoes climbing swiftly skywards to the north-west. Three huge explosions then overwhelmed his part of the prison, followed quickly by three more. All was concussion, dust and darkness.

The guards' quarters were demolished, and many were killed as they sat at lunch, perhaps as many as nine of the twenty guards (French and German), including the German governor, Eugene Schwarzenholzer, who, according to the *Daily Express* reporter Laurence Wilkinson, who described the raid some months later, was 'a short, fat, 48-year-old bully and drunkard'. Schwarzenholzer was decapitated. Standing next to him when he was killed was

Gaston Brasseur, arrested only that morning for allowing messages to be smuggled in and out of the prison, who was unharmed. Probably all of Smith's wave's bombs detonated in the guard's quarters, against the opposite (i.e. western) wall, or bounced out of the prison entirely. It seems that it was one of the bombs from the second New Zealand wave that damaged the German-occupied Hospice St-Victor (some 600 yards to the south-west), the direction and speed of the attack providing momentum to the bombs that allowed them to skip across the hardened earth like flat stones skimmed across a pond.

In the swirling sensation of the moment, eardrums bursting and lungs choking, a brief silence settled over the prison. Before long the cries of the injured began to be heard, rising through the gritty gloom. Grabbing hold of his senses, Dr Antonin Mans discovered to his surprise that some instinct had led him to put on his shoes, and he caught himself saying aloud: 'Come on, my little Antonin, it's time you were off!' As silence settled over the stricken prison it did not take long for the survivors to realise that an opportunity had been presented to them to escape. With the dust still swirling, grimy figures pushed their way through broken doors and over piles of rubble.

One of Sismore's hopes was that the concussion of the bombs would force cell doors from their frames and free their occupants. Alas, the same concussion that offered hope to many was the cause of death to others. Those who were able to struggle from their confinement nevertheless did so rapidly. Standing outside the prison next to the road, Dominique Ponchardier helped running prisoners to find sanctuary:

> They fled blindly, out of the ruins. Some of them we directed to the houses nearby that were ready to shelter them, others hid as best they could. The people who lived near the prison, most of whom had been given no warning of the raid, were wonderful. But God knows, they must have been afraid . . .

Two things had caused the extensive damage: first, the intensity of the bombing (which was necessary if doors and windows were to be shattered), and second, the fact that the stores of grenades had been hit, so that they blew up and burst all over the place.

Among those who managed to escape were seven men and a woman who had arrived in the prison the day before. They were due to be tried before the Gestapo court in Amiens on terrorism offences on 26 February. None were ever recaptured by the Germans.

On the floor above Mans, Jean Beaurin shared a cell with three others. His mother, who had urged Ponchardier to find a way to free her two sons, had herself been arrested. Fishman suggests that she deliberately got herself imprisoned at the prison gates by abusing the guards and insulting the Führer, in order to warn her sons of the impending attack. However it happened, Beaurin confirmed that he had received Ponchardier's message that an attack was imminent:

We heard the planes overhead, then suddenly I realised that the bombs were dropping on the prison. I turned to the others and shouted: 'Look out! They're here!' Then I saw a second plane fly over, but the blast hurled me down from the window. The window was shattered, and the walls cracked open. I had been hurt in an eye and an arm, and I saw that my cell mates were spitting blood; they too had been caught by the blast. I grabbed a sheet and bit on it as hard as I could . . .

The *résistant* Marius Couq was in Cell 27 with his friend Liétard and two other young prisoners, both only nineteen years old: Terreux and Guelton. Marius was hungry, and had been listening to the sound of Otto's key in the doors and the soup being poured into the cans. A sudden screeching noise overhead sounded as though a meteor were flying over the prison:

I climbed on to my bed and looked through the window, which was so tiny that we could only see a small square of sky, hoping that I might see something of the planes. A sudden blast flung me back into the cell – they were dropping bombs on the prison itself! Liétard had been injured in the face, and myself in the hand. We crouched in the corner of the cell for shelter. The noise was infernal, and bomb after bomb exploded, each seeming nearer than the last. It was getting hard to breathe at all in the thick, suffocating, blinding dust. And all the time there was the crash of falling masonry, and screams of terror from the women's quarters. We thought our last moment had come. Then the sound of the planes drew away into the distance. We peered round our cell, which seemed as if it was suspended in mid-air. There was no longer a roof over our heads, and the floor looked as if it might collapse at any minute.

The *résistant* Maurice Genest (*Henri*) had been imprisoned since May 1942 after being sentenced to penal servitude for life by the Nazi-run 'Special Court' in Amiens. He had been in contact for some time with both Roger Collerais and René Chapelle about the possibility of a Resistance-led *coup de main*-type attack on the prison, and had proposed a method in September 1943 in which a large explosion outside the prison would offer a diversion to the guards. He had previously smuggled out information to Chapelle giving details of the German guards and their rosters. The prison in fact had very few guards: Genest recorded that in addition to the French warders there were only six armed German soldiers on duty during the day and four at night. There did not seem to be more than twenty Germans inside. It would not be impossible, he judged, to overwhelm these guards if the attackers were audacious enough. At the time of the attack, Genest was in solitary confinement.

At a few minutes to noon the hungry Raymond Vivant was preparing for his meagre lunch in his cell, No. 16:

I had 'laid' my table in readiness for lunch on the plank that was fixed to the wall: a yellow and blue cloth, a pink toothglass, my platter, and the fork and spoon which had also come in the suitcase. The German guards always seemed impressed by this display I made each meal-time – it had something of the order that they were conditioned to admire. I had just taken off my jacket to go and wash my hands, when there was suddenly the deafening roar of planes flying very low overhead, followed by a tremendous explosion. At first I thought a German plane must have crashed just outside, and was rejoicing gleefully to myself when the first explosion was followed by several others. Instinctively I crouched for protection in the corner of my cell, while the window shattered to pieces. The left wall of the cell suddenly gaped open, and the air was filled with dust. I didn't move, and by now I was thinking that there must be an aerial battle going on overhead, and that planes were crashing to the ground with their bomb loads. But as soon as the dust cleared a little, I saw that my cell door had been torn from its hinges. The corridor outside was a pile of stones and smoking rubble! To the right, the prison buildings seemed to be still intact, but to the left I could see my way open to the country, the snow-covered fields stretching as far as the eye could see! A wide gap had been torn in the high surrounding wall . . .

It didn't take me long to make my mind up. How many times I had paced up and down in my cell, concocting wild plans of escape – and now here was my chance, heaven-sent! I couldn't see my coat and hat anywhere – probably whisked away by the blast from the explosions. But there was no point in hanging about looking for them now. Scrambling over the debris as best I could, I reached the breach in the wall at the same time as three or four other prisoners who were seizing their chance to escape.

Henri Moisan, a *résistant* and friend of Antonin Mans, remembered the bells in a neighbouring church chiming noon. An agricultural broker, he had collected information on fortifications and

troop movements during his visits to rural farms and passed them
to André Tempez. He too was hungry and awaiting lunch:

> As I wait for the so-called soup, I am reading. Suddenly I hear the
> noise of powerful engines approaching . . . A violent explosion
> shatters our window panes. Frightened, we step back towards our
> cell door. Explosions follow, one after the other in quick succes-
> sion. I suddenly feel myself going down with the debris as the
> building disintegrates in a mass of bricks, concrete and beams. I
> find myself a few metres lower down, buried under the rubble,
> dazed and stunned, but without quite losing consciousness.
>
> I am boxed in, squeezed on all sides, and bruised. I feel incap-
> able of any movement. I choke and am unable to breathe properly
> because of the crushing weight on my chest. I do not know if I am
> wounded. My mind is in a daze. The bombing goes on and I feel
> lost.

On the ground, the waiting Dominique Ponchardier had only six
men with him: Edouard Rivière, a young man of twenty from the
OCM named Renel, and four men from René Chapelle's FTPF
réseau. Unfortunately, and not for want of trying, *Eugène* could not
deliver on his promise, possibly because of the limited time
Ponchardier had given him to alert his members to the impending
attack. It was hardly enough for the task, and as Ponchardier
subsequently admitted the 'helpers were overtaken by events'.
Nevertheless, even before the dust had begun to settle over the
crippled prison Ponchardier writes that they rushed to help the
escapers, 'opening the doors and loading the prisoners either into
trucks, the homes of those who lived in the neighbourhood, or
further helping them flee by their own means'.

> We were getting more than we had bargained for. The first bomb
> had made a breach in the surrounding wall, but it was quite
> impossible for us to get inside the prison, where bombs were still

exploding. Finally the planes drew off, and we floundered through the dust and the smoke and the fire. But dozens of civilians were doing the same, and the chaos was indescribable. So much for our fine plans! We couldn't find the prisoners we were helping to escape, and kept running into terrified Boches who were creeping out of their shelters; everyone was firing on everyone else in the confusion . . .

High above the prison, flying his protective air patrol in his No. 198 Squadron Typhoon out of RAF Manston on the very tip of the Isle of Thanet in Kent, Flight Lieutenant R. A. Lallemant, DFC, Royal Belgian Air force, watched the drama unfold below him, as the final wave of Mosquitoes thundered away after dropping their bombs. He reported that he saw clearly a number of vehicles drive up to the holes in the prison wall during the attack. He worried, in fact, that they would be hit by the third squadron if it deployed against the prison:

One bomb bounces on the frozen ground, rebounds and goes through the jail without exploding. At the same time 'F for Freddie' comes back to the jail, very low: about 500 feet. He is master of ceremonies. He orbits the jail and evaluates the destruction . . .*

On the northern side, there is also a hole in the rear wall of the jail and some prisoners escape that way, some run in the fields towards the large snow covered plain, extremely visible, black on white, and very vulnerable as there is nowhere for them to hide. From here, things start getting worse. Some people have just left the waiting cars, engines turning. In this cold I notice the smoke and the vapour coming out of the exhaust pipes at the rear of the cars on the road to Amiens.

---

* Lallemant likewise appears to confuse 'O for Orange' with 'for Freddie'.

Flying his Mosquito as part of No. 21 Squadron, Philippe Level recalled:

> Suddenly, in the silence, we heard the voice of Pickard: [sic] 'Red, red, red . . .' So the mission was over. It had succeeded. We flew over Amiens, the town dominated by its cathedral. Ahead, to the left, we could see the cloud of smoke, and drawing nearer we could distinguish what looked like hundreds of ants moving on the white snow. All was well. Our friends were escaping.

The entire attack was over in four minutes, although Wickham's aircraft made three passes over the prison after the two initial bomb runs had been completed, the first at 12.07 p.m. at medium level (3,000 feet), the second two minutes later at 400 feet and then a third and final pass at 12.11 p.m. at 200 feet. In an interview for the BBC Iredale recorded:

> We could all see a cloud of smoke and dust behind us. We knew we had hit the target but my only worry was – had we killed the prisoners as well as their guards? Next day we saw the films taken by the recce boys who followed us in with their cameras. We had succeeded all right, the walls were breached and we had blown both ends off the main building. You could see the first of the released boys running away from the prison after they had got through the holes in the wall. The Squadrons were rather pleased, that of all the bombs dropped by another section and mine, only one went astray.

Lee Howard's report indicates that he and Wickham could see that the attack had been a success and that a third strike by No. 21 Squadron was no longer necessary. But they had not heard Pickard's call to cancel the third wave, so Wickham gave the code words 'red, red, red' himself. On hearing the signal to abort, No. 21 Squadron turned for home.

Wickham and Howard reported a very large breach in the north wall, with a hole to the east of this and a hole in the main building. Damage was also seen to the east end, but no details could be given. Evaluation of their film confirmed that there was a breach in the eastern wall, two breaches in the north wall and a large breach at the junction of the western and northern walls. Inside the prison the junction of the north and east wings on the north side was badly damaged, as was the northern end of the north wing.

As soon as they could, Ponchardier and his men rushed into the dust and the smoke, which glowed red with fire. The door of Jean Beaurin's cell had been torn from its hinges. He tried desperately to escape:

> The four of us helped to kick it down, though each fresh explosion knocked us off our feet. Eventually the door broke open, and we rushed out onto the landing. Everything seemed smoke and blood and ruins. For a moment I looked for my mother and brother, but I knew that like everyone else they would be trying to make their escape. Maurice Holville saw me on the landing, and hand in hand we made for the way out. With several other friends we ran for the wall at the spot which we had been told would be breached.

He was only to learn much later that his brother had been killed, and his mother wounded. The Germans later sent her to hospital at Amiens, where Marcel Holville, Maurice's brother, came to collect her.

Marius Couq remembered:

> We broke through our cell door with the aid of our stool, and were confronted with a horrifying scene of desolation ... the opposite wing of the prison was a pile of ruins. We could hear groans of pain on all sides, and men were fleeing, blood-stained and wide-eyed with fear. We did what we could to help the

wounded. In the midst of it all, one man remained calm, bending down here and there to bandage an injury.

It was Dr Antonin Mans. The cell into which he had first been placed, on the second floor, had been destroyed and its new inmate, M. Gruel, killed. His cell door on the first floor had been torn from its hinges:

> I put my nose outside. The roof of the hall had completely disap-peared, and there was an indescribable heap of debris. The stair-cases had been utterly demolished. A strange atmosphere of silence and emptiness hung over everything. I went out into the hall, over to the north-east corner and through the old Gestapo offices, which had been completely demolished. Someone later told me that they were full of dead men lying under the tables, but I didn't see them. I felt stunned. The only idea I had in my head was that I had to escape. I had got as far as the courtyard when I heard someone calling me: 'Doctor, come and let us out.'

Mans recognised the voice of his *OCM* colleague Captain André Tempez. Looking up, he realised that he was caught in a first-floor cell. Somehow, he couldn't remember exactly how, he found himself armed with a key, clambering up the broken stairs to let Tempez out. The same key happened to open other cell doors, so it came in useful that day. Rubble and bodies lay everywhere. Raymond Bonpas, a member of *Alliance* who had been im-prisoned in Cell 24 since his arrest on 4 January 1944, recalled that the keys had been found on the body of a dead German. Bonpas had been injured by flying glass, but together with his friend André Pache managed to slide down the broken staircase.

Returning to the hall, Mans found lying on the ground floor the mortally wounded body of Madame Colette Platel, from Albert, her legs crushed by a block of concrete, life rapidly drain-ing from her as her husband held her head, weeping in fear and terror. Imprisoned for a month on a charge of printing leaflets, she had been due for release that afternoon, and her husband George had been in the hall awaiting her discharge.* The sight immediately convinced Mans: as a doctor he would stay and look after the injured, whatever the consequences for himself when the Gestapo returned. When Tempez heard Mans's decision to stay, he likewise decided to forgo escape in order to look after the injured.

Completely unforeseen by Ponchardier, an entire group of *résistants*, who faced certain death at the hands of the Germans for their underground activities, now determined selflessly to stay on in the prison. Tempez was joined too by Gendarme Achille Langlet (who was badly injured), Couq, Terreux, Guelton, Litard and Clément Leboeuf among others. They helped Dr Mans set up a makeshift operating table, and before long, with only the most rudimentary equipment, Antonin Mans found himself cutting, sawing and sewing, the muck, dust and blood a physical accompaniment to the ringing in his head from the noisy and unexpected violence that had descended with sudden fury on the prison. Other prisoners, offered the chance of escape, decided to stay for fear that their families would suffer reprisals from the Germans. One such was Léon Gontier, later to be deported and die at Neuengamme concentration camp, near Hamburg, the resting place of many deported *résistants français*.

All the while Tempez and the others were desperately clawing at the rubble in an effort to free those injured and trapped. Jean Bellemère, an Amiens solicitor arrested for tampering with the seals of German documents, who was buried in a cellar under an enormous heap of stones and iron, was only freed the following day. He died in Amiens Hospital a week later. Robert Bibaut, who had smuggled information to his sister that found its way to London, was also killed. The German NCO, Otto, had been killed

---

* Mme Platel died later that day in Amiens Hospital.

in the first blast, while the two young Belgian *résistants* accompanying him with the midday soup had miraculously survived.

It was clear to Dr Mans that most of the German guards had been killed at the start of the attack. He attempted to assist a number as they died of their wounds. One lightly injured German NCO came stumbling through the rubble threatening him with a sub-machine gun. Mans calmed him and bound his wounds. He then realised that it was 1 p.m.; nearly an hour had passed since the attack. Renel, one of the men Ponchardier had collected, managed to make his way into the prison and, finding Mans, urged him to flee – he had a car outside for that purpose. Mans turned him away, insisting that he remained with his patients. He asked the young man to ring his wife to say that he had survived the attack. Renel went away, weeping, but honoured Mans's request, and within the hour Madame Mans knew that her husband was safe.

The bombing had caused mayhem, and unintended casualties. But those *résistants* who managed to stumble through the rubble to safety, when given the opportunity to reflect on their situation, were in no doubt about the consequences of the raid for them, personally. 'You saved my life,' Maurice Genest remarked years later. He had been dug out of the rubble after three hours, and escaped while being escorted to hospital. He knew that he was not long for this life, waiting in solitary confinement for execution – 'I was already condemned to death by the Gestapo.'

André Pache agreed:

The bombing saved my life, that's for sure. My cell mates and I would have gone in front of the firing squad or have been deported had it not been for the bombing. Deportation was the best that I could have hoped for.

FIFTEEN

What Dr Odile Regnault saw

Ponchardier left the prison at 12.30, after guiding a considerable number of prisoners to the breach in the wall and taking thirty of them off in a lorry. It was too dangerous for anyone to linger for long in the vicinity of the prison if they had no good reason to be there, and Ponchardier was high on the Gestapo's most-wanted list. Unfortunately, in the confusion he and his small group of assistants could not find the two men they most wanted to find: Jean Beaurin and Maurice Holville.

It took quite some time for the German authorities to realise that the prison had been attacked. At the onset of the air raid the population, including the Germans, had run for the shelters, and once the attack had passed, the Civil Defence organisation concentrated on the railway station, assuming that it was the target, as it had been so often in the past. It was not until 2 p.m. (2.30 p.m. in some accounts) that the first Germans from outside the prison managed to reach it from the town, along with the Civil Defence teams who had made their way from the station. Leading them was Dr Mans's medical colleague and fellow *résistant*, Doctor Odile Regnault. In André Tempez's absence, the Civil Defence organisation in Amiens was being run by Raymond Dewas, who, when he heard the news of the attack, telephoned Regnault, an assistant to Dr Mans, and a secret member of the *OCM*. She recorded her impressions of the prison:

I was full of admiration for the accuracy of the bombing. The left wing, where the Germans were quartered, was entirely demolished: one bomb had scored a direct hit on the guard room and the gateway. Many Germans were killed. In this part of the prison all the cell doors had been blown to bits, and the prisoners' quarters damaged by the deflagration. Outside, the surrounding wall – an extremely high wall bristling with broken glass – had been hit, and prisoners had been able to pour through the breach into the surrounding fields. In the snow-covered courtyard, a nauseating smell was coming from a large hole. Blackish water and faecal matter were running in all directions: one of the bombs had scored a direct hit on the cess-pool. A gaping hole in the wall led to the Germans' quarters. There all the cell walls had collapsed, and men lay groaning under the debris. I was thankful to find that Dr Mans, who had been imprisoned in this part of the building, was safe and sound. He could easily have made his escape, but his first care was for the injured. Not only the prisoners, but several Germans, owe their lives to his care that day. In the face of suffering, nationality ceases to be a barrier . . .

Despite the obvious humanitarian mission to which he had set himself, the arriving Germans forced Dr Mans to cease his ministrations, and marched him, together with twenty other recaptured *terroristes*, to temporary custody in the nearby German hospital, a converted French barracks, under armed escort.

Dr Regnault took the opportunity to have a good look around. She found Raymond Vivant's cell and, seeing no sign of his body, assumed correctly that he had made good his escape. She then found the body of another man she knew from her medical circles. She probably also knew of his work for MI9:

It was Doctor Robert C A Beaumont, who had been imprisoned a few days previously. His death must have been instantaneous, for his head had been crushed by the falling masonry. But in any case he had been charged with the most serious offences, so he would inevitably have been condemned to death.

Dr Regnault was forced to watch whilst men died in the rubble, there being no heavy-lifting equipment available to free them. Those digging for the dead and injured initially had only their hands to work with, though picks and shovels made their appearance during the afternoon. Henri Moisan still lay under his pile of bricks, unable to move and finding it hard to breathe:

> I can hear the sinister chorus of groans. All those buried who are still conscious are crying out, either through pain or to attract a rescue team. Some time passes but I have no idea how long. I ration my shouts to conserve my breath. Suddenly I notice a light, I hear voices becoming gradually more distinct, and at last I understand. They are my rescuers. My shouts have attracted them and one of my fingers sticking out of the debris has guided them . . . Taking great care to prevent a further cave-in, the rubble is removed, my head is freed, and then my body. My legs are pinned under the ceiling, a mass of concrete which, but for a miracle, should have smashed my limbs. I am freed at last, and among my rescuers I recognise one of my prisoner friends, Louis Sellier. He could well have escaped during the ten or fifteen minutes it took the Germans to throw a cordon around what was left of the prison. He had waited at all costs to help in my rescue. For his trouble and his loyalty he was later deported to Germany. Praise be to God, he came back.

Marcel Debart, a *résistant* who had rushed to the prison to see what help he could offer, was horrified to see what he described as a 'terrible massacre', noting that 'the Germans were mad with rage'. Dr Regnault also noted the indifference of the newly arrived Germans to the suffering: they were interested only in recovering their most important 'terrorist' prisoners, dead or alive. She noticed that the Vichy *préfet* of the Somme, the hated collaborator Pierre Le Baube, had arrived to view the scene with an SS accomplice:

The Germans seemed indifferent to all this human suffering, and concentrated on bringing in more and more police and tightening their cordons. Baumann, chief of the Gestapo in Amiens, along with his interpreter Lucienne Den, made a careful inspection of each corpse as it was dragged out of the ruins and carried away on a stretcher. They would take away the cloth with which, out of respect for the dead, the rescue workers had covered the body. They laid the corpses out in a row in a shed belonging to a nearby café. Then another member of the Gestapo would set about taking the most elaborate identification measures, even taking the fingerprints of the dead . . .

Baumann contemplated one of the corpses for a long time, then turned to me and indicated the dead man with a dramatic gesture: this, he said, was the *sous-préfet* of Abbeville . . . I took care not to undeceive him. 'Lucienne', the interpreter, made a good deal of commotion. She read aloud the names of the prisoners, questioning them as they were brought before her, giving orders to right and to left. Forgetting that I was standing nearby, she toyed with a revolver that she had brought out of her pocket. I drew away to a discreet distance – it was vitally important that she should never know I had picked up her true relationship with the Gestapo.

Ambulances began to arrive, to take the most urgent cases to hospital. Outside the prison had gathered a crowd of anxious families and inquisitive people, all severely controlled by a police cordon. Those prisoners who had survived the bombing were taken under escort to the fortress, which from then on became the special prison for Resistance members.

Henri Moisan was one of many brought out of the rubble alive, but looking half dead:

I am laid on a stretcher, still a bit groggy but nevertheless conscious. I am given an injection and something to drink. I try to move carefully. I am delighted that nothing seems to be fractured, only superficial injuries to the face, head and hands, making for a very bloody picture. With an eight-day beard, the dust covering my body and my clothing in shreds, I looked like a dying man. I meant to keep it that way. Stiff on my stretcher with my eyes half closed, the Germans took one look at me and lost interest. They only enquired where I was being taken. The Civil Defence people, both men and women, were on the scene before the Germans arrived with ambulances. They succeeded in helping a few of the injured survivors to escape. It is too late for me. In any case I am in no fit state to walk. I am lifted up into an ambulance. The nurse who has taken me in charge, instead of taking me to hospital, takes me to Dr Filachet. He tells the Gestapo that the hospital is full and has no more room. Dr Filachet is my brother-in-law.

This was my salvation. I expect to be recaptured by the Gestapo at any moment, but during the following weeks such alarming bulletins are issued about my health that the Gestapo decide to give me up as a bad job. To help them in this decision, the bombing of the prison has given the administration authorities enough headaches as they try to identify the victims and search for the escapees. I am more or less forgotten.

Dr Regnault carried on the work of recovery until 20 February, when there were no more cries for help from men buried in the rubble. She observed that the Germans' fury against the Resistance still raged:

During the following days, I had to visit the hospital several times. I found Baumann there, and his interpreter, continuing his interrogations at the bedside of the wounded. He told me how much he admired Dr Mans for his heroic and selfless conduct during the bombing, and assured me that the German authorities, 'who always acknowledge and appreciate such courage', would certainly liberate him before long.

In all, ninety-five Frenchmen were killed, and eighty-seven wounded. A funeral service for the victims was held in the cathedral, where all the coffins, borne by young men of the Civil Defence, were gathered in the choir. It was a poignant ceremony . . . I noticed that one of the coffins was draped with the Tricolour. The Red Cross workers formed a guard of honour.

Monseigneur [Lucien] Martin, in a short but moving address, expressed his sympathy to the families of the dead men, and referred to 'This unforeseen and mysterious catastrophe'. The *préfet* of Vichy [Pierre Le Baube], a well-known collaborator, was present at the service in full uniform, with the idea of scorning the RAF by paying homage to its victims. He was forgetting, of course, that many of the dead men had been members of the Resistance.

After a good deal of fuss from the Gestapo, who were afraid that there might have been some trickery with the dead body, Doctor Beaumont was taken away to be buried in his own country, but not without [Lucien] Pieri, a sinister traitor who had joined up with the Gestapo, opening the coffin for a last time to check on its contents.

Pieri had been responsible for many of the arrests in the Somme, and was reckoned one of the most odious and despicable of all the collaborators in Picardy. His cruelty repelled even the Germans, and they despised him; he was executed a few weeks before the Liberation.*

Raymond Bonpas was phlegmatic about the casualties. '*C'est la guerre*,' he commented many years later. 'I knew I was risking my life [serving in the Resistance].' He had one consoling thought for

---

* Jack Fishman interviewed Jean Cayeux, a shy schoolteacher in his twenties, who assassinated Lucien Pieri in 1944 on orders from the FFI.

the RAF pilots who, he believed, would have grieved at the loss of life they had unwittingly inflicted during their heroic rescue mission, which he and his fellow prisoners had discussed before the raid even got under way. During 1943, the inhabitants of Amiens had seen all kinds of Allied aircraft in the skies above Picardy. 'We wanted the English to do it, not the Americans,' he reflected. 'If the Americans had done it, they would have dropped one bomb on the prison and the rest of Amiens would have been destroyed. That's what we French people thought.'

SIXTEEN

The escape of Raymond and Jane Vivant

This is the story that Raymond Vivant gave to Gilbert Renault.

I set out away from Amiens, running fifty metres then walking the next fifty, and so on, to conserve my strength. As I walked I sucked a lump of sugar. One of the other prisoners was keeping up with me: 'I was dumped in there for fiddling the Boche petrol,' he explained. 'I'm making for Albert where I've got some pals.' We had covered only about a kilometre or so when I spotted some German soldiers ahead; if we went on we would run straight into them. Nor was there anywhere to hide and wait for nightfall . . . and besides, I knew well enough that the Gestapo would be sending their police dogs after us. It was freezing cold too – snow and ice everywhere. I decided to turn back and make for Amiens, where I had friends who would shelter me, and so I started back along the main road.

A cyclist was overtaking me, and I hailed him: 'Would you lend me your bicycle?' The man hesitated, but then, indicating the foodstuffs and the bread on his carrier, he said: 'Sorry, mate, but they're waiting for me at home.' With which he disappeared as fast as his legs would pedal him. Next I met three young girls who were wandering along the road, laughing and chattering among themselves. When they saw me they stopped dead in their tracks and gazed at me as if they couldn't believe their eyes. It was only then that I realised I was covered in grey dust from head to foot. I approached them and asked: 'Would you be kind enough to brush me down, Mesdemoiselles?' Willingly they cooperated, and soon I looked a little less like a flour-covered Pierrot.

Soon I had to pass the prison itself. Even from a distance I could see that there was a good deal of disturbance going on: relief teams, civilians and German soldiers were scurrying to and fro before a gaping crowd. Confidently I strolled past, and all seemed to be well, for I reached the crossroads from which the main road runs to the station, and no one had so much as given me a second glance. But even as I was congratulating myself on my success, a car suddenly drew up and a young woman leapt out – the young woman who had been present when I had first been interrogated [Lucienne Den]. Harshly she shouted a few words in German, and I picked out 'Alive . . . *sous-préfet*!' At once I was surrounded by three Germans, each armed with a sub-machine gun and yelling all kinds of threats, which fortunately I could not understand. The young woman forthwith ordered the soldiers to take me back to the prison, and so, my tail very much between my legs, I was marched back the way I had come. My guards took me into a factory not far from the prison, where I found myself in the company of several others who had been recaptured after a brief taste of freedom. A young man came over to me: 'Monsieur the *sous-préfet* of Abbeville?' I looked at him. His face seemed vaguely familiar, but I couldn't place him. 'Don't you remember me?' he asked.

'I'm afraid that . . .'

'I'm the secretary of the police superintendent at Abbeville.'

I remembered that he had been arrested several months previously, but he was a lot thinner now, and had also grown a beard. 'What are you doing here, *Monsieur le sous-préfet*?' I smiled at the naivety of his question. 'It's quite simple,' I told him. 'I too have been arrested . . . I tried to escape just now, but the Boches caught up with me.'

A young girl who had heard what we said came up to me: 'You are the *sous-préfet* of Abbeville?'

'Yes, Mademoiselle.'

'Is there anything at all I can do for you?'

'Certainly. I'd very much like a little water to rinse my hands.' I had just noticed that my left hand had been injured slightly in the explosions.

'Come,' said the young woman, who I learned was Mademoiselle Christiane Lecaillet. Turning to a German guard, she spoke a few words to him, then led the way into the house, which was through the gateway. I followed her, and we were in turn followed by the German, but I closed the door firmly in his face when we entered the house. For some reason he didn't press his point, and stayed outside waiting for us.

'Please tell me if there is anything you would really like me to do,' urged Miss Lecaillet. 'Please tell me if there's anything you need, whatever it is.'

'There is one thing, Mademoiselle – I should very much like to get a message through to my wife. She will probably be interrogated soon, and I want her to be sure to deny that we were ever visited in Abbeville by either Courvoisier or Clerc.' Courvoisier had formerly been in charge of the *OCM* in the Nevers region, while Clerc had followed me as head of operations in the Somme district.

'Right, I'll see to that,' she assured me.

'And there's one more thing, Mademoiselle. Is there any way of escaping from here?'

'The only exit is by the door we have just used, and that is always guarded. But there's a yard at the back. If you could manage to jump over the wall, then you might get away.'

'I'd get over the wall all right!'

'Then you'd go on for about three hundred metres, and take the third road on the left, rue Labarre. Go straight to number 127, where my parents live. Tell them you're a friend of Christiane's and they'll shelter you.'

No sooner said than done. I made my way through a corridor into the yard, and with the biggest leap of my life I got over the high wall and picked myself up on the other side. There wasn't a German in sight, only a passer-by who looked rather astounded at my sudden apparition. I began to run up the street, thinking inconsequentially that it wasn't a very good idea to be dashing about like this in the snow without a hat and coat. I came up to a workman who was talking to a child on his doorstep, and stopped: 'Will you help me, friend . . . I've just escaped from the prison and the Boches are after me. I don't want them to recognise me – can you lend me your cap to disguise me a bit?'

The man didn't answer me, but opened the door and shouted: 'Where's my old cap?' A woman's voice answered: 'I don't know where you put it – it wasn't me that put it away.' The man turned and, still without speaking to me, held out to me the cap he had been wearing. I thanked him and began to run for it again.

I had only gone a few metres when I heard little footsteps behind me, and the child came panting up clutching the old cap: 'Here's the old one, can I have the new one back!' It certainly was an old cap at that, and looked as if it had had many a rough passage in life.

At last I arrived at 127 rue Labarre, knocked on the door and hurried inside. The family was sitting down to a meal, and my sudden arrival caused them no small bemusement. 'I've been sent here by Christiane,' I blurted. 'I'm an escaped prisoner, wanted by the Germans. I wonder if you could help me to get back to the centre of Amiens without using any of the main roads – the Germans are patrolling them and recapturing us.'

Madame Lecaillet, just like the mother of a family, first thought of inviting me to join them at table, but I wasn't hungry, excitement seemed to have blunted my appetite. I asked her husband whether he had an old overcoat he could lend me. 'I've got an old overcoat all right, but it would hardly go round you I'm afraid.' Madame Lecaillet had an idea though, and hurried off without more ado, to return a few minutes later with her brother, a chap as large as myself. He was carrying a black overcoat on his arm, which he offered me, saying: 'I hope this will fit you.'

'But you haven't got any papers!' cried Madame Lecaillet, who thought of everything. Without fuss, her brother produced his wallet, and gave me his own identity card: 'Here's my card. The photo's not exactly a likeness, but you should be able to manage with it.'

'Your cap really is a bit too battered,' contributed Monsieur Lecaillet. 'Take this black hat here.' Then, putting on his overcoat, he added: 'I'll come with you. Where is it you want to go?' I gave him the address of two Resistance friends. 'They're in the Resistance? Don't you think it likely that they'll have been questioned since your arrest? No, no. I'll take you to someone I know.'

And so we set off. M. Lecaillet took his bicycle with him to save time on his way back. Soon, in the distance, I could see a German roadblock. I asked M. Lecaillet to lend me his bicycle, thinking that the Germans would be less likely to ask for my papers, as they would hardly expect to find one of their escaped prisoners cycling peaceably along. My heart was beating nineteen to the dozen as I came up to the group of Germans, but my hunch proved a good one – they let me pass without so much as a single question, whereas M. Lecaillet had to produce his papers.

A few moments after this we went into the house of a very friendly-looking woman, whose husband was the head of public transport. 'I've brought you a friend,' said M. Lecaillet. 'Hide him well: he's in trouble with the Boches.'

The good woman agreed without question, and prepared a soothing cup of coffee for me. I also asked her to unpick the initials that were embroidered on my handkerchief and my shirt. M. Lecaillet said goodbye, and was on the point of leaving when a young woman arrived unannounced. I noticed that M. Lecaillet looked worried when she came on the scene, but he said nothing and went away.

Three-quarters of an hour later Madame Lecaillet knocked on the door and came in. 'Come with me!' she said urgently. So once again I started to cross Amiens.

'Would you mind if I took your arm?' I asked Madame Lecaillet. 'The Germans wouldn't dream of suspecting such a debonair-looking couple.' She smilingly agreed, and told me that the young woman who had unexpectedly arrived just as M. Lecaillet had been leaving had the reputation of being something of a gossip, so that M. Lecaillet had been uneasy about letting me stay any longer in the same place.

'Instead I'm taking you to some good people that we can be sure of, called Boutvillain. There I know you'll be safe.'

When we reached their house, we were welcomed by a man who was clearly kind and loyal. 'Come in, come in,' he said, 'you must make yourself at home here. I've heard your story, and we're very glad that we can give you shelter.'

We went into the kitchen, and Mme Boutvillain offered me the traditional coffee. Madame Lecaillet left, assuring me once more: 'You'll be all right here.'

'Have you any identity papers?' asked M. Boutvillain. I showed him my card borrowed from Lecaillet's brother-in-law. 'That's fine, but we must do something about getting your own photograph on it.' Within the hour it was done – a friendly neighbour helped to replace the betraying photograph with one of myself.

'It's getting late,' said M. Boutvillain. 'We have a relative coming to stay tonight, and I think it would be better if he didn't know you were here.' So I was given a tasty meal, and was just about to retreat to my bedroom when the visitor arrived. To save the price of the railway ticket, and to make sure of arriving at Amiens – for the lines were often cut in those days – he had walked the fifteen miles from his home to the town. He was obviously astonished to see me there, but M. Boutvillain passed me off as a regimental friend of his from Toulouse, saying that I had come to deliver some material in the Somme area and had made a slight detour in order to see him again. It was news to me when he concluded by saying that I was setting off very early in the morning for the Midi again, but I took my cue and made this my excuse for retiring to bed. The Boutvillains showed me to my room.

'But where are you going to sleep yourselves?' It hadn't taken me long to discover that there were, in fact, only two rooms in their tiny house.

'Don't you worry about us,' they assured me. 'We shall be all right there.' There was a mattress on the landing, with an odd blanket. They wouldn't listen to my objections, saying: 'You're the one who needs sleep tonight. Make yourself comfortable in our room, and forget about everything else.'

I had to give in, but I warned them that at dawn it was more than likely that the Germans would be searching the houses and that . . .

M. Boutvillain laughed quietly. 'You can sleep in peace. I know those Boches. When they're on the brink of defeat they'll leave Amiens with their tails between their legs. Otherwise they won't hesitate to shoot anyone they can lay hands on. I haven't forgotten the 1914–18, I haven't! So I've arranged a little hiding place . . . you'll see, there'll be no chance of them finding you there, even if they do come and search the house. So good night, and sleep well!'

It didn't take me long to fall asleep. Early in the morning Boutvillain tapped on my door. I had to cross the yard, go into his carpenter's workshop and climb up into the attic above. There, right against the roof, was a hiding place quite impossible to detect, accessible only by ladder. True, it wasn't particularly comfortable, for you could hardly stand upright and the cold was so intense that stalactites of ice hung from the slate roof. But my host had put several layers of straw down, and gave me a blanket and an enormous tent canvas, in which I rolled myself up and waited to see what would happen. Every two or three hours, Boutvillain came and visited me, bringing a hot drink or some books to help the time to pass more quickly. But I was hardly in the mood for reading.

During the morning, Christiane Lecaillet arrived to give me news of my wife [Jane]. She had been at the *sous-préfecture* when the prison had been bombed, and the chief secretary had come to let her know that I was safe and sound. She had gone straight away to Amiens to see the German authorities, and protested vigorously to the officer who received her: 'I know what it is – you've been storing all your ammunition and war weapons too near a civilian building!'

The German was furious: 'No, Madame! The prison has been bombed by English planes to help some of your "Resistance" leaders to escape! Your husband took the chance of running away, instead of staying to help the wounded!'

My wife went round the various centres where the prisoners were being temporarily held, and met Dr Mans and others, including Tempez. M. Stenne, who was informed of the escaped men at the prefecture, told her: 'I found your husband's hat in the cell next to his own. When I saw his initials on it I was afraid that he must have been killed. But it's all right – you needn't worry: I know now that he has escaped and that he is safe and sound.'

With this assurance my wife returned to Abbeville, and decided not to go to the *sous-préfecture* but to lie low in the home of some friends of ours. Unfortunately she ran out of petrol, and as soon as she stopped at the *sous-préfecture* she found the place surrounded by *Feldgendarmen*. Two officers came up to her.

'Madame, we must arrest you!' the Hauptmann solemnly informed her.

'In that case,' answered my wife, 'you will have to let my daughter Claudine come into prison with me. I refuse to leave her alone in your hands – she's only ten years old!'

The Germans didn't care for this idea. 'Madame,' said the Hauptmann, 'we are not barbarians. We do not arrest children!' My wife remained adamant, and the Boche finished by telephoning the Feldkommandantur, and had a long conversation in German. The outcome was that my wife won the day: she could stay in the *sous-préfecture*, but must consider herself a prisoner. 'And you must promise to warn the police if your husband tries to get in touch with you,' added the Hauptmann as he left.

Many of our friends, all loyal Resistance members, offered advice to my wife, urging her to get away as soon as she could. The Germans had left someone on guard outside the house to check all comings and goings, but they had forgotten to give any instructions about the official car belonging to the *sous-préfecture*. So it was that my wife and Claudine crouched down in the front of the car, and slipped away the very next day. She drove straight to Amiens and had a heated conversation with Pierre Le Baube, the Vichy *préfet* of the Somme, telling him off in no uncertain terms for having done nothing about my imprisonment. She gave some money to Mademoiselle Solange Lecaillet, a member of our network who worked at the prefecture, for her to give to me. Then, telling the chauffeur to go to the Kommandantur and tell them that Madame Vivant had disappeared, she took the train for Paris.

It was M. Boutvillain who brought me the money from my wife. 'She has gone to Paris,' he said, 'meaning to stay with your friend Madame Ducombeau, and she wants you to join her as soon as you can.' The idea was all right, but there remained the technical problem of how to get me a railway ticket, for which a special admission slip was required, showing that the journey was necessary. 'Don't worry, I think we'll get you off all right tomorrow morning,' said M. Boutvillain. 'We'll see to it straight away.'

That evening, while I was in the kitchen with my friends, a young man came in, a plumber by the looks of him, who was due to travel to Paris the following morning to attend the funeral of one of his relatives killed in a raid. 'You can trust me,' he said. 'We're all patriots here. We'll come and call for you at about six-thirty in the morning, and you'll be on the seven-thirty train.'

The next morning, at the prescribed hour, the whole family, five of them, arrived. I was to take the place of the sixth person, a cousin of the dead woman. They told me her name, her Christian name, something of her situation and her background. Remembering my

Gestapo interrogation, I disguised my give-away white 'desk' hands by plunging them in a bowl of old fat, and then rubbing them over with ashes, breaking a few nails to complete the effect. I swapped my black hat for one of Boutvillain's caps, and borrowed a pair of steel-rimmed spectacles. I was barely recognisable.

At the station, the telegram summoning us to the funeral was examined, and then we were given our tickets and took our seats in a third-class compartment, waiting for the departure time. On the platform I could hear the heavy tread of the *Feldgendarmen* who were there to prevent any escaped prisoners from leaving the town. At 7.30 a.m. there was no sign of the train leaving. At 8 o'clock, 8.30 a.m., 9 o'clock we were still here . . . Finally, to my unbounded relief, we drew out of the station at 9.15 a.m. . . . I heard later that the engine shed had been hit by machine-gun fire, and that it had taken them the best part of two hours to find a machine in working order. At Beauvais two passengers joined us, and while we ate some of our packed food, they talked about the raid on the prison: 'The *sous-préfet* was killed, you know,' they assured us. 'They found his body under the debris, and he's been buried in the military cemetery . . .'

A few miles beyond Beauvais, the train suddenly stopped. Resistance members had blown up the track. So we had to reverse some distance, and make a long detour which lost us several hours.

Eventually, at 4.30 p.m., we reached the Gare du Nord. Safely through the barrier, I said goodbye to my 'family', thanking them warmly for all their help, and took a cycle-taxi to the house of a Resistance member, Madame Claude Salvy. Fortunately she was at home.

'What is it you want?' As soon as I spoke, she recognised me. 'What! . . . is it you!' The first thing she did was to run a hot bath for me! Before long I was reunited with my wife and my daughter . . . We sent Claudine to stay with our cousins, the Chevalliers, and then my wife and I were free to go on with our clandestine fight. But that's another story.

SEVENTEEN

The journey home

In London Gilbert Renault spent the morning of 18 February 1944 in the BCRA's Duke Street offices, the snow that lay deep on the streets turning quickly from its pristine whiteness to a dirty brown mud by the scurrying crowds. He was talking in his tiny office with André Manuel, who had been left in charge of the London office while André Dewavrin was in Algiers. Renault was briefing Manuel on the progress of his plans for Operation *Sussex*. He had just returned from Algiers himself, where he had been recruiting Free French volunteers for the task of operating behind enemy lines during the reconquest of their country.

Darkness was already falling at 3 p.m. when the quietness of the day was broken by the sound of a commotion in the corridor. The door burst open to reveal the unmistakable bulk of Squadron Leader Philippe Level. Still clad in his flying clothes, he had hurried to London after arriving back at Hunsdon after the raid. 'He seemed very much out of breath,' Renault recalled, 'and, leaning heavily on Manuel's desk, one word escaped his lips: "Pickard!" He continued "He hasn't come back! You must get a message to France immediately, they must find him. They must do everything they can . . . You will, won't you?"'

It appears that Pickard and Broadley's aircraft was intercepted by Focke-Wulf 190s as they followed No. 464 Squadron while the Australians prepared to undertake the second and final wave of attacks on the prison. As Ian McRitchie completed his attack at 12:06 he saw Pickard's aircraft leave northwards.

No Allied eyes witnessed the tragic demise of this extraordinarily brave and experienced crew. As the crash site was a mere seven miles north-east of Amiens, the most likely sequence of events is that while following the rear of Bob Iredale's squadron on their attack run their Mosquito was jumped by two FW190s, one of which was piloted by Feldwebel Wilhelm Mayer of Jagdgeschwader 26, on combat air patrol in the region at the time, flying from a base at Grévillers, 32 miles north-east of Amiens near Bapaume.*

Pickard and Broadley's flight path indicates that instead of turning left towards the prison after circling over Glisy in line with the remainder of the Australian squadron, they continued to fly north-east, either in an attempt to shake off their pursuers or because the aircraft had already been hit and damaged by cannon fire and was therefore difficult to manoeuvre. Lee Howard, circling in the FPU Mosquito to the north-east of the prison during the attacks, records that he saw Pickard at this time, but does not report any pursuing or attacking enemy aircraft. Eyewitnesses north of Querrieu (five miles north-east of the prison on the road to Albert) then described the FW190s diving at the low-flying Mosquito. It appears that the FW190 angle of attack was such that Pickard and Broadley were unable to see Mayer before explosive cannon shells began ripping into their fuselage. It would have taken the aircraft no more than two minutes, flying at 230 miles per hour, to find itself north of Querrieu. It is likely, therefore, that no more than two minutes after the Australians completed their run over the prison – at 12:08 p.m. – F for Freddie crashed into farmland directly north of the hamlet of Saint-Gratien, seven miles north-east of the prison.

When, in the wake of the German retreat, Squadron Leader Edward Houghton of No. 2 Group arrived in Amiens to investigate

---

* 7th Staffel (7/JG26).

the circumstances surrounding the raid, he recorded that on Saturday 9 September he visited the crash site and interviewed a number of French civilians who saw the demise of F for Freddie:

After the bombing of the prison was completed, 1 Mosquito flew ENE towards Querrieu (2062) and Berencourt (2266). It is possible that the machine was already slightly damaged, although still under control, from small arms fire emanating from the German hospital near the prison. A farmer, Monsieur Dourfaut, at Montigny (2166) saw a single-engine enemy aircraft on the tail of the Mosquito and saw the Mosquito's tail shot away, whereupon the Mosquito spun in, the tail falling at 178662 and the engines and forepart at 175663. Empty cartridges which had fallen from the enemy fighter were recovered by a farmer at 198645.

The son of the mayor at Saint Gratien, Monsieur Gagnard-Pinket, went out to see the crash and found both occupants burnt up. On one body he found a motor licence with the name John Allen Broadley (Group Captain Pickard's navigator) and his body had the back of the head broken open. The other body was too burnt up to be recognisable but there was a shoulder strap with 4 stripes . . .

Two hours later a party of Germans arrived who sent them away. They went out next morning and found the bodies still there with no guard and so brought them back into the village and had coffins made. Later that day the Germans returned with oak coffins and admonished the French for interfering. The mayor's son marked the German coffin containing the remains of Broadley with 4 scratches. The Germans took the coffins and buried them in the cemetery at St Pierre, just east of Amiens Prison (120595). A friend of the Mayor watched the internment and the graves are in the British part of the cemetery.

A young French woman, Giselle Cagé, who had removed Pickard's wings and ribbons from his jacket at the crash scene, posted them to his widow in early 1945. She described to Ian Hamilton, Pickard's biographer, how she rushed to the crash site with other villagers, including her husband Gabriel and her father:

> Through the smoke we could see two dark shapes between the engines. We thought they must be the airmen. With long sticks cut from the wood the men pushed and pulled. It was extremely dangerous as the heat was making the bullets explode and go off in all directions. At last they were able to bring the bodies out of the fire and they laid them out on struts of wood from the aeroplane.
>
> I went and retrieved their parachutes and wrapped them in them myself. Captain Pickard still had some scraps of clothing and I cut the wings and ribbons from his jacket to make it more difficult for the bodies to be identified by the Germans. The clothes of Lieutenant Broadley had been completely burned. They were just ashes when he was pulled from the fire. The bodies had not been burned, just a little swollen from the heat, and the wounds had no blood showing at all. Their faces were black from the smoke. I have never seen photographs of Captain Pickard or Lieutenant Broadley, but I certainly remember their faces well.
>
> We are certain that the two men had been killed by shock on impact. They had remained in a sitting position and one of them had his two arms raised and his hands half clenched. He must have been holding the two handles in the cockpit, no doubt. Perhaps in order to spread or allay the shock. The aeroplane was low over the wood when it flipped and they struck the ground at once.
>
> The bodies were taken to the Mayor's house at Saint Gratien and guarded by the French for as long as possible.

It appears that too little Typhoon cover was available to protect Pickard and Broadley at the time that they were bounced by the

FW190s. The task of the Typhoons during the raid was to prevent enemy aircraft from interfering with the attack, especially from those that might scramble from nearby Glisy, but it is clear that escorts could not protect each and every aircraft and that Pickard's aircraft, flying to the rear of the attacking Australians, was picked off simply because F for Freddie was the last in the group and therefore most vulnerable.

There is a more melancholy side to the story of the Typhoons. The Royal Belgian Air Force pilot Flight Lieutenant R. A. Lallemant was to testify in 1990 that, contrary to the official RAF records of the time, only slightly more than 60 per cent of the Typhoons tasked for the operation managed to lift off from their bases at RAF Manston in Kent and Westhampnett in Sussex to support the raid. Others took off, but decided in the poor weather that there was no chance of rendezvousing successfully with the Mosquitoes and abandoned the mission, landing safely at RAF Tangmere in Sussex.*

From this point on the raiding force began to take casualties, as the aircraft made their way, singly and in small groups, for the safety of the English Channel. In addition to the loss of Pickard and Broadley the Mosquito flown by the Australian Ian McRitchie

---

* Four squadrons of Typhoons were in fact instructed to support the raid, two from RAF Westhampnett (174 and 245) and two from RAF Manston (198 and 3). No. 3 Squadron was responsible for escorting the Mosquitoes to the target area, and No. 198 Squadron was to escort them back to their bases in England. The latter squadron was due to meet the attackers over Amiens, and the Westhampnett squadrons were to undertake escort duties from Littlehampton. At this remove in time, it is not possible to be definitive about how many of the available Typhoons tasked to deploy against Amiens actually arrived to provide the required top cover and escort protection. The squadron records indicate that Nos. 3, 174 and 245 Squadrons had eight aircraft each, and No. 198 Squadron had six, although at any one time only six aircraft would deploy from each. This meant that there were a total of twenty-four aircraft available to fly the support mission that day. However, an evaluation based on the conflicting evidence suggests no more than 15, or 62 per cent, actually completed their tasks over Amiens: six aircraft from 245 Squadron, three from 198 Squadron, none from three Squadron and six from 174 Squadron.

and navigated by the New Zealander Flight Lieutenant Dick ('Sammy') Sampson was struck at low level – perhaps 100 feet – by anti-aircraft fire near the village of Villeroy (two miles south-west of Oisemont and 25 miles west-north-west of Amiens). Sampson was killed instantly and McRitchie somehow managed to land his aircraft on snow-covered fields despite travelling at well over 200 miles per hour and his body being peppered with 26 separate wounds. Taken by his German captors for treatment in Amiens Hospital several days later, much of the talk was about the raid. He kept his mouth shut. He spent the remainder of the war as a prisoner in Germany.

Two of the escorting Typhoons also failed to return. One, piloted by Canadian Flying Officer J. E. Renaud, was attacked by a FW190 over Poulainville and riddled with 20 mm cannon shells, although Renaud was able successfully to land close to the Amiens–Doullens road. Wounded in the knee, he was taken into hospital at Amiens before also spending the rest of the war as a prisoner in Germany. A second Typhoon, flown by Flight Sergeant Henry Brown RAF, was observed to have been hit by flak and continue towards the English Channel, but did not reach home. The aircraft was never found.

Anti-aircraft fire also struck a number of aircraft making their way back to England, and several aircraft had to make emergency landings at airfields on the south-east coast of England. 'Titch' Hanafin had been forced to leave the attack before reaching Amiens. His crippled aircraft had then been hit by flak south of Oisemont, 24 miles west of Amiens, at about 12:05 p.m., and Hanafin badly injured. A bursting shell had struck him in the neck. Although in great pain and with the right side of his body increasingly paralysed, he nevertheless attempted to nurse the aircraft home. His navigator, Pilot Officer Frank Redgrave, gave him morphine injections. With their role in the raid complete, Arthur Dunlop and Max Sparks were flying due west when they caught up with Titch Hanafin limping home, and heard him ask Wing

Commander 'Black' Smith on the radio: 'Smithy, will you escort me, I'm on your port side.' Dunlop recalled:

> We didn't know what this meant at this stage but the Wing Commander left the formation and went to escort Titch Hanafin who had been shot in the neck on the way to the target and who had one engine on fire. He hadn't been able to get to the target because he was paralysed on one side and losing a lot of blood so Wing Commander Smith escorted him home. We had been going too far westward and would come out too close to Dieppe, a heavily defended area, and so we turned very sharply as soon as Wing Commander Smith had left to turn to starboard.

It was then that German flak also managed to hit Sparks and Dunlop, slamming into the wing on the outside of their port engine Dunlop:

> The next few moments or minutes . . . we didn't know whether we were flying or on our way down. I thought Maxie had been hit and said to him 'Are you all right, let me have it.' He shouted to me 'Wind the trimmer' so I wound the trimmer. He said 'More, more' so I wound the trimmer as hard as I could and the wing came up and we were then out over the sea and heading towards home.

They landed at Ford, a mile west of Littlehampton. What Dunlop did not say was that one of their aircraft's wheels collapsed on landing. The aircraft was a write-off. They watched others limp in:

> The next one to come in was No. 2. As he came in his undercarriage flicked back and the next moment he was up the runway on his belly. Titch Hanafin then came in and rolled on up the runway going on and on and on. The engineer officer was with us saying 'Pull your undercarriage up' but eventually he stopped right at the extreme end of the runway. The others came in then one by one.

We were debriefed at Ford where we were told that Group Captain Pickard and Flight Lieutenant Broadley were missing but they had heard Group Captain Pickard call out to tell 21 Squadron that their bombing was not necessary and to go home. They also suggested that we shouldn't write up our log books with the target and that we shouldn't discuss the target with anybody and that was that. The rest of the Squadrons then took off and went back to Hunsdon.

For most other returning aircraft the flight home passed without incident. The New Zealander Bob Fowler shot up a lorry that was part of a very large convoy travelling towards Amiens: he had the satisfaction of seeing it burst into flames. Except for the ever-present flak, most other return journeys went smoothly. Philippe Level:

The return trip was uneventful – we crossed the French coast at the same spot, flying at something like three hundred miles an hour when we dipped down to fly low over the Channel. We landed at the aerodrome with all our bombs still on board, and were the last crews to get into the interrogation room. On all lips was the same question: 'Have you seen F for Freddie? Do you know what's happened to Pick?'

In London there was no immediate response to Level's anguished question to Renault in the Duke Street offices of the BCRA. Indeed, the loss of the aircraft was unknown to the *résistants* on the ground, who were not paying any attention to what was going on in the air. In England the initial hope was that although the aircraft had been shot down, the crew might have emerged intact, and within a short while would be languishing, but safe, in a POW camp. In fact, Pickard and Broadley were the first casualties to enemy fire, crashing just at the point of success. All of the enemy-inflicted damage on the raiders occurred during the return journey.

The entire raid took no more than two hours and twenty minutes, the aircraft landing at Hunsdon or emergency strips along the coast of England between 1:10 and 1:20 p.m. When Pickard's and McRitchie's aircraft failed to return to Hunsdon the following day it became apparent that both aircraft had been lost over France, together with two of the accompanying Typhoons. Their loss was deeply felt. When the truth became known, Gilbert Renault spoke for both his RAF and his BCRA friends and colleagues:

> As we wept for the victims of the raid in which he paid with his life, so we wept for Pickard, loyal and generous Pickard and his companions. Pickard was a great loss to England, for he was a rare and gallant knight. But it bound our countries the more closely together that this knight of the air should lose his life in this mission, joining in death the Frenchmen he loved and for whom he was ready to die. The best men are not often left to build the future: they have bought it with their lives.

When, in October 1944, the announcement was made of the death of Pickard and Broadley, that seemingly indestructible partnership, Max Sparks recalled that the news came as a 'terrific shock' not just to the 2nd Tactical Air Force but also to the RAF in general. An attempt by his friends to submit Pickard for the award of a posthumous Victoria Cross petered out not because of any official resistance but because he, together with his friend 'Bill' Broadley, and countless other young men in the skies over Europe, were considered to have died doing their ordinary, day-to-day, gallant duty.

Charles 'Pick' Pickard was a legend to the men and women of the Resistance, a man whose exuberant, larger-than-life character represented for them a modern-day John Bull whose dogged refusal to bow to tyranny gave them hope of liberty. Few operational servicemen in Britain had a richer relationship with the entire sweep of senior members of de Gaulle's Secret Service – André Dewavrin, Gilbert Renault and André Manuel. The French trusted him, and he was their friend. This can be seen very clearly in the comments made about him by Dominique Ponchardier, for instance, and was exemplified by the letter to *The Times* on 2 November 1944 by the *résistant* René Massigli, who before the war had been France's ambassador to Turkey:

As one of the many Frenchmen whom the RAF pilots helped to escape from France in the recent years of affliction, may I be allowed to pay to Group Captain Pickard my tribute of admiration, gratitude and regret?

The time has not yet come when it will be possible to reveal to the full what British airmen did in helping Resisting France. So much courage was demanded of them, so much ability and endurance when, on a moonlit night, they had to discover, somewhere in the French countryside, the field or glade that was 'target for tonight'. Among these admirable men Group Captain Pickard was one of the greatest.

Yesterday, as I was reading the thrilling story of the flight to Amiens, where he had a rendezvous with death, I was vividly reminded of the steady bravery, of the indomitable energy, of the boundless devotion to duty of the pilot who, although petrol was running low, tried with so much dogged obstinacy on a certain night of January 1943, to discover the field where he was briefed to drop a Frenchman and to pick up another. That night the homeward bound passenger was Pierre Brossolette who a few months later was to fall into the hands of the Gestapo and commit suicide rather than let out any of the secrets in his possession. Among the brave country-folk who had escorted me to a field there was one, probably the best as well as the youngest, who was to lose his life last August on a Maquis battlefield. The men of the French Resistance will never forget that Group Captain Pickard, after giving them so much help in so many ways, at last gave up his life to rescue some of their fellow-fighters.

Philippe Level remarked: 'The memory of Pickard was constantly with us. He had been our leader, and we had loved him.'

EIGHTEEN

Les évadés

With the honourable exception of those who, like Dr Antonin Mans and André Tempez, were determined to stay with the injured, most *résistants* grasped the opportunity offered to them to seek their freedom through the gaping holes in the walls of Amiens Prison. Some, like Jean Beaurin, spent time looking for friends and relatives in the rubble before making good their own escape. Men and women scattered far and wide, as far as their legs could carry them. In some instances vehicles were found to transport a number away, but the support offered the escapers was, of necessity, slender.

Dominique Ponchardier had made what limited preparations he could, and appears to have had at least one lorry and several cars available, hidden in side streets. At his prompting the indomitable Madame Vignon, supported by Madame Barré, collected heavy coats ready to equip any escapers. Lieutenant Marceau Laverdure, who was in the central Amiens gendarmerie when he received a telephone call saying that the prison was being bombed, immediately called two fellow members of *réseau Zéro*, Michel Dubois (a local building contractor) and Gendarme Edouard Robine, asking them to assist the escapers in any way they could. Jumping on his motorbike, he raced towards the dust cloud rising above the prison.

When the three men arrived they recorded a scene of devastation and confusion. Thinking quickly, Dubois was able to take about forty prisoners and secrete them in a series of old caves, once used for mushroom growing, in the Saint-Pierre area of the town, just over a mile away, but with a single entrance known only to the local inhabitants. During the First World War, and during the German invasion in May 1940, the caves had been used to shelter the population from the shelling that devastated large parts of the town. The local police ran many risks in helping their fellow *résistants*, and were under constant suspicion by Le Baube, Baumann, and the local chief of the Milice, M. Pechon. Angered at the large numbers who were successfully remaining at large, Pechon ordered raids in the following weeks on the homes of those officers he considered to be sympathetic to de Gaulle. Michel Dubois, for example, and the five evaders he was still harbouring, only just managed to escape when the Gestapo came knocking on 8 April. They went to hide with Madame Vignon.

As the afternoon of 18 February progressed, Laverdure organised many of the ambulances, trying where possible to ensure that wounded ordinary prisoners were sent to Amiens Hospital, while *résistants* were dispatched to clinics across the town, such as the private clinic of 48-year-old Dr Jean Poulain and his son Pierre, which had fifteen rooms on the rue Victor Hugo. It was staffed by sisters of the Order of the Bon Secours de Paris. Secret cellars under the clinic had previously been used to hide Jews hiding from their persecutors, as well as wounded *résistants*. It was quickly prepared to hide escapers. With the help of the sisters, the Poulain brothers hid a number of these in the clinic itself, disguising them in bandages. In the event the Gestapo had their hands full, and they were not molested.

Likewise other men and women associated with the Resistance threw themselves into the effort to assist prisoners to escape, or to bind their wounds. The remarkable Perdu medical family, who ran their own clinic in the town, made their way to the prison to offer what comfort they could. Dr Gérard Perdu and his brother Jean François were both surgeons, and their uncle, Dr Christian Perdu, was deputy mayor of Amiens. They were all close friends of Dr Robert Beaumont, and had the tragic task of identifying his body.

Many members of Dr Mans's Civil Defence organisation were *résistants*, and so had dual responsibilities that day. Two of Dr Regnault's colleagues were Robert Pecquet (*Charles Julian*), the chief technical adviser to the organisation, and Monseigneur Chanoine Duhamel, the chaplain. Both made straight for the smoking ruins. A total of eighty men and twenty women of the Civil Defence helped search for bodies and survivors, but mostly relied on their hands to move rubble. François and Raymonde Vignolle, Dr Mans's two assistants, also arrived, in part to see what they could do to find him.

By 3 p.m. the Germans, Milice and Gendarmerie had set up roadblocks round Amiens and checks were mounted on all roads. Sweeps and checks were made of roads and houses, picking up escapers who had not succeeded in merging unseen into the town to find sanctuary from their pursuers. It was this length of time more than anything else that allowed many escapers to remain permanently at large. Armed patrols searched the streets, houses, vehicles, trains and premises over the coming hours and days, but the hugeness of the task meant that there were too few troops available to secure every exit from the town. However, the cold weather was a significant problem for ill-equipped escapers attempting to survive outdoors for any length of time without shelter, warm clothes and food. Claire Normand had been imprisoned for her work assisting Allied flyers to evade the German authorities. She and three others found themselves hiding in the garret of a house that already billeted two unsuspecting Germans in the rooms below. German aircraft scoured the snow-covered terrain in concentric rings running out from Amiens Prison in an attempt to identify the tracks of prisoners escaping unsupported through the snowy countryside, and collaborators kept a watch out for anything unusual in their areas. As Le Baube triumphantly declared in his reports, many prisoners were quickly recaptured.

But many also got away. Jean Beaurin escaped with two of his cellmates, Louis and Gilbert. They went first to Louis's house near the suburban railway station of Saint-Roch, where Beaurin left them after giving them some money, and Gilbert and Jean carried on via train to Beaucamps-le-Vieux. They didn't have enough for the fare, but an understanding conductor allowed them to continue. From Beaucamps-le-Vieux they found their way to the home of a member of the *Sosies* named Armel. He found them both a safe house near the Luftwaffe base at Poix.

Maurice Holville likewise found his way to the station at Saint-Roch. He first walked the mile and a half to the home of Madame Deloiseaux, part of a family with no Resistance links. He knew her because his brother was in the same bronchial ward at the Hôpital du Nord as her husband. She fed him. She also walked to the hospital and told Holville's father, who was visiting his brother, to come and help him escape. At 6 p.m. Holville's father arrived at Madame Deloiseaux's house with fresh clothing and cautiously they caught a train from Saint-Roch to Mers-les-Bains. Their destination was the home of his sister, Madame Renée George, who lived some nine miles from the seaside town. They arrived successfully, to find that another escaper had reached the house before them.

A number of escapers made their way directly to the railway station in Amiens, where the 48-year-old French station master – M. Germain Bleuet, a member of *Zéro* who had worked with Dr Mans's *OCM* and Holville's *réseau* in the past – helped them to merge into the background, dressing them as railway employees. Bleuet, claims Fishman, was one of the men warned in advance of the likelihood of an attack on the prison. He was to lose his life for his Resistance activities, and possibly for his role in the Amiens escape.

Madame Beaurin was taken to the Hôpital du Nord with a head injury. When he discovered that she was there Maurice Holville urged his father to rescue her, before the Gestapo attempted to hold her as a hostage for her son. They managed to spirit her out of the hospital that night, after initial treatment, to a house close to the hospital, after which she was moved to the village of Beaucamps-le-Vieux. There, coincidentally, she was cared for in the same family home in which her son Jean had first stayed after his escape. They missed each other by a matter of hours, but Madame Beaurin was comforted to know that at least one of her sons was safe. She had no information, however, about her other son, Roger Lheureux.

All five men who shared the cells in the prison with Pierre Bracquart managed to escape. Bracquart had initially stayed in the prison after the attack to find his fiancée, Elaine Guillemont, while the other four managed to make their way through to the Route d'Albert. Bracquart found Guillemont lying motionless in the rubble, blood seeping from wounds to her head. He carried her into the street and walked to the Route de Corbie, but found himself exhausted and could go no further. Risking their lives, he knocked on a door, and was given immediate sanctuary. After receiving a drink, and with Elaine a little revived, they made their way through the town, past a patrol, and towards his parents' house. There, the family doctor, Dr Beauvillain, diagnosed shock and a fractured temple. At 11 p.m., two hours after the start of curfew, they risked German patrols and made their separate ways to friends' houses on the other side of town, as the Gestapo had Bracquart's address and were bound to call in due course. They were then able to escape in unexpected style, personally escorted from Amiens in a reserved railway carriage belonging to Pierre's uncle, who was Principal Controller of the railways and, along with many SNCF employees, an active *résistant*. They melted into Paris and survived to the liberation.

The other four members of Bracquart's cell came from Péronne, 28 miles away. The only one of them with identity papers and cash was 30-year-old Gratien Bocquet. The others were Emile Malezieux (an insurance agent in his fifties), Alexander Grisentello (a café proprietor also in his fifties) and twenty-year-old Léon Rat. Stumbling coatless through the snow, they made their way across the fields in the direction of Albert. They walked the seven miles to Daours across the frozen fields, and later that night managed to catch a train east towards Péronne. Just before 10 p.m. they jumped from the slowly moving carriage, just short of Péronne, which they had been warned was swarming with Germans. Bocquet made it safely to his parents-in-law's house. A few hours later he was guided by his mother-in-law through the darkness to a hunting hut hidden in the middle of the Somme marshes.

Sympathetic members of the Gendarmerie also looked after some of the escapees by keeping them imprisoned in local police cells, on the basis that it was safer for them there than on the run. Gendarme Chief Lamont held three recaptured escapees in the little gendarmerie at Saint-Sofleur: Julien Michel, a saboteur almost certainly destined for the firing squad, Henri Foy and Roland Caron, who worked in support of the OSS's escape and evasion line (MIS-X), the US equivalent of MI9. After three days in the cells Lamont took the three men, under supposed police guard, to Lille, and released them into the hands of a local *réseau d'évasion*, where they were hidden overnight in a brothel. Given new false papers, they joined three US airmen the following day on a train heading for Paris. From Paris they reached Toulouse, where they were looked after by an escape line run by the remarkable 61-year-old Marie (*Françoise*) Dissard, a survivor of the Pat line, who still organised evaders and escapers across the Pyrenees. Françoise employed mainly Spanish, Basque or Catalan mountain guides, and used high mountain passes and smugglers' routes because they were much less intensively patrolled by the Germans. This made them very physically demanding, and a feat of endurance for escapers and evaders weakened by weeks and sometimes months of privation. The three Americans successfully got to Spain.

Likewise, Warden Gaston Brasseur, fearful of rearrest, walked out of the hospital and cycled away with his wife and fourteen-year-old daughter. He went first to his wife's house in Fouencamps, near Boves, but was so badly injured that he needed further medical treatment. He was taken by his friends to hospital, where he was well enough bandaged to avoid recognition by Baumann and Lucienne Den. He avoided recapture and survived.

A group of men escaped from Amiens by hiding in the boats that brought market garden produce into the town from the region's *hortillons*, wetland gardens. In this way Georges Danielou, Vincent Miller and Roland Avy made good their escape. Still further escapers managed to get out of the town disguised as mourners at the funeral ceremonies put on by the local authorities to bury eighty-seven of the dead on 23 February. Father Janin (an escape-line organiser who was in Raymond Bonpas's cell, and who had also escaped from the wreckage of the prison), together with sixteen other escapers, mingled with the crowds of mourners, and joined the various corteges as they made their way, unmolested by the Germans, to various cemeteries around the town. From there they disappeared into the countryside. They included the *résistant* Roger Delassus, a US pilot evader called 'Martin', and a group of ordinary burglars, together with Richard Joliot, Guy Bayard and the bank robber Joseph Metz.

The Pas-de-Calais was now heavily fortified, with many forbidden zones, in preparation for an Allied invasion. Joliot, Bayard and Metz, unaware since their incarceration of just how much had changed, were caught in a minefield and killed as they attempted to go cross-country to Bapaume.

A number of those who managed to flee into the countryside slept in a shelter at the Commonwealth War Graves cemetery at High Wood (Bois des Foureaux) on the night following their flight from Amiens (23 February). Their intention was to make their way to Bapaume or Arras, to make contact with any one of Father Janin's escape-line friends. During the evening they encountered a young woman named Claire, whose British soldier father had been killed just before the Armistice in 1918. She worked as a *passeur*, an escape-line assistant who helped guide escapers or evaders to their safe houses.

The strong local *réseau d'évasion* came into its own following the mass escape. Until early 1944 most escapers and evaders had to travel south across France and make their way over the Pyrenees to reach Spain using routes pioneered by the Pat line under Guérisse and the *Comète* line, both of which had been broken up by vigorous German activity in 1943. In 1944 a new line, the *Shelburne* line, set up to ferry men by boat from the Channel beaches, provided another (if temporary) option. Their safe houses in Amiens included a number of brothels; another establishment in Poix, run by Madame Irène and Madame Paulette, was exclusively reserved for members of the Luftwaffe. Irène's fiancé was a Free French pilot serving in the RAF.

MI9 undertook nine rescue operations from Sous-Kéruzeau beach in Saint-Brieuc bay (also known as Plage Bonaparte) in northern Brittany to England between January and August 1944. In the official history of clandestine sea operations between Britain and Brittany, Brooks Richards describes how twenty-five passengers were embarked on MGB 502 under the command of Lieutenant Peter Williams RNVR and safely returned to Britain on 16 March 1944. On 19 March 1944, twenty-five airmen and a French agent were embarked on MGB 503, commanded by Lieutenant Mike Marshall RNVR. A total of fifty passengers were therefore ferried to safety under the noses of the Germans during these two operations. The official records of American escapers and evaders, the MIS-X lists, contain the names of thirty-nine US flyers evacuated by MGB from Brittany on these two voyages. The difference in numbers will most likely have been made up of *résistants*, some of whom may have been escapees from Amiens.

After the bombing, eleven days later, a handful of prisoners who helped rescue wounded comrades were pardoned and released, including Achille Langlet and Raymond Bonpas. But it was clear that the Gestapo would never show clemency to any of those perceived to be leaders of the 'terrorist' movement. In October 1944, just outside Arras, a mass grave was discovered. It contained

260 bodies, including that of 47-year-old Captain André Tempez and many of those who had elected to stay behind to succour the wounded following the raid. Recompense for their selflessness was a bullet. Others whose bodies were discovered in that gruesome pit included 58-year-old Colonel Alfred Touny and the Amiens station-master, 47-year-old Germain Bleuet. Arrested on 8 March 1944, he was sent to the Citadel at Arras and was shot on 5 April.

Epilogue

On Sunday 29 October 1944, soon after Canadian troops and armour had swept the Germans from Amiens after four and a half years of occupation, the Air Ministry in London released the story of the raid. One of many newspapers that reproduced the account, Glasgow's *Sunday Post*, published on its front and back pages on 29 October 1944 a detailed story under the headline: 'RAF Save Condemned Men: Strangest Story of the War'. The article was a heavily edited version of a press release given to the media by the RAF's Director of Public Relations. What remained hidden at the time, and what no one seemed interested in asking, however, was why the raid had been kept secret since February. Operational security – not allowing the Germans to learn any more about the raid than they could themselves deduce from what happened – was the primary reason, given the likelihood of similar attacks by the RAF in the future. The war was still far from over. But there was another reason. As has been seen, the British Secret Intelligence Service was actively managing a wide range of espionage networks in France, on its own behalf as well as for the Free French. The very existence of the SIS was a state secret, and was to remain so for decades – NCND (neither confirmed nor denied) in the shorthand of Whitehall and St James's – and that alone was enough to draw a blanket over its involvement in military operations abroad in the territory of a friendly (though occupied) state.

Another reason perhaps for the delay in announcing the loss of Pickard was that the death of such a high-profile figure was not news the Air Ministry wanted publicised. The authorities in Whitehall were concerned to ensure that the official version of the story of that momentous day in February reached the world in a format that was as controlled as possible, before it could become distorted by journalists piecing it together from local gossip. There does not appear to have been any fear that the role of MI6 might somehow be revealed in the affair, rather that the rationale for the raid, in the face of potential criticisms about the scale of French casualties, needed a calm and lucid explanation. It would not have been acceptable, for instance, for accusations to arise that the RAF had staged the raid for the purpose of releasing *British* subjects from the prison when so many innocent French men and women had perished in the attack.

London wanted to ensure that the world received a central truth (though the real audience was the French public and its government-in-exile), which was that it was Frenchmen who had requested the raid to free other Frenchmen, men and women involved in acts of resistance against the Nazis, and that the raid in overall terms was considered by these same Frenchmen to have been successful. There was certainly no need to reveal anything about the role of MI6 in the affair, or anything of the relationship between the various French underground networks and Britain's Secret Intelligence Service, or indeed of the possibility that British SIS or SOE agents had been beneficiaries of the strike. The question about MI6's involvement never arose.

The problem for London was that while the desire of French *résistants* to release other French *résistants* from German captivity and the certain fate that awaited all captured *terroristes* was understandable, it hardly seemed a compelling rationale for an attack. After all, large numbers of *résistants* were languishing in prisons across France, not to mention those in concentration camps in Germany and the east, but no effort had been made to release *them* in the dramatic style of the Amiens raid. If, however, it was obvious to Allied observers that a large-scale massacre of *résistants* was about to take place in the prison, and that the French Resistance itself was determined to prevent this slaughter, this might offer adequate justification.But was there a mass execution planned for the day after the raid? There is no evidence in the historical record to this effect. Yet the reality remains that those arrested for 'terrorist' crimes by the Germans were facing a bleak future. To go by the German record in the past, most of them were destined for death, either by firing squad or by deliberate neglect in a concentration or labour camp.

The evidence appears to suggest that somewhere along the way, the original information received in London from the Resistance, to the effect that 'many of the prisoners would in due course of time be executed', acquired a subtle shift so that it specified a precise number of executions (120) due on a certain day. In order to reach a valid target-acquisition judgement, the military recipients in London of the Resistance request (in the Air Ministry especially) would have asked two main questions of detail: 'How many *résistants* are to be executed?' and 'When are the executions expected?' The fact that it looks as though the process of asking and answering these questions added spurious clarity to Ponchardier's entreaty does not invalidate the core request. In any case, Gilbert Renault's account makes no inflated claims, suggesting that Ponchardier's motivation was limited to saving a young communist *résistant* named Jean Beaurin, who had been told that he would be executed on 20 February. It should be noted, however, that in his account Ponchardier recorded that twelve prisoners, 'including Jean Beaurin, had been due for execution on the 20th February' and in a statement made in 1953 he confirmed that a *résistant* named André Leroy was told on 17 February that he was to be shot two days later.

Renault argued that Ponchardier and his colleague René Chapelle were determined to save Beaurin at all costs. Jean

Beaurin, whose father had already been deported to Germany, had been arrested at the end of December 1943 for the possession of counterfeit ration cards. His half-brother brother Roger Lheureux had been arrested a month before for stealing a bicycle. When Jean was arrested it appears that the Germans did not at first understand whom they had caught, even though the work of the notorious French counter-agent Lucien Pieri had caused severe damage to the local branch of the FTPF to which Beaurin belonged. Both young men were in fact active in sabotage activities; they had played a role in derailing several German troop trains and in repeated attacks on the railway network (see Appendix 4). When arrested Jean had been consigned to the criminal section of the prison. Once the Germans learned his true identity he was taken before the special court in Amiens and told by the judge that he would be executed within weeks.

Thus it seems that a degree of deliberate exaggeration took place, going back to the original orders given on 18 February to the men of 140 Wing who were to fly the mission, namely that 120 *résistants* were soon to be executed and needed rescue. In February 1944 someone, perhaps in the Air Ministry, believed that to justify such an attack, the numbers at risk had better rise. When it came to the public announcement of the raid in late October the RAF's Director of Public Relations (DPR), keen to ensure the publicity of this good news story, was only too happy to accept this earlier, if much inflated, figure. However, the fact that the evidence reveals that the execution of perhaps twelve *résistants* was imminent, not 120, does not in any way undermine the rationale for the raid. It merely demonstrates the spin that some well-meaning individual exerted when the 'object' paragraph of the orders was being drafted in the headquarters of 2nd TAF in February 1944. In any case the truth was that the chance of survival for any '*terroriste*' prisoner was judged to be near-zero. In this sense, therefore, those who deliberately exaggerated the number of prisoners awaiting execution were actually correct: it was only a matter of time.

A further consideration was that in addition to releasing deserving *résistants* from almost certain death, the raid also freed other undesirables – common criminals and those imprisoned for serious crimes unrelated to the war – such as murder and rape. This unhappy consequence of an otherwise laudable operation was not a subject the leaders of Free France in Algiers wanted to publicise in France itself, for fear of losing some of their public support. The Vichy regime had long claimed that the forces of de Gaulle were mere bandits and separatists for whom a lawless France would further their political ends. An attack on a prison, a basic element in the structure of a law-abiding society, did not play well to this propaganda, no matter how pure the intentions behind it.

It is not known exactly how many prisoners were in Amiens at the time of the raid. The official versions are contradictory, and vary between 700 and 820, with between 180 and 190 men and women recorded as *terroristes*. On the day following the raid M. Heannot, the divisional police commissioner, drafted a report for the attention of both German and French ministers in Paris in which he calculated that there were some 820 prisoners, 640 jailed by the French and 180 by the Germans. He recorded that the German authorities appeared 'to have recaptured many from the prison and dug out thirty', presumably alive. He also noted that it 'has not as yet been possible to make an exact census of prisoners as the archives were destroyed'.

At that moment there were 37 confirmed dead, including two doctors, M. Goyot and Robert Beaumont. Crush injuries, however, meant that only six or seven bodies had by that stage been identified. Ninety-two had been injured, including Jean Bellemère, all of whom had been transported either to the town's hospital or to a number of private clinics. M. Heannot noted that a 'large number of prisoners have benefited from the bombing by escaping', although this number included all those, like Antonin Mans and André Tempez, who had decided not to escape. By the time he drafted the report, he recorded that of the 640 French 'criminals' counted as held in the prison at the time of the raid, 163 occupied temporary accommodation in a factory at Faubourg de Hem, a suburb 3 miles away. A further fifty prisoners, presumably *terroristes*, were being 'looked after' by the German authorities in the Citadel, while eighteen women were held elsewhere. It is clear, therefore, that by the end of 19 February 1944 a total of 460 prisoners, or 56 per cent of the pre-attack muster, remained unaccounted for by the German authorities, and of the 180 'important prisoners' (i.e. *résistants*), 130 (72 per cent) were still at large.

Some, Heannot correctly surmised, would be lying 'under the enormous mounds of material', but he could not be certain about the numbers. He reported that Raymond Vivant had disappeared and that a woman had been killed at her home in the rue Voltaire. Perhaps in an attempt to win some measure of regard from the authorities, he made a specific note of the selflessness of those prisoners who had relinquished their opportunity to escape in order to provide succour to the wounded:

I should signify the exemplary behaviour of certain prisoners who, after the event, cooperated actively with some of the other prisoners. Among them, particularly, Doctor Mans, André Tempez and Gendarme [Achille] Langlet of the Nesle Gendarmerie Brigade [a town 38 miles south-east of Amiens].

A massive manhunt was launched later in the afternoon of the day of the raid, although it is clear that the authorities took some considerable time to organise themselves, time that proved invaluable for many escapers. Regular German troops were mobilised to join those of the Milice (under the command of the local chief,

Pechon), Gendarmerie and other uniformed forces. Fascinatingly, Pierre Le Baube knew by instinct that the underground movement was at the heart of the attack. In his report he gave vent to his suspicions, unwittingly touching on the truth of the situation but knowing nothing of the detail, except to suggest that an RAF raid on the prison had been an open secret among Resistance circles for some days:

> The police services and the gendarmeries of my department have carried out active searches with a view to laying their hands on prisoners who profited from the bombing by escaping. In the hour that followed, they arrested 165 prisoners, of which 22 were apprehended by police at Amiens, Péronne, Villers-Bretonneux, and in other localities. Police security detectives arrested 18 prisoners, 9 during the day, and 9 in the night. Moreover, 56 prisoners who had been imprisoned by the Germans were recaptured by French police. Several of these prisoners were women. The total of prisoners retaken was 284, and this figure kept on increasing as various prisoners' homes were known to the police and other services.
>
> I consider that the possibility of bombardment and its consequences were known to M. Melin [M. l'abbé Melin], in charge of the mission to the regional Prefecture, as he had been forewarned by about 14 hours by the Somme's Director of Civil Defence.

As the days went by a clearer picture slowly began to emerge. On 21 February Heannot reported that thirty houses situated in the neighbourhood of the prison had suffered bomb damage, as had the pavilion of the monastery of St-Victor, which the Germans were using as a hospital. Seventy-seven bodies had been recovered and 78 injured hospitalised. He noted that M. Gruel, chief of the *préfet*'s office, had been killed. One hundred and ninety-seven 'criminals' had been recaptured, together with 74 (54 male and 20 female) *résistants*.* On 26 February the police reported that they had recovered 83 bodies from the ruins and that eight injured remained in Amiens Hospital from the original 88 who had been hospitalised. Of those who had escaped, 208 French civil prisoners and 56 *résistants* had been recovered. The final number of dead, recorded Dr Odile Regnault, was 95. The 26 February report indicated that the total number of original prisoners was 712, among them 190 *résistants*, and of whom 518 (73 per cent) had been recaptured, leaving 194 (27 per cent) at liberty. Of the 190 *résistants* originally in the prison, therefore, over a week later 134 were missing, dead or injured.

The exact number of those who had avoided recapture is impossible to determine, but if the same proportions of dead and injured across the entire prison were to apply to these prisoners, the number of dead *résistants* would have been 25, and the same number injured. With 50 casualties, therefore, this means that around 84 *résistants* would have secured their liberty on that momentous day, most of whom permanently escaped Nazi clutches, to play important subsequent roles for the British and Free French secret services in the ongoing intelligence and guerrilla war across northern France, and in support of the Second Front that would open up with D-Day on 6 June, four months later. At the same time the man on the ground who made the raid possible, Dominique Ponchardier, reported that German counter-espionage efforts were severely hampered in the months following the raid as escaped *résistants* were able to take revenge on the traitors who had turned them in.

---

* In a second report that day, Heannot reduced the number of prisoners originally in the prison from 820 to 700. There seems no reason for this reduction, except perhaps to reduce the embarrassment faced by the Vichy judicial authorities at the scale of the escape. It is possible that the discrepancies in the numbers existed because the larger number included prisoners temporarily incarcerated in the Citadel, taken there for detailed questioning by the Gestapo and therefore absent from their cells in the *Maison d'Arrêt*. We are unlikely ever to know.

But it also meant that many died. The concerns in London about the risk of what would today be called 'collateral damage' were borne out in the attack. In retrospect, more 500-pound bombs were dropped during the attack (forty were dropped in total) than were strictly necessary for the task of cutting through the walls and blasting open the doors of the prison, and several of these ploughed through their intended target without exploding. Ninety-five prisoners were killed, mainly by bombs going through or bouncing beyond their intended targets, and this is bound to cast a shadow over what was otherwise a flawless operation.

The reasons for using so many bombs were a mixture of technology, insurance and weather. Low-flying aircraft could not drop bombs that exploded on impact without jeopardising themselves, so all bombs dropped at low altitude needed to be fitted with delayed-action fuses. Equally, even so-called 'precision' bombing at the time was often so inaccurate that it was usual to leave a margin in order to make sure that enough bombs would strike the target.

Unintended damage and unwanted casualties from aerial bombing remained a perennial problem for Allied planners during the war, even from precision raids. Thundering at a mere 20 or 30 feet above the ground against a tiny target at upwards of 300 miles per hour called as much for luck as for judgement when it came to placing 'dumb' (i.e. unguided) bombs* with any accuracy even the most carefully planned and executed attack was likely to cause unintended casualties where targets were sited in built-up areas. The harm inflicted on innocent French civilians by Allied air attacks was in fact an issue of considerable political import in 1944, and one of the suspected causes of official French antipathy to the Amiens raid. During the war 68,778 French civilians were killed by Allied bombing, 7,458 in 1943 alone.

---

* The first guided free-fall bomb was not invented until 1972.

In the immediate aftermath of the raid Dominique Ponchardier, in hiding outside Amiens, knew little of its impact or effects, Nevertheless, on the basis of what he knew he sent a message to MI6 on 23 February to thank London for the raid:

> I thank you in name of comrades for bombardment of prison. The delay fixed for the attack was too short; we were not able to save all. Thanks to admirable precision of attack the first bombs blew in nearly all the doors, and 150 prisoners escaped with the help of civilian population. 12 of these prisoners were to have been shot on the 19th. Bombing was too violent; 37 prisoners were killed, some of them by German machine guns. 50 Germans also killed. To sum up it was a success. No plane down over AMIENS, but we are having pilots looked for.

When he sent that note, Dominique Ponchardier didn't realise how inaccurate and understated his figures were. Neither he nor René Chapelle knew the full panoply of events they had set in motion, nor their actual outcome. It has been suggested that this message was a fraud, manufactured by MI6 as part of an elaborate cover and not sent from France at all. However, the context and language demonstrate that Ponchardier was the author, or at the very least that the message came from France.* Ponchardier's last

---

* The number of prisoners to be shot (twelve) does not align with the estimate provided by the Air Ministry to 2nd TAF ('approximately 120') in the orders on 18 February, a figure that was clearly exaggerated, either by the Air Ministry or by MI6, but does tally exactly with subsequent records of the attack by Dominique Ponchardier. If the message came from the same source as the inflated numbers, the number of those to be executed would have been increased to accord with that in the earlier message. Ponchardier had consistently argued that the execution of twelve prisoners was due to take place within a few days. Second, the total number of escapees, which could not have been manufactured, was recorded here at 150; actually it was initially many more, although the number of recaptures was high. Third, the report stated that the blast effects of the bombs were substantial, which accords with reality, but which would not have been known in this detail by the RAF or the Air Ministry at the time. In all respects, this message can clearly be shown to be genuine.

sentence clearly provides an answer to the question sent to him by
Gilbert Renault following Level's emotional intervention: where
was Pickard? Ponchardier had not been informed that an aircraft
had come down over Amiens. The melancholy news from Saint-
Gratien had yet to reach his hiding place.

Ponchardier's message was the first direct indication from
France that the raid had been successful. Sir Stewart Menzies
immediately sent on a note to Tubby Grant at the Directorate of
Intelligence at the Air Ministry, who had the following note sent to
Leigh-Mallory's HQ:

> I have been asked by 'C' to express his gratitude and the gratitude
> of his officers for the attack carried out on Amiens prison on 18th
> February, and also their sympathy for the relatives and comrades
> of the air-crews who were unfortunately lost.
>
> Before writing I wished to ascertain what the result of the
> attack had been. This has taken some time; however, we have now
> received certain messages from France . . . I should be grateful if
> you would pass the above 'Highly Secret' information to Air Vice-
> Marshal Embry.

Air Marshal Sir Trafford Leigh-Mallory wrote to Embry:

> It turned out more successful than I hoped, and your people are
> to be congratulated on the wonderful Job they did. As an oper-
> ation it certainly was an epic. It was a tragedy that we lost Pickard,
> but I hope that we may see him before long.

Embry replied:

> It is most satisfactory that we should have released so many.

It remains unclear whether the members of 140 Wing who took
part in the raid were given this information. Most recalled,

nevertheless, their profound satisfaction at knowing that they had managed to break down the walls of the prison, and that the raid had given the inmates the greatest possible chance of escape.

The attack remained a mystery to the Germans, and to most Amiénois. The occupying powers set out at once, in print and by word of mouth, to belittle the attack, and to suggest that the Allies had nefarious motives for mounting the raid. One persistent rumour, almost certainly started by the Germans and still current today, was that the RAF had deliberately bombed the prison to kill Frenchmen and women who held vital secrets, and who needed to be silenced before they talked. The RAF, in this fabrication, came not as saviours but as executioners.

German ignorance of the reasons for the raid is not surprising. One key fact about Allied espionage activities in northern France in late 1943 and early 1944 is that the Germans had no idea how much the Allies knew about their operations. In France, the Gestapo and Abwehr between them proved remarkably adept at sweeping up Resistance networks, lifting *résistants* for interrogation, or pushing them directly into the Night and Fog of the Reich's liquidation machine. They proved far less adept, as it proved, in grasping the extent to which their own secrets had been unravelled, not by *Ultra* or signals intelligence, but by the 'Mark I eyeball' of the man and woman on the ground spying for their country against the hated occupiers and persecutors. The extent of Allied penetration of the V1 programme, for instance, or of the secrets of the Atlantic Wall, was quite unknown to the Germans.

Ponchardier was later to remark, in terms that would have been entirely supported by Gilbert Renault, that the attack was much more than an act of war: it was also an act of profound solidarity between the free peoples of Britain and the subject peoples of France. It freed relatively few *résistants*, and did nothing to reduce the length of the war, but in its symbolism it was a powerful statement of commitment by the Allies to the cause of resistance which,

Ponchardier asserted, was 'very precious at the time'. He concluded that although the losses of Pickard and Broadley and the other aircrews were regrettable, 'its material and moral reach in my opinion went far beyond the simple region of Amiens'. It is hard to disagree with this conclusion. Operation *Jericho* took Allied support for the underground a step beyond the moonlit ventures of agents in Lysanders to a violent act of war in direct military support of the Resistance. In so doing, it provided a foretaste of the massive aerial rearmament of the Maquis in southern and central France that would take place in the coming months. Amiens demonstrated that the Allies considered the Resistance to be an important military component of victory, and the growing recognition of this created a tsunami of pride and heightened morale across Resistance networks the length and breadth of the country, as rumours of the spectacular attack spread by word of mouth and underground newspapers. In practical terms, on the streets of Amiens where confusion and even hostility towards the Allies was felt in the days and weeks that followed the attack because of the large number of casualties, news that the raid had been designed to free patriots, and that the much-liked Raymond Vivant was one of those who had made their way to freedom, did much to allay the inevitable anger.

Even by the time of his 1946 interview it was apparent that Dominique Ponchardier still had little grasp of the consequences of the raid, either in terms of casualties suffered or of prisoners freed. This is not surprising, as he was on the run at the time of the raid and did not stop running until the liberation, evading his pursuers by a whisker.

Almost as soon as Amiens was liberated in August 1944 the RAF sent Squadron Leader Edwin Houghton, an Intelligence Staff Officer from No. 2 Group, who worked for Pat Shallard, to investigate the circumstances surrounding the raid, and in particular to find out just what had happened to Pickard and Broadley. He arrived in Amiens on 4 September 1944. Houghton's report, and the way he conducted himself, proved strangely naïve. He had not been briefed by the Air Ministry or MI6 as to the origin of the request for the raid. Given the standard demands of security this is not surprising, but he could have learned much simply by talking in the first instance to Basil Embry before he left for France, or to someone reasonably close to the source of the original request from France. Even a short conversation, for instance, with Gilbert Renault at the offices of the BCRA in Duke Street would have enlightened him, and spared him some of the time he wasted in Amiens. Instead, he seemed to believe that he might be able to pick up the story by talking to people on the street there.

In the event, Houghton learned next to nothing. Interviewing Dr Marchoire, who had been the local chief of the French Forces of the Interior from mid-1944 (and a close friend of Dr Robert Beaumont), he discovered that there was a general mystery in Amiens as to the reasons for the raid. Marchoire told Houghton gently that this was unsurprising: the Resistance networks worked in watertight compartments; only those directly involved with an operation would know anything about it, and fewer still would know anything more than the vaguest details. The best *réseaux* – the ones that survived – were by nature completely secret, even from each other: asking people in the street the whys and wherefores of the raid would merely have drawn blank stares.

Once the request had been sent to London, only a few people in the BCRA would have known about it (Gilbert Renault and André Manuel primarily, André Dewavrin being in Algiers at the time), plus a few MI6 staff (Kenneth Cohen, Claude Dansey, Airey Neave, Neil Whitelaw and perhaps Biffy Dunderdale). The 'need to know' principle meant that no more than a handful of people would ever have known the origin of the request, and its route from the field in France to the Air Ministry in London via the offices of MI6 in Broadway.

Nevertheless, Marchoire knew enough about the fragile state of local *réseaux* in late 1943 to appreciate the certainty that the call to release prisoners had come from Amiens, concluding that it 'was probable that the request had come from within the prison through our agents'. What history does not reveal is whether Dr Marchoire even knew of Maurice Genest, for instance, or of Dominique Ponchardier. From his comment to Edwin Houghton it appears not, although he did correctly guess the origin of the call for help: inside the prison itself. With such a sketchy picture of events, Houghton was bound to reach the wrong conclusion in his final report:

> One point was clear – that the most important prisoner to escape was a Monsieur Vivant, the Sous Préfet of Abbeville, who was arrested by the Gestapo on the 14th February, 1944. Monsieur Vivant is now in the Ministry of the Interior, in General de Gaulle's Government.
>
> I think it probable that we were asked to carry out the attack mainly to effect his escape. Monsieur Vivant was a key member of the Resistance at Abbeville and probably had in his possession important secrets of the Resistance Organisation.
>
> From all sources it was clear that the population of Amiens had wondered why the attack had been carried out, more particularly since the section of the prison occupied by Political prisoners was the most seriously damaged; but that within a few days, when it became known that Monsieur Vivant had escaped, together with so many other Political prisoners, the attack was generally applauded.

Houghton's visit was groping in the dark, his report an investigative failure. Finding no definitive origin for the request to attack Amiens Prison, he concluded that the aim was to release Raymond Vivant, neglecting to recognise that in fact Vivant had been arrested several days after the decision to attack the prison had been made.

This seems to have been an error repeated by Jack Fishman. The one point about which Dr Marchoire was clear, however, was the general support given to the raid, despite the casualties, when the local populace heard that Raymond Vivant had been freed.

There have been accusations that Dominique Ponchardier manufactured evidence of his involvement in the raid, perhaps in order to disguise the reason for the attack. Such a claim is preposterous. Historically, the credibility of Ponchardier's evidence relating to his role in the raid on Amiens Prison on 18 February 1944 is unassailable. His 1946 deposition is in the French National Archives, as is his brother's (two years previous), together with those by René Chapelle and Edouard Rivière, which confirm and corroborate his claims. The memoirs of his mentor within *Gilbert* also attest to Ponchardier's role in the Amiens affair, something that has been in the public domain ever since Georges-André Groussard published his memoirs in 1964. If Ponchardier's claim to be the author of the request was matter-of-fact, it is because it was true. This was confirmed in part by his involvement in a French production of a film telling the story of the raid, a production that received considerable support from the Air Ministry in London and the RAF, including the visit in 1946 to attend the premiere at the Palais de Chaillot and celebrate the success of the raid by the Air Minister and Sir Basil Embry. At the event British and French dignitaries met ex-members of the *réseau Sosies*, including Dominique Ponchardier, Edouard Rivière and René and Maria Chapelle. Ponchardier's role was accepted unequivocally by all involved, French (BCRA and Vichy) and British. Entitled *Opération Jéricho*, the film received a considerable level of support from the RAF, although Ponchardier personally detested it for some of its crass exaggerations (such as *résistants* being depicted reconnoitring the prison wearing rabbit skins, for instance).

Ponchardier's role was accepted unquestioningly by Raymond Vivant (who, Gilbert Renault recounted, had authorised the first call to London for a raid), as well as by Philippe Level and René Chapelle. In 1950 he developed the story and his involvement in it in more detail in a novel entitled *The Paving Stones of Hell*. On the tenth anniversary of the raid a reception was held in Paris at which the French Premier, M. Joseph Laniel, was guest of honour alongside Air Chief Marshal Sir Basil Embry, who was then Commander-in-Chief of Allied Air Forces Central Europe. Once again Ponchardier was the principal guest. No one who knew anything about the raid was in any doubt as to the role he had played.

In 1953 Ponchardier attested further to the work of one of the members of the *Sosies*, André Emile Leroy:

I, the undersigned Dominique Ponchardier, Companion of the Liberation, administrative receiver of the 'Réseaux de Renseignements et d'Action' 'Sosies', 'Pre-Sosies' and 'Gilbert', certify that Mr André Emile Leroy, born on 24 May 1919 at Daours (Somme), worked in close cooperation with one of my colleagues, Mr Chapelle, alias Pépé, from 15th February 1941 until 18 November 1943 in the Department of the Somme. On this date he was arrested and incarcerated in Amiens Prison, where he was condemned to death on 17 February 1944 with his execution set for 19 February 1944. He was freed the day before his execution through 'Operation Jericho' which I carried out on 18th February 1944.

Made in Paris on 13th January 1953.

Gilbert Renault wrote up the story in 1955 in a book entitled *L'opération Jéricho* and conducted extensive interviews of those involved. These notes sit today among Renault's papers in the museum Le Mémorial de Caen.

Between 1978 and 1982 the late Jack Fishman interviewed virtually all the surviving participants in the story. This evidence, from people in positions of responsibility in Geneva, Berne and London, corroborates the essential narrative of the story and removes any

doubt that a Resistance group in France – the *réseau Sosies* –
formally asked its SIS handlers in London for action to be taken to
free its own and other prisoners in Amiens Prison.

But why did London pay this request any attention? The context
of early 1944 makes this clear. In early 1944 the Resistance had
becoming a strategic priority in the Allied war effort. Even six
months before it was, arguably, merely a tool in Allied strategic
deception (such as Operation *Cockade* and *Starkey* in 1943, precur-
sors to Operation *Fortitude South*), a small element in the acquisi-
tion of target intelligence in France and the primary mechanism
for giving sustenance to the resistance impulses which London
hoped would grow as the war progressed. They had suffered grievously. Now, however, months from the cross-Channel invasion, it
was critical that the Resistance was fully prepared to contribute to
its success. Churchill recognised this, telling Anthony Eden on
Christmas Day 1943 that he was willing to talk to the various
members of the resistance groups, rallying them to the cause of
defeating Germany rather than contemplate fighting among themselves in a struggle for power in post-war France.

Gilbert Renault was in no doubt that the raid had been designed
as a boost to Resistance morale. Speaking of the mass slaughter of
résistants in the Reich's concentration camps, he wrote:

> It was to save the prisoners from a fate like this that 'Operation
> Jericho' took place. News of this great endeavour on the part of
> the RAF spread swiftly through the ranks of the Resistance move-
> ment, giving the men new courage and the will to be ready to do
> all they could on the eve of the landings on the coast. It had been
> the proof that the Allies had not forgotten us.

There seems little doubt that one of the motivations for a raid was
to raise the flagging spirits of the resisters in the region, and to
demonstrate that their work and sacrifice was understood by
London, and appreciated.

It is possible that London may have also considered an attack on Amiens advantageous in terms of its support for the Operation *Fortitude South* deception, in persuading the Germans that the British wanted to release a *résistant* or *résistants* who, entirely unbeknown to the Abwehr or Gestapo, had a role to play in the impending invasion. Any activity within the Pas-de-Calais or its general area was a bonus for the complex deception the Allies were running in preparation for D-Day. While not the rationale for the raid on Amiens Prison, the attack was nevertheless grist to this mill. All additional activity carried out in this region by the Resistance and RAF during the pre-invasion period would have added to the general view in German military circles that the Pas-de-Calais was to be the location for the invasion (this point is stressed by Chester Wilmot and repeated by John Terraine). But this was a fortuitous by-product of the plan, not its *raison d'être*.

It happened that the British government found itself under immense pressure at that moment to increase the scale of its support to the Resistance. The subject involved the Prime Minister, the War Cabinet, the Chiefs of Staff Committee in London and the Joint Chiefs of Staff in Washington, as well as the Secret Intelligence Service (MI6), and marked a fault line in late 1943 and early 1943 between the British and their Free French allies. In the run-up to Operation *Overlord*, the programme called Operation *Sussex* was under way, designed to reinforce the existing Resistance networks across France. If these networks were incapacitated by the Germans then the role of the Resistance before and during D-Day would be substantially lessened, especially their ability to target essential communication links such as railways to prevent the Germans sending troops by rail to reinforce their defences in Normandy.

One of the consequences of the raid was to enable the freed *résistants* to kill those traitors and German agents who had been responsible for the demise of so many of their colleagues in the first place. In Ponchardier's memoirs he argued that he had seen a

German report about the 'massacre of German secret agents [that] followed the liberation of prisoners; to such a point that the German units/services [were] disrupted for ... nearly two months in this sector and ... [it saved the lives of] numerous resistance workers.'

Pickard's raid demonstrated convincingly to all observers (the Air Ministry, RAF and presumably, MI6) that Resistance groups could receive succour from such attacks, and as a result several notable raids followed Amiens. In April 1944 a Mosquito attack destroyed the Dutch central population registry to prevent the Gestapo getting access to information about the racial background of the Dutch population as part of the Final Solution. Then, on 31 October, in Professor M. R. D. Foot's words: 'three squadrons of Mosquito bombers made a low-level attack on a line of terrace houses, forming part of the university of Aarhus: they picked out individual houses in the row, burnt up the Gestapo files, and had the luck to kill over 150 officers in conference'. All of these attacks were planned by Ted Sismore. Tragedy, however, accompanied a similarly spectacular attack on 21 March 1945 (Operation *Carthage*). Eighteen Mosquitoes struck the landmark art deco Shell building in central Copenhagen, a six-floor block with prisoners on the top floor and Gestapo agents, files and collaborators in the rest, which the Gestapo had taken over and attempted to camouflage with green and brown paint. Twenty-seven prisoners escaped, including two members of the 'Freedom Council', and the Danish resistance was saved. Over a hundred Germans and collaborators were killed, although the local Gestapo chief, Dr Karl Hoffmann, and all his senior officers were absent at a colleague's funeral at the time. But tragedy marred success. A Mosquito in the first wave came in so low that it hit a tall pylon, swerved, and crashed into a school: the following wave saw the conflagration and mistakenly bombed the school. Eighty-six schoolchildren and eighteen adults died, including many nuns, with 156 wounded.

A balanced judgement of the effect of the Amiens raid is presented by Professor Matthew Cobb who, echoing Dominique Ponchardier, concludes that: 'Despite the dead and injured the attack restored French morale by showing the power of the Allied military machine and its concern for the fate of the *résistants*.' This was the ultimate triumph of the young men of many nations (British, Australian, New Zealand, Belgian, Canadian and French) who flew in the attack squadrons of 140 Wing that momentous day. The New Zealand official historian sums up the achievement of these aircrews:

> . . . as a result of careful planning, accurate navigation and fine precision bombing, this mission to Amiens was to rank among the most memorable daylight raids of the war . . .

So ended one of the many gallant episodes in which the RAF helped and encouraged patriot organisations on the Continent. It was indeed a worthy gesture, for the men and women who worked in those organisations – French, Dutch, Belgian, Polish, and Norwegian alike – displayed great courage. Many frequently risked their lives to help Allied airmen shot down over enemy territory, and those who were betrayed or captured suffered cruelly at the hands of the Gestapo. The whole of their work forms an epic story in itself. Much of it will never be told. But at least let their amazing courage and quiet heroism be remembered.

Gilbert Rémy did not for once romanticise the raid, or the reasons for it. He knew that it would be controversial, especially if prisoners were killed and common criminals allowed to escape their confinement. Yet he saw these casualties as the unfortunate but inevitable consequence of a vicious war between the forces of tyranny and those of freedom. In his account of the operation he was honest enough to admit that when he heard of the toll the raid had taken he wanted to blame Ponchardier for his role in asking for it:

> When it was established that Group Captain Pickard and his insepa-rable navigator, Flight Lieutenant J. A. Broadley, D.S.O., D.F.C., D.F.M., only twenty-two and a Yorkshireman like his chief, were

dead; when I learned that 'Operation Jericho' had caused the loss of another Mosquito and its crew, as well as one of the escorting Mustangs [*sic*]; when I heard that the attack on Amiens prison had caused ninety-five dead, many of whom had been members of the Resistance, and eighty-seven wounded – then my first thought was that it would have been better had Ponchardier never started the idea.

But on mature consideration he believed that this attitude was wrong, and gave three reasons for so thinking:

Among the prisoners who escaped, in spite of the energetic search that went on day and night by German police and gendarmes, many would certainly have been condemned to death. Thanks to these escaped prisoners, who were immediately in touch once again with the Resistance movement, it was possible for them to identify at least sixty Gestapo agents. German counter-espionage in the whole region became comparatively useless, and thus many arrests were avoided that would otherwise doubtless have been made. Finally, and most important, the secret armies of the Resistance had been shown that the Allies were not forgetting them. Supposing that the operation had been a total catastrophe, that all the prisoners had been killed without exception, still the knowledge that the Allies had been prepared to risk valuable lives and material in coming to the rescue of their comrades would have served its main purpose of reassuring all members of the French Resistance.

In the spring of 1943 I had myself asked for a similar raid on Fresnes prison, to save a dozen of our men who were due to be shot. The proposition was seriously considered, but proved impractical. Had it taken place, I was running the risk of losing my mother, five sisters and my brother, who were all in Fresnes prison, although it was unlikely that they would themselves be shot. Nevertheless, I should not have been the less grateful to the R.A.F. for risking its men and its planes in a dangerous mission, in order to save the lives of twelve of our men. I know well enough how heart-rending it is to think of Madame Platel, who had been due to be freed, dying of terrible wounds in the arms of her husband, or of the young Amiens solicitor who died after agonised hours of waiting, or of the funeral service in Amiens cathedral when ninety-five coffins lay side by side in the choir.

I remember that, after the first raid on the port of Bordeaux at the close of 1940, which resulted from messages I had sent informing the Allies that there were German submarines in the Bacalan docks. I was plunged in misery when I heard how many victims there had been among the civilians. But, at that rate, I should logically have refrained from sending any information whatever to London, and even wanted the Allies to make no landing on the Normandy coast, since it was obvious that terrible devastation would be the result. All of which would boil down to preferring slavery to freedom.

I hate war, war that is so blind and brutal, war that, like all means of force, proves nothing in the end. But invasion is also a means of force, and one's duty is to oppose it, to do everything within one's power to get rid of the invader, even if it means the deaths of innocent people.

Without the work that was carried on every day by our under-ground networks, it is possible that France would still be waiting for her Liberation today. What would have become of our men, women and children if the Nazis had had time to consolidate their position and keep us under their yoke? I had far rather have seen my children die there and then, than watch them being taken from me, first their bodies, then their souls.

By the beginning of 1944, the state of our networks was becoming precarious. Arrests, executions and deportations were becoming more and more frequent.

News of this great endeavour on the part of the R.A.F. spread swiftly through the ranks of the Resistance movement, giving the men new courage and the will to be ready to do all they could on the eve of the landings on the coast. It had been the proof that the Allies had not forgotten us.

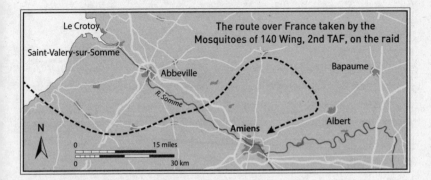

Le Crotoy

Saint-Valery-sur-Somme

Abbeville

R. Somme

The route over France taken by the
Mosquitoes of 140 Wing, 2nd TAF, on the raid

Bapaume

Amiens

Albert

N

| 0 | 15 miles |
| 0 | 30 km |

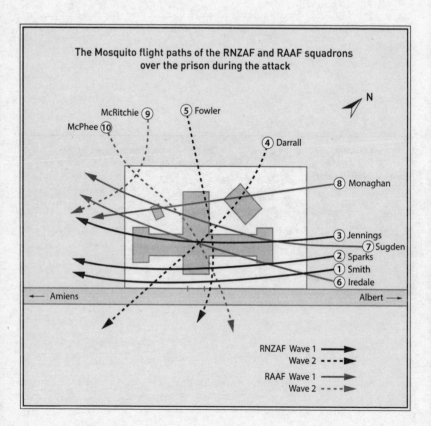

The Mosquito flight paths of the RNZAF and RAAF squadrons over the prison during the attack

N

McPhee ⑩
McRitchie ⑨
⑤ Fowler
④ Darrall
⑧ Monaghan
③ Jennings
⑦ Sugden
② Sparks
① Smith
⑥ Iredale

← Amiens
Albert →

RNZAF Wave 1 ——▶
Wave 2 - - - -▶
RAAF Wave 1 ——▶
Wave 2 - - - -▶

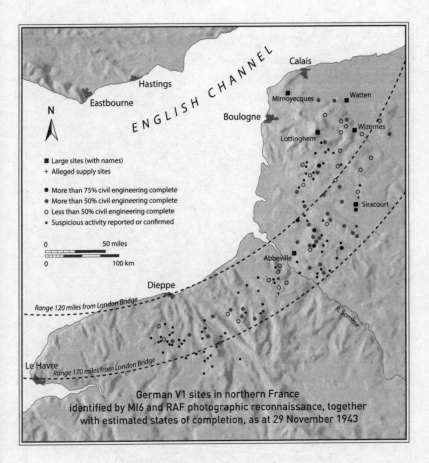

Hastings

Eastbourne

ENGLISH CHANNEL

Calais

Mimoyecques

Watten

Boulogne

Wizernes

Lottinghem

N

■ Large sites (with names)
+ Alleged supply sites

● More than 75% civil engineering complete
● More than 50% civil engineering complete
○ Less than 50% civil engineering complete
• Suspicious activity reported or confirmed

0   50 miles

0   100 km

■ Siracourt

Abbeville

Dieppe

Range 120 miles from London Bridge

R. Somme

Le Havre

Range 170 miles from London Bridge

German V1 sites in northern France
identified by MI6 and RAF photographic reconnaissance, together
with estimated states of completion, as at 29 November 1943

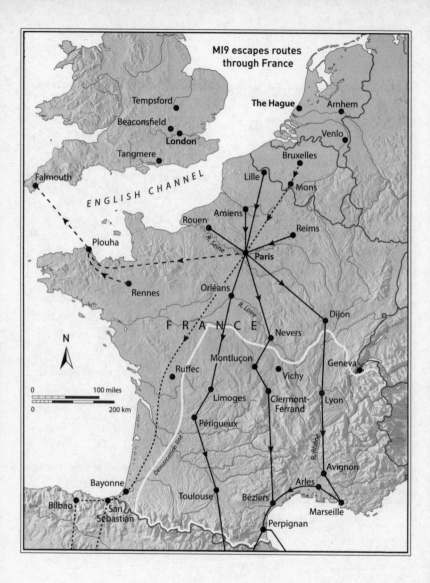

MI9 escapes routes
through France

Tempsford

Beaconsfield
London
Tangmere

Falmouth

ENGLISH CHANNEL

The Hague   Arnhem

Venlo

Bruxelles

Lille   Mons

Plouha   Amiens

Rouen   Reims

R. Seine   **Paris**

Rennes   Orléans   Dijon

R. Loire   Nevers

F R A N C E   Geneva

N   Ruffec   Montluçon

Vichy

0   100 miles   Limoges   Clermont-   Lyon
0   200 km   Ferrand

Périgueux   R. Rhône

Avignon

Demarcation line   Arles

Bayonne   Toulouse   Béziers   Marseille

Bilbao   San   Perpignan
              Sebastián

APPENDIX 1

Confusion or conspiracy?

In a BBC *Panorama* documentary shown on 19 April 1982, Colonel Maurice Buckmaster, the long-retired former head of F Section of the Special Operations Executive (SOE), was challenged by the interviewer, Michael Cockerell, as to whether SOE was behind the famous jail-breaking attack by RAF Mosquito fighter-bombers on Amiens Prison at noon on 18 February 1944. The interview had been prompted by the recent publication of Jack Fishman's *And the Walls Came Tumbling Down* and his publication of a letter dated 2 March 1944, addressed to Air Vice Marshal H. E. P. Wigglesworth, Senior Air Staff Officer (SASO) of the Allied Expeditionary Air Force (AEAF) and written by Group Captain L. G. S. Payne, MC, AFC RAF, a member of the Directorate of Intelligence in the Air Ministry. It began:

> I have been asked by 'C' to express his gratitude and the gratitude
> of his officers for the attack carried out on Amiens prison on 18th
> February, and also their sympathy for the relatives and comrades
> of the air-crews who were unfortunately lost.

'C' was Major General Sir Stewart Menzies, head of the Secret Intelligence Service (SIS), more commonly known as MI6. A startled Colonel Buckmaster denied any involvement by F Section. As well he might. The interviewer had made the common mistake, when considering the direction of underground activities in France during the war, of failing to grasp the difference between two of the French-focused elements of SOE, F and RF Sections, and also of confusing SOE's work alongside the French underground with that of MI6. It was and remains an easy error to make, if that indeed was what had happened. It seems more likely that the interviewer knew the distinction very well, but by his line of questioning was attempting to catch Buckmaster out.

The programme's agenda was somehow to prove that a secret lay behind the raid, a secret that the British establishment had attempted and was still attempting to hide through its supposed refusal to release documents hidden in the archives of MI6. In an article written for *The Listener* on 29 April 1982 Cockerell lamented that the 'secrets of war are still as secure after 40 years'. The programme did not stop to consider the possibility that there was nothing else to say about the raid, either because there were no remaining British archives to scour, or because the truth was already in the public domain. But that would have meant that the BBC had nothing to report, and that would have made dull television.

The evidence shows beyond reasonable doubt that the raid had in fact been authorised by the Air Ministry and undertaken by the RAF at the behest of MI6, on behalf of one of the latter's many secret intelligence networks (*réseaux*) that were operating at the time against the occupying German forces in France, and not by SOE. At least one Resistance network, and possibly more, sent repeated messages to London urging action. The evidence also suggests that MI6 were encouraged to consider the raid by their colleagues in the BCRA, with whom they worked closely throughout the war.

The revelation in 1982 about the involvement of the Secret Intelligence Service did not in fact reveal anything new to experts in the subject, although it was the first time that MI6's involvement had been directly referenced in an official document about the raid. MI6's involvement could, nevertheless, have been easily deduced from material in what was then the British Public Records

Office (now the National Archives at Kew) and freely available in the Hôtel de Soubise, the home of the French National Archives in Paris. In addition, there was any amount of published material relating to MI6's wartime operations available, including the auto-biographies in French and English of a number of important Resistance leaders going back to the 1950s (such as those of Georges-André Groussard, Gilbert Renault, Marie-Madeleine Fourcade and Paul Paillole), as well as three separate legal depos-itions by two of the Resistance leaders responsible, the brothers Pierre and Dominique Ponchardier, dated September 1944, 26 October 1946 and 13 January 1953. While the opening up of the MI6 records – if any still exist – would be a boon for historians of this period, it is fair to say that both archival and published mat-erial in France going back to 1944, written by the men who conceived and initiated the raid, helps compensate for (although not replace) the lack of official records in Britain, and enables the construction of an accurate picture of the respective roles in the Amiens affair of the French Resistance, the Free French Secret Services (and those of Vichy), and of MI6.*

The fact that the BBC interviewer in 1982 had not compre-hended the role of MI6 in the affair (except perhaps in an under-hand way) is testament to the success of the organisation in remaining in the shadows. In the meantime it was the exploits of SOE that loomed large in the public imagination and received most of the attention for underground operations in occupied Europe. Without the oxygen of publicity, the extent of MI6's intelligence-gathering activities (in contrast to the noisy setting off of 'bangs' by SOE), and any implications of this activity in terms of military operations – except insofar as this information had been released as part of wider deception operations, such as

---

* The strong likelihood is that no MI6 files on the raid remain. Duncan Stewart, latterly the SOE adviser to the Foreign and Commonwealth Office, confirmed as much in a letter to Sebastian Cox, head of the MOD's Air Historical Branch, on 3 August 1999.

Operation *Fortitude South*, for example – has been quietly forgotten as the years have passed.

One of the problems with operating in any kind of information vacuum is the temptation it poses for otherwise well-intentioned people to fill gaps in the historical record with ill-evidenced notions of their own. The story of the Amiens Prison raid in recent years has been no exception. The 'revelation' in 1982 of MI6's involvement prompted a flurry of speculation, in film and books, that questioned the 'real' reason for the attack and suggested some nefarious purpose by MI6, some of which has subsequently found itself in print, and of course in more recent times on the Internet. It has led some at worst to suspect some form of cover-up and at best to describe the affair, as do M. R. D. Foot and J. M. Langley in *MI9, Escape and Evasion 1939–1945*, as 'mysterious'.

In one sense Foot and Langley's description is apt. There is not, for example, a clear and unequivocal official record laying out the rationale for the raid, only a rather jumbled piece concocted by the RAF's Director of Public Relations in October 1944, many months after the event (see Appendix 5). But on the other hand there is no mystery at all, merely *secrecy*. The French networks and operations deep in the heart of enemy territory run by Britain's SIS, in conjunction with the Free French secret service, were not in the habit of advertising their activities, some of which involved the most spectacular coups (the discovery of the V1 rocket programme, for instance) ever secured in the history of espionage, and achieved in the face of severe personal danger for many scores of dedicated French patriots and directly employed British agents of MI6 and RF Section. The truth is that at stake in February 1944 were the lives of a number of French men and women, and possibly those of other nationalities as well, who had been instrumental in opening a priceless window into France that enabled London to have sight – if perhaps through a glass darkly – of secret German plans for the bombardment of Britain, and to whom a debt of honour was owed.

Unfortunately the gaps in the official record have not always been seen for what they represent – the necessary product of operational secrecy – and have led, bizarrely, to claims that the raid was a cover by MI6 for other purposes. This distortion is a common theme in intelligence studies – an occupational hazard, as it has been described to me by one insider. One account of the raid, which has received more prominence than it deserves, even claims that the official RAF version is 'sheer lies', that the Resistance did not ask for the raid, that the operation had nothing to do with releasing *résistants* and was instead part of the Allies' complex strategic deception plan designed to mask the true target of the forthcoming invasion of France. It even suggests – preposterously – that there is no evidence to support a genuine Resistance dimension to the raid, despite the overwhelming and publicly available evidence to the contrary.

There has been some surprising support given to these ideas. Professor M. R. D. Foot had initially accepted that the purpose of the raid, as he explained in *Resistance* in 1976, was 'to try to rescue some resistance leaders . . .' Prompted by the BBC in 1982, however, he apparently changed his mind, and suggested that the raid was in fact designed to support the deception plans that lay at the heart of Operation *Fortitude South*. This idea was subsequently taken up and elaborated by others. Was what has become known to the world as Operation *Jericho* a gigantic hoax dreamed up by the schemers in the SIS at Broadway House in St James's, a cruel fabrication that resulted in the loss of many innocent French lives, as well as those of four gallant airmen shot down during the mission?

No. The truth of the events of 18 February 1944 remains grounded firmly in the freely available historical record, and this book is a careful exposition of this evidence. The account of the raid does not need to be gilded by conspiracy to make it any more remarkable than it was in reality. At the same time as the BBC documentary was being aired in Britain, Television New Zealand also commissioned a documentary from Limelight Productions entitled *Dead on Target*, which interviewed three of the surviving *résistants* who were inside the prison when the first of the New Zealand Mosquitoes thundered overhead, as well as a number of *résistants* on the outside. All three – Maurice Genest (*Henri*), André Pache and Raymond Bonpas – were active in networks at the time of their arrest that were all feeding intelligence to MI6.*

The New Zealand documentary (presented by Ian Johnstone) frankly made a far better fist of it than the BBC, by refusing to be swayed by the temptation to present flimsy though headline-grabbing suppositions from half-complete archives. The truth is not hard to find, if only one knows where to look, and is not side-tracked by fantasy on the way.

---

* Paché had been arrested following a failed plan to destroy 500,000 litres of industrial alcohol at a plant in northern France on Armistice Day, 11 November 1943.

APPENDIX 2

Nacht und Nebel Erlass
(Night and Fog Decree)

The Führer and Supreme Commander of the Armed Forces
SECRET

Directives for the prosecution of offences committed within the occupied territories against the German State or the occupying power, of December 7th, 1941.

Within the occupied territories, communistic elements and other circles hostile to Germany have increased their efforts against the German State and the occupying powers since the Russian campaign started. The amount and the danger of these machinations oblige us to take severe measures as a deterrent. First of all the following directives are to be applied:

I. Within the occupied territories, the adequate punishment for offences committed against the German State or the occupying power which endanger their security or a state of readiness is on principle the death penalty.

II. The offences listed in paragraph I as a rule are to be dealt with in the occupied countries only if it is probable that sentence of death will be passed upon the offender, at least the principal offender, and if the trial and the execution can be completed in a very short time. Otherwise the offenders, at least the principal offenders, are to be taken to Germany.

III. Prisoners taken to Germany are subjected to military procedure only if particular military interests require this. In case German or foreign authorities inquire about such prisoners, they are to be told that they were arrested, but that the proceedings do not allow any further information.

IV. The Commanders in the occupied territories and the Court authorities within the framework of their jurisdiction, are personally responsible for the observance of this decree.

V. The Chief of the High Command of the Armed Forces determines in which occupied territories this decree is to be applied. He is authorised to explain and to issue executive orders and supplements. The Reich Minister of Justice will issue executive orders within his own jurisdiction.

APPENDIX 3

Georges Charraudeau, *réseau Alibi*

Paul Cousseran of *réseau Alibi* suggests that Georges Charraudeau was involved in the Amiens affair. Through his connection with Colonel Georges-André Groussard, Charradeau was made aware of the work of the *réseau Sosies*, and of the Ponchardier brothers. The suggestion was that, as with the *Sosies*, a number of *Alibi* agents and *pianistes* were imprisoned in Amiens Prison, and a number had been executed there and elsewhere. According to Cousseran, Dominique Ponchardier faced 'great reluctance' in London at the prospect of an operation against the prison, and he asked Charraudeau for help with persuading MI6 of the importance – even if only symbolic – of such a raid. While the claims of Charraudeau's involvement are not independently verifiable they make circumstantial sense. Airey Neave acknowledged that considerable debate took place in MI6 about the merits or otherwise of responding to the request from France to undertake a raid against the prison, and for Dominique Ponchardier to approach the head of *Alibi* to get him to support the pressure on London would have been a natural step to take.

In addition, Gilbert Renault records that Dominique Ponchardier sought the permission of the senior Resistance representative in the region to ask London to mount a raid on the prison. By late November 1943 this man was Raymond Vivant, the *sous-préfet* of Abbeville and – with the imprisonment of Dr Antonin Mans and Captain André Tempez – now the regional head of the *OCM*. This, too, makes sense. Since mid-1943 the Resistance networks in the region had been more or less collaborating, with centralised structures assisting in command and control, and in the planning and conduct of operations. While these relationships could be fragile (the FTPF, for instance, refusing any form of external control), it is true nevertheless that leaders of the disparate *réseaux* were talking to each other. Dominique Ponchardier would have realised that his chances of successfully persuading London of the merits of his scheme were remote if he did not at least have the sanction and support of the senior Resistance representative in the region.

Cousseran suggests that the involvement with Charraudeau was decisive, and that the messages to London were sent to MI6 from the *Alibi* boat connections with England from the Île Grande in Brittany. He also names the MI6 contact in London for *Alibi* as 'Captain Thomas', whom he met when he was in London. Independently, Dominique Ponchardier in his memoirs refers also to a 'Captain Thomas' as his contact in London, confirming that Ponchardier's liaison was with MI6. Without access to the archives it is impossible to be definitive about who this man may have been, but the notes provided by Charraudeau refer directly to him as Lieutenant Neil Whitelaw of MI6, who worked to Kenneth Cohen, and who accompanied most of the MGB runs arranged by Charraudeau to Brittany. It seems more than likely, therefore, that Ponchardier and Charraudeau were linked to MI6 through one man, their case officer Neil Whitelaw.

APPENDIX 4

Train sabotage in the Frévent sector, Pas-de-Calais, 1941–3

23/10/1941	150 m of telephone line cut between Brias and St-Pol*
26/3/1942	Attempted sabotage of switching equipment at Tincques station (failed)
2/4/1942	Attempted sabotage of railway lines at Brias station (failed)
15/5/1942	Railway line blown up between Albert and Beaucourt-Hamel: derailment stopped traffic for seven hours
22/6/1942	Railway line cut with explosives at Monchy-Cayeux
12/7/1942	Railway line cut at Beaucourt-Hamel: derailment stopped traffic for seven hours
14/10/1942	Attempted sabotage of railway lines near Auxi-le-Château
7/1/1943	Rails unbolted from the line St-Pol, Sains-Bouvigny
6/3/1943	Rails unbolted at Beaucourt-Hamel: derailment completely blocked the line until 9 March
17/9/1943	Rails unbolted between Bouquemaison and Frévent: derailment blocked the line at Rebreuviette until the evening of 18 Sept

---

*   Extracted from 'La Résistance dans le Ternois', a personal account of the activities of a group of *résistants* in the Pas-de-Calais, handwritten by one of the participants, M. René Guittard, in September 1986, courtesy of Keith Janes. Jean Beaurin was party to a number of these attacks.

29/7/1943   Rails unbolted at Beaucourt-Hamel: derailment and
              collision of military train completely blocked the line
              until 30 July

28/8/1943   Rails unbolted at Miraumont: derailment completely
              blocked the line until 30 August

19/9/1943   Eighty telephone lines cut between Frévent and Fortel:
              stopped service until the morning

28/9/1943   Rails unbolted at Frévent: derailment stopped service
              until noon 29 September

29/9/1943   Derailment between St-Pol and Frévent: service inter-
              rupted until 16.00 hrs on 1 October

4/10/1943   Rails unbolted between St-Pol and Wavrans: engine and
              11 wagons derailed and service interrupted until 18.00
              hrs on 5 October

7/10/1943   Rails unbolted between Frévent and Fortel: derailment
              and service interrupted until 22.00 hrs on 9 October

15/10 1943   Rails unbolted between Frévent and Fortel: derailment
              and service interrupted until 16.00 hrs

20/10/1943   Rails unbolted between Frévent and St-Pol: derailment
              of German military train and service interrupted until
              18.00 hrs on 21 October

25/10/1943   Attempt to set fire to hydraulic works at Auxi station
              (failed)

8/11/1943   Rail maintenance tools stolen from Auxi

23/11/1943   Rail maintenance tools stolen from Conteville

25/11/1943   Rails unbolted between Fortel and Auxi: derailment
              interrupted service until 26 November

31/11/1943   Rails unbolted between Auxi and Conteville (no result)

DPR's press release, October 1944

Some of the confusions that have grown around the Amiens raid were caused by an exaggerated piece of prose published by the RAF Director of Public Relations in October 1944 for propaganda purposes. It was never meant to be a statement of historical fact, true in every detail, but rather an opportunity to make up for the propaganda deficit of not announcing the raid when it actually happened. The war was still being fought, but with Amiens now in Allied hands the story would inevitably emerge, and the general thrust of the British account needed to be presented to the media. Its function was to spin a clear, exciting and ultimately triumphant description of the victory of (British) good over (Nazi) evil. A press release was no place for ambiguity, whether in terms of the precise detail of the source and content of the original request, or of the deliberations by the SIS, the Air Ministry and the RAF (in that order) as to the nature of the British response, if any.

The message the DPR wanted to get across was the clear request from the patriots in France for help, the scale and nature of the threat facing the men and women incarcerated in Amiens Prison (which was representative of all other Gestapo prisons across Nazi-occupied Europe), and the decisiveness, skill and success of the Allied/British response. The difficulty is that the piece has become the foundation for all subsequent myths about the raid, and gave rise to questions about its origin because some have read far more into it than was ever intended, assuming (wrongly) that if this was not a statement of fact, it must therefore be an attempt at dissimulation. In fact, it was neither. Rather it was an attempt at what we might recognise today as public relations or media spin. It read:

Mosquitoes are to attack the prison at Amiens in an attempt to assist more than 100 prisoners to escape. These prisoners are French patriots condemned to death for assisting the Allies. This was the briefing one day of air crews at an Allied Expeditionary Air Force intelligence room, and it was the prelude to an epic operation by the Royal Air Force. For security reasons it has not been possible until now to give a full account of the exploit. Frenchmen were lying in the jail awaiting death for their brave efforts in the Allied cause. Some of them had been condemned for assisting Allied flyers to escape after they had been brought down in France. It was clear that nothing less than a successful operation by the R.A.F. to break down the prison walls even at the risk of killing some of the patriots they wished to rescue – would afford these men any reasonable prospect of escape.

The R.A.F. undertook this exacting task, accepted the risk of killing people who, in any event, were to be put to death by the enemy, and eventually learned that as a result of their attack on the jail, many prisoners escaped and considerable casualties were caused among the German guards.

The prison was a cruciform building in a courtyard, surrounded by a 20 feet high wall, some 3 foot thick. The yard was fenced internally to segregate the prisoners while they were at exercise. Accuracy in attack was regarded as essential, for whereas on the one hand the walls and buildings required to be breached, on the other, in order to reduce casualties to a minimum, it was important that the least possible force should be used.

The jail was guarded by German troops living in a special wing, location of which was exactly known. The attack had to be sufficiently discriminating to ensure that decisive force was used against this part of the building. The time factor, too, was important, for the escaping men were to receive valuable assistance by patriots from outside if these patriots could be warned of the exact time of attack.

The task, therefore, called for secret and detailed planning, and a model of the prison and its surroundings was made from photographs and other information already in the Air Ministry's possession. Thus, in planning and briefing every aspect was studied.

To carry out this exceptional operation, the task was entrusted to a Mosquito wing of the RAF Second Tactical Air Force comprising British, Australian and New Zealand squadrons, and including RCAF airmen, commanded by Group Captain P. C. Pickard DSO and Two Bars, DFC, one of the most outstanding and experienced bomber pilots in the RAF. It was decided to allocate two fighter squadrons for escort duties from a fighter group that played a memorable part in the Battle of Britain.

The task added to the many difficult and daring operations which the Mosquitoes of the Second Tactical Air Force have performed – operations which have included the destruction of the single-building German Headquarters of Civil Administration in the centre of the Hague, numerous enemy army barracks or chateaux converted, for occupation by German troops in France, a headquarters in the field, electric power stations and other targets which demanded the most exacting precision attacks.

Of all those operations, however, the Mosquito air crews counted as most intricate the action against the Amiens prison on 18th February 1944. On the morning of that day the aircrews rose before dawn for their very careful briefing, to find the airfield covered with snow and low cloud, and with little prospect of clearance.

Once the plan was outlined, the crews, the most experienced from each squadron, were determined to press home their attack in spite of the adverse weather. It was obvious that the prison walls must be broken in at least two places to enable any escape whatever to be made. At the same time, both ends of the main

building had to be hit to release the prisoners from their confinement. Accordingly, the first wave of six aircraft was detailed to
breach the wall, on its north-east and north-west perimeter. The
second wave of six aircraft was to divide and open up both ends of
the jail, and to destroy the German guards' quarters. A third wave
was available should any part of the plan miscarry.

To obtain the accuracy required, it was necessary to bomb
from deck level and each wave had to be so timed that the results
were achieved in their right sequence and to avoid casualties by
collision over such a small target. A Mosquito was allotted to the
operation to make film and photograph records of the attack.

It was an hour before midday when the squadrons left their
snow-covered airfield to rendezvous with their fighter escort on
the south coast of England, from there the formation flew at sea
level to the French coast, swept round the north of Amiens and
approached their objective along the straight Amiens–Albert
road on which the prison is located. The second wave, on
approaching target, saw that the first wave had been successful.
Through the dust and smoke of the bombing the corners of the
jail were seen, enabling an accurate attack to be made. This, too,
was so successful that Group Captain Pickard, circling the target,
was able to send the third wave home without any necessity for its
attack. The photographic Mosquito, making three runs over the
objective, saw the breaches in the wall, the ends of the building
broken, prisoners running out through the breaches, Germans
lying on the ground and, on the last run, some patriots disappearing across the snow on the field outside the prison.

The operation was not completed without losses, however, for
two Mosquitoes, one of which carried Group Captain Pickard
and his navigator, Flight-Lieutenant J. A. Broadley, D.S.O., D.F.C.,
D.F.M., of Richmond, Yorkshire, were shot down by enemy fighters, as also were two of the fighter escort. Saddened as they were
by this loss of their leader and other colleagues, the aircrews who
took part in the operation felt that the sacrifices had not been in

vain when it became known that a high percentage of patriots had escaped. Although, as was unavoidable, some of the patriots were killed by German machine-guns as well as by bombs, it is known that the Germans themselves suffered casualties from the attack.

Since the successful liberation of France and subsequent relief of Amiens by the Allies, it has been possible to collect certain details, particularly of our losses, which had hitherto been unobtainable. All that was originally known of Group Captain Pickard's fate was that his aircraft was last seen circling over the prison slightly above the height at which the three waves of Mosquitoes were attacking.

His purpose was to decide whether or not sufficient force and accuracy had been achieved by the first two waves and to order the reserve wave to attack or withdraw, accordingly. It was for this reason that he had detached himself from the main formations to a position from which, though it was dangerous, he could best see and direct the operations.

It now seems certain that when he had ordered the last wave to withdraw without dropping its bombs, he saw one of his Mosquitoes brought down by the fierce light flak put up by the German defences. Determined to investigate the crash, to discover the fate of the crew, he was himself 'bounced' by a pair of F.W.190s sent up to intercept our aircraft. Caught thus pre-occupied, and detached from the friendly fighter escort, which by then was covering the withdrawal of the main formations, he fell victim to the enemy fighters.

He was shot down a few miles from Amiens and his body, with that of his navigator, was subsequently recovered by friendly villagers, who had seen the whole action. The Germans forced the villagers to hand over the bodies but were unable to prevent them attending the burial in the cemetery alongside Amiens prison.

As soon as his comrades reached Amiens after the invasion, seeking news of the aircrews' fate, the villagers presented them with photographs of the graves and a few personal belongings which they had secreted from the Germans for the months before the invasion in order that his identity and that of his navigator might be established

Tragic though Group Captain Pickard's loss is, there is consolation in the knowledge that it occurred while he was leading probably the most successful operation of his gallant and brilliant career.

The attack on Amiens prison will remain one of the most memorable achievements of the Royal Air Force.

APPENDIX 6

140 Wing statistics

Squadron	No. 487	No. 464	No. 21	FPU	Total
Mosquitoes detailed	6	6	6	1	19
Mosquitoes took off	6	6	6	1	19
Completed sorties	5	6	4	1	16
Aborted sorties	1	–	2	–	3
Missing	–	2	–	–	2

APPENDIX 7

After the battle

The Ponchardier brothers survived the war by a whisker. By the time of the raid they had already been betrayed, and were being hunted down by both the Milice and the Gestapo. After several close scrapes they were both arrested by withdrawing German troops near Belfort in August 1944, but managed to escape on the night of 7 September 1944 by killing their sentries. Dominique ended the war aged twenty-seven with, amongst other honours, the Cross of the Liberation, the Légion d'Honneur, and the Croix de Guerre with four citations.

With the onset of peace he enjoyed a varied and successful career in industry, diplomacy and literature. Under the pseudonym Antoine Dominique he created the famous 'Gorilla' series of spy fiction in France, making a name for himself as an accomplished and prolific author. During the war in Algeria he was a government adviser countering the Organisation de l'armée secrète (OAS). He was Ambassador to Bolivia from 1964 to 1968, and High Commissioner of the Republic of Djibouti from 1969 to 1971.

Pierre Ponchardier had joined the French Navy in 1927 and held the rank of Lieutenant. After the war he rejoined the service and was responsible for establishing the SAS B or Commando Ponchardier, active in 1945-6, then dissolved. He died as a Vice Admiral in 1961 in a plane crash in Senegal.

Dominique Ponchardier was astonished by the repeated questioning about Operation *Jericho*, asserting that his work in securing
the attack on the prison was nothing to the intelligence he helped
provide, with his colleagues in the *Sosies* and *Gilbert réseaux*, about
the V1 programme in the region. He became mildly irritated by
the questions that were raised from time to time in France about
the origins of the raid, and eventually stopped answering questions
about it, replying: 'Gilbert Renault has explained it all, perfectly
well. There is nothing else to be said.' He would have been horrified
at the conspiracy theories that have emerged in more recent times.
His book *Les Pavés de l'enfer*, published in 1950, describes how he
asked London for help. The British awarded him an MBE for his
wartime intelligence work. He maintained many of his wartime
friendships in the years that followed, and attended all the Amiens
anniversary services and parades. He died in 1986 and was buried
in Villefranche-sur-Mer.

Il était un véritable héros de la France, et de la liberté.

Select bibliography

Imperial War Museum, London, Department of Film

OPS 20/1–3	6 December 1942: Attack on Philips Radio Works, Eindhoven
OPS F 20/21	3 December 1943: 464 Squadron RAAF attack on Mur de Bretagne
GEN 10/1	18 February 1944: 140 Wing attack on Amiens Prison
OPS F 199	31 October 1944: 464 Squadron RAAF attack Gestapo HQ, Aarhus, Denmark
OPS F 257/8	21 March 1945: Fighter Command attack Gestapo HQ, Copenhagen
MGH 4114	1994 *Channel 9 Australia*

Imperial War Museum, London, Sound Archive

8901	Charles Patterson
12399 Reel 1/2	Arthur Dunlop
2236 Reels 4/5	Irving Smith
11754	Irving Smith
10988 Reel 2	Edward Sismore
12421 Reel 5	Duncan Taylor
2240	Maxwell Sparks
33555	Frank Wheeler

The National Archives, Kew, London

HS 6/311	SOE's relations with French governing authorities
HS 6/327&8	Main and local resistance and partisan groups: EAM (Independent French)
HS 6/330-4	Resistance movements and partisan forces in France
HS 8/1002	British Circuits in France, Major Bourne Patterson
WO 165/39	Main HQ diary of MI9
WO 208/3242	Crockatt's Historical Record of MI9
WO 208/3268	MI9 Bulletin
WO 208/3298–3348	MI9 Evasion Reports
WO 208/3314/1366	Evasion Report of Flying Officer TAH Slack, 41 Squadron RAF
WO SPG 884	Evasion Report of Private Conrad Lafleur, Mont Royal Fusiliers
CAB 69/6	A note by the Minister of Economic Warfare, 1 January 1944
CAB 79/63	JIC (43)325(0), 1 August 1943
CAB 120/827	Note from Churchill to Hastings Ismay, 10 February 1944
Air 14/708	Co-ordinated Operations Bomber and Fighter Commands (Circus Ops) vol. III, April 1943 – August 1944
Air 14/1195	ORS Day Raid Reports, No. 2 Group
Air 24/1525	2nd TAF Appendices –Tactics, Photo. Technical, Armaments, Jun 43 – Dec 44
Air 24/1528	2nd TAF Appendices – Operational Research, Jun 43 – Dec 44
Air 25/23	No. 2 Group Bomber Command. Operational Record Books, 1941–43
Air 25/195	No. 11 Group
Air 25/208	No. 11 Group
Air 26/204	140 Wing/Airfield HQ Operations Record Book, Dec 43 – Oct 47

Air 27/34	3 Squadron Operational Record Book (microfiche)
Air 27/263/4	21 Squadron Operations Record Book (microfiche)
Air 27/1109	174 Squadron Operational Record Book (microfiche)
Air 27/1170/1	198 Squadron Operational Record Book (microfiche)
Air 27/1482	245 Squadron Operational Record Book (microfiche)
Air 27/1924	464 Squadron Operational Record Book (microfiche)
Air 27/1935	487 Squadron Operational Record Book (microfiche)
Air 27/2117	613 Squadron Operational Record Book (microfiche)
Air 29/481	Film Production Unit
Air 37/14	No. 2 Group Review of Operations – 1944–45
Air 37/15	No. 2 Group Attack on Amiens Prison – 18 Feb 44
Air 37/16	No. 2 Group and its Work of Tactical Bombing – A Lecture by Sir Basil Embry (AOC) to RAF Staff College
Air 37/23	No. 2 Group
Air 37/35	Attack on Shellhaus, Copenhagen.
Air 37/36	Attack on Gestapo HQ at Aarhus – 31/10/44 – 3/11/44
Air 37/45	2nd TAF photos
Air 37/806	2nd TAF targets
CAB 121/311	French Resistance Groups from 12 January 1944

The Air Historical Branch, RAF Northolt, London
21 Squadron RAF
Attack on Amiens Prison

The Fishman Papers
The French National Archives, Paris*

3/AJ2	BCRA (*CND* (31–33))
72AJ/80/IX	*Réseau Sosies*
A/5/I	Report of Edouard Rivière
A/8/I	Report of Dominique Ponchardier October 1946
A/9/I	Report of Pierre Ponchardier, September 1944
72AJ/35/IV	*Réseau Agir*
72AJ/35/VIII	*Réseau Alliance*
72AJ/37/V	*Réseau Bourgogne*
72AJ/38/I to 72AJ/38/V	Opérations aériennes du Bureau central de renseignements et d'action (BCRA)
72AJ/56/I to 72AJ/56/III	Francs-Tireurs et Partisans Français (FTPF)
72AJ/58/II	*Réseau* Gilbert
72AJ/81/XII	*Réseau* Zéro-France
72AJ/82/I to 72AJ/82/IV	Services spéciaux — Activités du commandant Paul Paillole
72AJ/83/I to 72AJ/86/I	Office of Strategic Services (OSS)

Le Mémorial de Caen Museum
Papers of Gilbert Renault ('Colonel *Rémy*')

National Archives, Washington, United States
Record Group 338, Folder *Réseau* Burgundy, Box 1, Entry ETO MIS-X

Australian War Memorial, Canberra
AWM 54 Item No: 81/4/97 – History of 464 Squadron 1942–1945
AWM 54 Item No: 81/4/112 – No. 464 (Australian) Squadron Diary, RAF Station Feltwell
AWM 64 Item No: 1/348 – No. 464 Squadron Diary

* Series 72AJ is the *Documentation du Comité d'histoire de la Deuxième Guerre Mondiale.*

AWM 64 Item No: 1/350 – Operational Record Book
AWM 64 Item No: 1/351 – No. 464 Squadron Diary
AWM 64 Item No: 1/353 – 464 Operations Reports
AWM 64 Item No: 1/354 – History of No. 464 Squadron – 1942–1945
AWM 64 Item No: 1/355 – Squadron Records, Dec 42 – Feb 44

Secondary Material

Albertelli, Sébastien *Les services secrets du général de Gaulle: Le BCRA, 1940–1944* (Paris: Librairie Académique Perrin, 2009)

Amouroux, Henri *La Grande histoire des Français sous l'Occupation,* vol. 8 (Paris: Robert Laffont, 1988)

Andrew, Christopher *The Defence of the Realm: The Authorized History of MI5* (London: Allen Lane, 2009)

Babington Smith, Constance *Evidence in Camera* (London: Chatto & Windus, 1958)

Bertrand, Gustave *Enigma, ou la plus grande énigme de la guerre* (Paris: Librairie Plon, 1973)

Bishop, Patrick *Bomber Boys: Fighting Back 1940–1945* (London: Harper Press, 2007)

Boog, Horst, Gerhard Krebs & Detlef Vogl *Germany and the Second World War,* vol. VII, *The Strategic Air War in Europe and the War in the West and East Asia, 1943–1944/5* (Oxford: Clarendon Press, 2006)

Bowman, Martin *Mosquito Fighter/Fighter-bomber Units of World War 2* (Oxford: Osprey Publishing, 1998)

—— *Mosquito: Menacing the Reich* (Barnsley: Pen & Sword, 2008)

Bowyer, Michael *No. 2 Group RAF: A Complete History, 1936–1945* (London: Faber & Faber, 1974)

Broussine, Georges *The Escapee of Free France* (Paris: Tallandier, 2000)

Campbell, Christy *Target London: Under Attack from the V-Weapons* (London: Little, Brown, 2012)

Cave Brown, Anthony 'C' *The Secret Life of Sir Stewart Menzies, Spymaster to Winston Churchill* (London: Macmillan, 1987)

Chanier, Yves 'Le Réseau CND-Castille', Mémoire de maîtrise d'histoire (Paris, X-Nanterre, 1995)

Clutton-Brock, Oliver *RAF Evaders: The Complete Story of RAF Escapees and Their Escape Lines, Western Europe, 1940–1945* (London: Grub Street, 2009)

Cobb, Matthew *Resistance* (London: Simon & Schuster, 2009)

Collier, Richard *Ten Thousand Eyes* (London: Collins, 1958)

Curtis, Michael *Verdict On Vichy: Power and Prejudice in the Vichy France Regime* (New York: Arcade Publishing, 2002)

De Gaulle Anthonioz, Geneviève *The Dawn of Hope: A Memoir of Ravensbrück* (New York: Arcade Publishing Inc, 1999)

Devigny, André *A Man Escaped* (Guildford, CT: Lyons Press, 2002)

Downing, Taylor *Spies In the Sky: The Secret Battle for Aerial Intelligence during World War II* (Little Brown, 2011)

Ducellier, J. P. *The Amiens Raid: Secrets Revealed: The Truth Behind the Legend of Operation Jericho* (Watton-on-Thames: Red Kite, 2011)

Dumas, Lucien *The Man Who Went Back* (London: Leo Cooper, 1975)

Eismann, Gaël & Stefan Martens (eds) *Occupation et répression militaire allemandes, 1939–1945. La Politique de maintien de l'ordre en Europe occupée* (Paris: Autrement, 2007)

Fishman, Jack *And The Walls Came Tumbling Down* (London: Macmillan, 1983)

Foot, M. R. D. *Resistance* (London: Methuen, 1976)

Fourcade, Marie-Madeleine *Noah's Ark* (London: George Allen and Unwin Ltd, 1973)

Franks, Norman *RAF Fighter Command Losses of the Second World War*, vol. 3 (Midland Publishing, 2000)

Galland, Adolf *The First and the Last* (London: Methuen, 1955)

Groussard, Georges-André *Service Secret, 1940–1945* (Paris: La Table Ronde, 1964)

Hasquenoph, Marcel *La Gestapo en France* (Paris: De Vecchi Poche, 1987)

Hollard, Florian *Michel Hollard, le Français qui a sauvé Londres* (Paris: Succès du livre éditions, 2007)

Irving, David *Mare's Nest* (London: Kimber, 1964)

Jeffery, Keith *MI6. The History of the Secret Intelligence Service, 1909–1949* (London: Bloomsbury, 2010)

Johns, Philip *Within Two Cloaks* (London: Kimber, 1979)

Jones, R. V. *Most Secret War* (London: Hamish Hamilton, 1978)

Kozaczuk, Władysław *Enigma: How the German Machine Cipher was Broken, and How it was Read by the Allies in World War Two*, ed. & trans. Christopher Kasparek (Frederick, MD: University Publications of America, 1984)

Langley, James *Fight Another Day* (London: Collins, 1974)

Lax, Mark & Leon Kane-Maguire *The Gestapo Hunters: 464 Squadron RAAF 1942–45* (Maryborough, Queensland: Banner Books, 1999)

Level, Philippe *Missions dans la R.A.F.* (Editions Mellottée, 1946)

Mangold, Peter *Britain and the Defeated French: From Occupation to Liberation 1940–1944* (London: I. B. Tauris, 2012)

Marshall, Bruce *The White Rabbit* (London: Evans Brothers, 1952)

Martelli, George *Agent Extraordinary* (London: Fontana, 1960)

Moore, Bob *Resistance in Western Europe* (Oxford: Berg Publishers, 2000)

Neave, Airey *Saturday at MI9* (London: Hodder and Stoughton, 1969)

—— *Little Cyclone* (London: Hodder and Stoughton, 1954)

Nivet, Philippe (ed.) *La Picardie occupée* (Amiens: Armand Colin, 2005)

Nowlson, James *Damned to Fame: the life of Samuel Beckett* (New York, Simon & Schuster, 1996)

Passy, Colonel *Souvenirs*, vol. I, *Deuxième Bureau, London* (Monte Carlo: Raoul Solar, 1947)

—— *Secret missions in France. November 1942–June 1943. Memories of BCRA* (Paris: Editions Plon, 1951)

Paxton, Robert *Vichy France: Old Guard and New Order, 1940–1944* (New York: Columbia University Press, 1972)

Perrier, Guy *Rémy: L'agent secret N°1 de la France Libre* (Paris: Editions de la Loupe, 2004)

Ponchardier, Dominique *Les Pavés de l'enfer* (Editions Gallimard, 1950)

Read, Anthony & David Fisher *Colonel Z: The Secret Life of a Master of Spies* (London: Hodder and Stoughton, 1984)

Reile, Oscar *Abwehr: Spying against France in 1935–1945* (Paris: Editions France Empire, 1970)

Renault, Gilbert *L'opération jéricho* (Editions France Empire, 1954)

—— *The Hands Clasped* (1954)

—— *Mémoires d'un agent secret de la France libre* (Editions France Empire, 1984)

—— *Réseau Comète* (Librairie Académique Perrin, 1967)

Riols, Noreen *The Secret Ministry of Ag. and Fish* (London: Macmillan, 2013)

Seaman, Mark *Bravest of the Brave* (London, Michael O'Mara, 1997)

Sellier, André *Dora Camp* (Chicago: United States Holocaust Memorial Museum, 2003)

Sisman, Adam *Hugh Trevor-Roper: The Biography* (London: Weidenfeld & Nicholson, 2010), p. 93.

Slack, Tom *Happy Is the Day – A Spitfire Pilot's Story* (Penzance: United Writers Publications Ltd, 1987)

Terraine, John *The Right of the Line: The Royal Air Force in the European War 1939–1945* (London: Hodder and Stoughton, 1985)

Thirsk, Ian *De Havilland Mosquito: An Illustrated History* (London: Crecy, 2008)

Thompson, H. L. *Official History of New Zealanders with the Royal Air Force*, vol. 2 (Wellington: Historical Publications Branch, 1956)

Vincent, David *Mosquito Monograph: A History of Mosquitoes in Australia and R.A.A.F. Operations* (privately published, South Australia, 1982)

West, Nigel *MI6: British Secret Intelligence Service Operations 1909–1945* (London: George Weidenfeld & Nicholson, 1983). Nigel West is the nom de plume of Rupert Allason.

Wilkinson, Peter & Joan Bright Astley *Gubbins and SOE* (London: Leo Cooper, 1993)

Wilmot, Chester *The Struggle for Europe* (London: Reprint Society, 1954)

Wolmar, Christian *Engines of War: How Wars Were Won and Lost on the Railways* (London: Atlantic Books, 2010)

Woodridge, John *Low Attack: The Story of Two Mosquito Squadrons, 1940–43* (Sampson Low, Marston & Co. Ltd, 1943)

Wylie, Neville *Britain, Switzerland, and the Second World War* (Oxford: OUP, 2003)

Magazines and Articles

Adrian Orchard 'Charles Pickard', *Old Framlinghamian*, 2006

Bent Pedersen 'The Aarhus Attack', *After the Battle*, no. 54, London, 1986

Pat Pointon 'They Wasted Amiens Jail', *Roundel*, vol. 6, no. 11, Dec 1954

John Reed 'Operation Jericho – The Amiens Raid', *After the Battle*, no. 28, London, 1980

Articles by Gary Bridger in *Aeroplane Magazine*, March 2012 and
    October 2012

Film

The Jail Breakers, www.britishpathe.com (Film 44801)
BBC Yorkshire Documentary, 2011, presented by Martin Shaw
Television New Zealand (TVNZ), *Dead On Target*, 1982
Great Raids of World War Two, episode 2, *Prison Busters*, 2003

Author's Note

The first question an historian always asks is: 'Where, and what, are the sources?' All of the varying and sometimes competing strands to a story need to be identified, evaluated and corroborated piece by piece before a balanced judgement can be arrived at, especially if there are gaps in the historical record, or if different pieces of evidence conflict. It is not always possible to come to a definitive determination in every instance, but a carefully argued case, fully substantiated by the available sources – especially when independent pieces of evidence corroborate one another – can offer a result in which, as in a court of law, the balance of probability points unequivocally in a particular direction.

The second question one learns to ask, in support of the findings of the first, is: 'What is the context?' In other words, what were all the varying strands of activity – political, military, economic, and military and so on – surrounding a specific event or events that might cast light on its provenance?

The purpose of the RAF raid on Amiens Prison on 18 February 1944, and the role of MI6 in the affair, therefore, has been deduced using these accepted principles of historical interpretation. This entails identifying and carefully sifting all the available evidence, including primary and secondary sources (interviews, reports, official and autobiographical accounts) and then testing each through corroboration before assessing the entire thesis in the light of the existing historical, military and political context. The full truth behind the raid *may* still sit quietly in the files of MI6 (although I doubt it), but without it enough solid material exists in the public domain for a careful historian to be able to add the fragments together to provide a convincing account not only of what happened, but *why*. What has been presented in this book is my personal interpretation of all the extensive evidence available.

In fact, the wide spectrum of evidence available on the subject of the Amiens raid is remarkable. Even without access to the still-closed files of the Secret Intelligence Service, the material available in the French and British National Archives, together with the wide array of reminiscences of participants, paints a detailed and convincing picture of the purpose and rationale of the raid. This is the raw material that has allowed me to paint the picture presented in this book. There remain many gaps, of course – history is too multi-dimensional for all of it ever to be fully uncovered – but where these gaps exist they are painted on my canvas in grey, rather than in colour. The lack of some detail does not invalidate the coherence of the picture as a whole. Perhaps future historians, with access to new material as it becomes available, might be able to fill in this detail where it is currently absent.

To enable me to come to the judgements I have made I am indebted to the remarkable first-hand accounts of those of the participants that survived. These include the memoirs of Dominique and Pierre Ponchardier, Dr Antonin Mans, Raymond Vivant, Philippe Level, Dr Odile Regnault, André Dewavrin, Colonel Georges-André Groussard, Marie Madeleine Fourcade, Henri Moisan, Michel Hollard, Colonel Paul Paillole, Jean Beaurin, Achille Langlet, André Paché, Maurice Genest, Raymond Bonpas, Edouard Rivière, René Lamps, Jean-Claude Beloeil, Etienne Dromas, Marcel Debart, Max Sparks, Charles Patterson, Merv Darrall, 'Black' Smith, Bob Fowler, Ian McRitchie, R. A Lallemant and Gilbert Renault. Their testimony (written and oral), taken together, paints the clear and unequivocal picture of MI6 participation in the French Resistance that I have presented in this book.

In many respects that testimony confirms the judgements made by the late Jack Fishman in *And the Walls Came Tumbling Down*. I owe a huge amount to Fishman, and to his son Paul, for allowing me to review the material Jack amassed in his exhaustive study of the raid. For the historian the problem with Fishman's book is the absence of any detailed references to his sources, which leads the reader to ask whether what they are reading is fact or fiction. This difficulty is exacerbated by what the historian Matthew Cobb describes as 'implausibly precise contemporary conversations', a feature also of Philippe Level's account. Level nevertheless was telling his and Dominique Ponchardier's tales, together with those whom he interviewed who had been in Amiens or in the prison at the time. Because of his immediacy to the story he can be forgiven these post hoc literary constructions, designed not to mislead but to bring the human element directly into his telling of a story. Fishman did exactly the same.

Jack Fishman undertook extensive interviews between 1978 and 1982, and interviewed an extraordinary array of people who were involved in the raid, including the primary British and French protagonists. I am grateful to him for his detailed interviews, which I have used profitably in my own research. Those concerned are Colonel Gilbert Renault, DSO, OBE; Air Chief Marshal Sir Basil Embry, GCB, KBE, DSO (3 Bars), DFC, AFC; Joseph Balfe (senior); Joe Balfe (junior); Colonel David K. Bruce OSS; Colonel Maurice J. Buckmaster; Commander Kenneth Cohen, CB, CMG RN; André Dewavrin; Donald Darling; Colonel Georges-André Groussard; Marie Madeleine Fourcade, OBE; John Haskell; Lt Col James Langley, MBE, MC; Captain André Manuel; Professor Justin O'Brien; Colonel Paul Paillole; Colonel G. H. Pourchot; Vice Admiral Edouard Rivière; Philippe Schneider, DSO; Sir Kenneth Strong, KBE; Mrs Francis Suter (widow of Sir Claude Dansey); François Thierry Mieg; Sammy Izard; Victor Pasteau; Violette Lambert; Sophie Glasser; Gendarme Achille Langlet; Gendarme Lieutenant Marceau Laverdure; Dr Albert Gérault; Dr and Madame Antonin Mans; François and Raymonde Vignolle; Raymond Vivant; Christiane

Lecaillet; Dr Jacques Dezoteux; Dominique Ponchardier; Jean Pierre Beaurin; René and Maria Chapelle; Maurice Holville; Raymond Bonpas; Liliane Beaumont; Gratien Bocquet; Pierre Bracquart; Jean Cayeux; Anne Marie Chedeville; Raymond Dewas; Sosthène Denis and his son Michel; Pierre Gruel; Madeleine Gandon (Dr Robert Beaumont's sister); André Loisy-Jarniere; Henri Moisan; Robert Pecquet; Dr Gérard Perdu and Dr Odile Catherine Regnault.

My research, however, does not support the idea that the primary aim of the mission was to free Raymond Vivant, nor that the role of the third Mosquito squadron was to destroy the prison if the first two squadrons were unable to blast holes in the walls to enable inmates to escape. Nor have I found any evidence to support the notion that specific MI6 agents were in the prison, and that this was one of the reasons why the raid received the support of MI6. There are many theories about the origin and rationale for the raid. One is that Amiens Prison held a number of arrested *pianistes*, men and women considered critical to the ongoing intelligence war in the area, which focused at the time on the massive reinforcement of the region in response to Berlin's belief that the Pas-de-Calais would be the location of the Allied invasion of Europe. These, and other theories, while interesting, are, in the absence of evidence, merely speculation. Instead, I am convinced that the raid was a simple response to the pressure put on London by Ponchardier's (and perhaps, although less likely, Pickard's) persistence. The extensive circumstantial and corroborative evidence demonstrates without reasonable doubt that the raid was conducted by the RAF in response to a plea from a *réseau* in the Somme, passed on by MI6, to rescue its comrades from the certainty of execution by the Germans.

The wider research for this book was dependent on a wide range of talented people, in both Britain and France. For their balanced perspectives on the material available I am grateful to the detailed research of Thomas Fontaine, Nicky Bird, Gaël Eismann, Rupert Allason ('Nigel West'), David Irving, Mark Seaman, Ian Thirsk, Mark Lax, Anthony Read and David Fisher (for their illuminating study of Claude Dansey), Chris Lethbridge, Guy Perrier Sebastian Cox and the Official Historian of MI6, Professor Keith Jeffery. Nicky Bird gave me information he had received from the one-time SOE Adviser to the Foreign and Commonwealth Office Gervase Cowell, which independently authenticated information provided by Paul Cousseran, late of the *réseau Alibi*. The historian Yves Chanier introduced me to the voluminous records in the Mémorial de Caen of Gilbert Renault (*Rémy*), a man who proved as commendable an historian and archivist as he was a spy. I have taken the liberty of using his accounts of Dr Mans's, Dr Regnault's and M. Vivant's stories for reasons of authenticity.

In Amiens Jean-Robert Fecan has provided an interesting slant on the story, claiming that the *pianiste* employed by Ponchardier to communicate with London lived in his childhood home in the Saint-Pierre area of the town, close to the prison. In the United Kingdom Professor Matthew Cobb, Nigel Perrin, Keith Janes (*Conscript Heroes*) and Duncan Stuart provided their usual standard of unstinting support, and read portions of the manuscript in draft. I am especially grateful to Andy Bird of the RAF Museum, himself a distinguished Mosquito historian, for his considerable assistance, to Sebastian Cox and his small team at the Ministry of Defence's Air Historical Branch, based at RAF Northolt, to Al Bridgwood and to Monica and Andrew Dale, grandchildren of Joseph and Madeleine Balfe. Gary Bridger of Auckland, New Zealand gave me invaluable material about Merv Darrall and the New Zealanders generally, and considerable encouragement along the way. Kim Stevenson, son of 'Steve' Stevenson and lifelong pal of Merv Darrall, also helped with information and advice. Caitlin Davies translated large numbers of pages of French text into impeccable English, at discount rates. Likewise I am indebted to the small army of Internet historians who every day reveal more of the detail behind the events in northern France during the war. Keith Janes's research into the story of the Balfe family through the MI9 and MIS-X files (and much more) offers considerable detail on this aspect of the resistance on the Somme, as does Jean-Pierre Husson's website on *Possum* and John Clinch's website on *Comète*. Fred Greyer, son of Dominique Edgard Potier, head of *Possum*, has unearthed the remarkable history of this *réseau d'évasion*, published at www.possumline.net

I am grateful to those authorities who gave me permission to use material in their possession, and to copy photographs and maps, especially the Imperial War Museum, the Australian War Memorial, the RAF Museum Hendon, Le Mémorial de Caen, and the Comptroller of Her Majesty's Stationery Office.

I have also been sustained by the encouragement of a remarkable band of Mosquito enthusiasts around the world, prominent among whom is the remarkable Glyn Powell QSM of Auckland, who built a Mosquito from scratch in his back garden. The results are remarkable, seen best in high definition at http://m.youtube.com/watch?v=Xvp2AeM68iM. I had the very great pleasure to be introduced to Glyn in Auckland in March 2014, and shown around his remarkable 'shed', home to his latest baby, NZ2308. To a whole series of wonderful people who made my stay in New Zealand in 2014 so enjoyable I offer my grateful thanks, not least among them Gary Bridger, Gary and Ali Morrison, Bryan and Kathy Long, Mark and Julie Davies, Gaye Oldham and Chris Fallows.

Last but by no means least I am indebted to my indefatigable agent, Charlie Viney, for his enthusiasm, patience and encouragement. This book, pushing back against the conspiracy theorists, was his idea.

Delving as I have done into dusty manuscripts and even dustier memories brings some dangers, although nothing of the kind or degree faced by those remarkable *résistants* and aircrew so long ago in Amiens and in the air above. I may, despite my efforts to prevent it, have made mistakes, either of fact or of judgement. If this is the case, I apologise in advance, and will rectify any errors in subsequent editions.

Index